Applied Conversation Analysis

Sara Miller McCune founded SAGE Publishing in 1965 to support the dissemination of usable knowledge and educate a global community. SAGE publishes more than 1000 journals and over 800 new books each year, spanning a wide range of subject areas. Our growing selection of library products includes archives, data, case studies and video. SAGE remains majority owned by our founder and after her lifetime will become owned by a charitable trust that secures the company's continued independence.

Los Angeles | London | New Delhi | Singapore | Washington DC | Melbourne

Applied Conversation Analysis

Social Interaction in Institutional Settings

Jessica Nina Lester
Indiana University

Michelle O'Reilly
University of Leicester

Los Angeles | London | New Delhi
Singapore | Washington DC | Melbourne

FOR INFORMATION:

SAGE Publications, Inc.
2455 Teller Road
Thousand Oaks, California 91320
E-mail: order@sagepub.com

SAGE Publications Ltd.
1 Oliver's Yard
55 City Road
London EC1Y 1SP
United Kingdom

SAGE Publications India Pvt. Ltd.
B 1/I 1 Mohan Cooperative Industrial Area
Mathura Road, New Delhi 110 044
India

SAGE Publications Asia-Pacific Pte. Ltd.
3 Church Street
#10-04 Samsung Hub
Singapore 049483

Acquisitions Editor: Helen Salmon
Editorial Assistant: Megan O'Heffernan
Production Editor: Andrew Olson
Copy Editor: Diane Wainwright
Typesetter: C&M Digitals (P) Ltd.
Proofreader: Liann Lech
Indexer: Marilyn Augst
Cover Designer: Candice Harman
Marketing Manager: Susannah Goldes

Printed in the United States of America

ISBN 978-1-5063-5126-1

Clipoard icon: Pixabay.com/Clker-Free-Vector-Images
Exclamation point icon: Pixabay.com/CreativeMerlin
Question mark icon: Pixabay.com/CreativeMerlin

This book is printed on acid-free paper.

18 19 20 21 22 10 9 8 7 6 5 4 3 2 1

• Table of Contents •

• Preface •

Aims of the Book

In this book, we focus on conversation analysis (CA), specifically applied CA, which offers important insights and perspectives about institutional talk. CA is a methodological approach that is rooted in the hermeneutic research tradition and is closely associated with the discursive turn (Tseliou, 2013). Broadly, language-based approaches include a range of methodological perspectives, including discourse analytic perspectives, rhetorical analysis, and conversation analysis, among others. The relatively recent critical "turn to language" has served to challenge positivist ideas about the way the world generally, and human interaction specifically, works. With this turn, language has become viewed as constitutive of social life, with increasing attention now being given to have language that creates and constructs reality. Applied CA is an especially useful methodology for understanding the implications of this turn to language, as it offers generative perspectives for applied fields and practitioners going about their everyday lives. Thus, when we developed this book, we sought to locate our discussions in relation to what applied CA might offer while intentionally working to craft a practical and accessible guide to planning and carrying out an applied CA research study.

Notably, a growing body of CA research has attended to varying institutional settings, including legal settings (e.g., Auburn & Lea, 2003; Stokoe, 2010), news and media settings (e.g., Hutchby, 2005), health care settings (e.g., Heritage & Robinson, 2011; Stivers, 2002), mental health settings (e.g., Hutchby, 2007; O'Reilly & Lester, 2017; Thompson & McCabe, 2016), and educational settings (e.g., Reddington & Waring, 2015; Waring, 2014), among others. Across disciplines and geographic locales, there is certainly a growing emphasis on applied research as well as research that may have an impact on practice. Thus, in this book, we argue that applied CA has much to offer in this regard. Over the last several years, CA has been growing in popularity, as evidenced by several journals devoted to publishing this kind of work, such as *Research on Language & Social Interaction*, and international research networks for scholars practicing CA, such as the *International Society for Conversation Analysis* and *Conversation Analysis Research in Autism*. Further, a growing number of conferences are designed to showcase CA research, including the *International Conference for Conversation Analysis* and the *Conversation Analysis and Clinical Encounters Conference*, to name just a few.

Who This Book Is For

This book is not discipline specific, and thus, across the book, we point to a range of examples from different institutional settings and fields. Consequently, scholars and practitioners within a range of fields will find the book relevant to their work and research, including those working in the areas of counseling, criminology, education, forensic science, health sciences, human geography, law, linguistics, marketing, media, mental health, social policy, social work, and sociology, among others. Further, we wrote this book with the hope that a range of audiences would find it accessible and useful to their work. As such, undergraduate students, graduate students (both master's and doctoral level), postgraduate students, and scholars (new or returning) of applied CA will likely find it useful. In addition, we also crafted the book with the intent of inviting practitioners to engage with the core principles and practices of applied CA.

Organization of the Book

This book is divided into three sections that reflect the core issues at stake when conducting a project using applied CA. The early sections of the book focus on context and planning, and are designed to facilitate the reader through the main decision-making processes that will inform the research. In this section of the book, the chapters provide an accessible introduction to applied CA and set the context for the reader by introducing the key principles and terminology used. Specifically, the early part of the book differentiates applied CA from pure CA, and considers the institutionality of the talk. Using case studies, activities, and useful examples, we guide readers through the challenges that they may face during the planning stages, incorporating some of the broader qualitative issues that are relevant to this qualitative approach, such as ethical concerns, proposal writing, developing questions, keeping a reflexive diary, and developing ideas.

The second section of the book focuses on the practical aspects of carrying out research using applied CA. This section of the book is designed to help the reader navigate through some of the complexities of doing fieldwork, recruiting participants, working with naturally occurring data, transcribing, translating, and sampling. Applied CA research has some specific ways of carrying out research that reflects its epistemological and ontological foundations as well as its methodological perspective, and these steps are provided in a practical way. For applied CA to be robust, the analysis should be conducted carefully and within the parameters of the approach, and these are explained. Other issues that may be relevant for some readers, such as the use of digital tools, are also included.

The final section of the book focuses on disseminating your research and considers the stages of a project once data collection and analysis are close to completion. The iterative nature of qualitative research broadly, and applied CA specifically, is recognized as we guide the reader through complex issues such as assuring quality in the approach. This is an area that has created some tensions in the qualitative community and among CA scholars, and this is considered to help readers draw their own conclusions. This is particularly important, as in a contemporary context, applied research now considers the evidence-based practice agenda, and this has been hugely influential in terms of funding and publishing research, and recognizing its value. Nonetheless, it is an agenda that has created tension and one that applied CA researchers must navigate. This relates to dissemination activities, and the book provides a specific focus on the different ways in which the applied CA research study might reach different audiences, including the dissemination through an educational qualification such as a dissertation/thesis. To consolidate the core messages, the final chapter provides examples of work in the field and highlights the importance of doing applied CA research.

How to Use This Book

The book includes a range of pedagogical activities, summaries for each chapter, interview boxes with experts, and learning points to highlight the main messages of each chapter. Notably, given that we developed this book to be a foundational text and therefore provide a basic platform for audiences to move on to other, more complex and sophisticated sources, we also include recommended readings at the end of each chapter. The pedagogical nature of the text serves to guide the reader through some of the more challenging aspects of doing this kind of research. Throughout the chapters, there are two boxed features:

Social interaction in sociological terms refers to the changing sequence of actions that occurs between individuals or groups of people—that is, the conversations that occur between people.

DEFINITION BOXES

Provide definitions and discussions of key concepts and terms used in CA research.

CA encompasses both a method and a theoretical approach (McCabe, 2006).

IMPORTANT POINT BOXES

Indicated by an explanation mark, these call out things to keep in mind as you work through the text.

• Acknowledgments •

*. . . we never write on a blank page, but always
on one that has already been written on*

—Michel de Certeau,
The Practice of Everyday Life

Indeed, no publication is ever written in isolation, as there are many people who contribute to its very making. Thus, we certainly have many people to thank for their support during the writing of this book. First, we thank our families for their support and patience during the writing process. Second, we appreciate the support from those working with SAGE Publications, who have been an invaluable source of advice. We are particularly grateful to our editor, Helen Salmon, for her helpful insights and suggestions throughout the development of this book.

We were also fortunate to consult with several PhD students (some recently graduated) on many of the chapters. We are grateful to:

- Alison Davies, who completed her PhD at the Open University United Kingdom in 2014;

- Katie Denman, who completed her clinical doctorate at Plymouth University, United Kingdom, in 2015;

- Chris Georgen, doctoral candidate at Indiana University, United States;

- Andrea Gomoll, doctoral candidate at Indiana University, United States;

- Victoria Lee, who completed her PhD at the University of Leicester, United Kingdom, in 2018;

- Suraj Uttamchandani, doctoral candidate at Indiana University, United States;

- Amber Warren, recently appointed assistant professor at University of Nevada, Reno, United States; and

- Francesca White, doctoral candidate at Indiana University, United States.

This book also benefits from many contributions from both new and experienced scholars in the field of applied CA who have provided interview responses related to specific topics included within the book. We are grateful to the following individuals for their contributions:

- Charles Antaki, Loughborough University, United Kingdom

- Tim Auburn, Plymouth University, United Kingdom

- Galina Bolden, Rutgers University, United States

- Paul Drew, Loughborough University, United Kingdom

- Alexa Hepburn, Rutgers University, United States

- Ian Hutchby, University of Leicester, United Kingdom

- Khalid Karim, University of Leicester, United Kingdom

- Nikki Kiyimba, University of Chester, United Kingdom

- Doug Maynard, University of Wisconsin, United States

- Trena Paulus, University of Georgia, United States

- Anita Pomerantz, University at Albany, United States

- Kathryn Roulston, University of Georgia, United States

- Trini Stickle, Western Kentucky University, United States

- Elizabeth Stokoe, Loughborough University, United Kingdom

- Tom Strong, University of Calgary, Canada

- Laura Thompson, Birkbeck University, United Kingdom

- Amber Warren, University of Nevada, Reno, United States

We would also like to acknowledge the input from SAGE's manuscript reviewers:

- Kate Anderson, Arizona State University, United States

- Michelle Lefevre, University of Sussex, United Kingdom

- Joanne McDowell, University of Hertfordshire, United Kingdom

- Chris McVittie, Queen Margaret University, United Kingdom

- Kathryn Roulston, University of Georgia, United States

• About the Authors •

Jessica Nina Lester, Ph.D. is an Associate Professor of Inquiry Methodology (Qualitative Research) in the School of Education at Indiana University, Bloomington. Dr. Lester has published over 50 peer-reviewed journal articles, as well as numerous books and book chapters focused on discourse and conversation analysis, disability studies, and more general concerns related to qualitative research. She is a co-author of the first edition of *Digital Tools for Qualitative Research,* published with SAGE. She has also co-edited a book focused on performance ethnographies (Peter Lang, 2013) and is currently co-authoring a book focused on applied conversation analysis with SAGE. More recently, Dr. Lester co-authored a research methods textbook with SAGE (*An introduction to educational research: Connecting methods to practice)* and served as the co-editor of *The Palgrave handbook of child mental health: Discourse and conversation studies* and *The Palgrave handbook of adult mental health: Discourse and conversation studies.* She is a founding member of the Microanalysis of Online Data international network, the Associate Director of the Conversation Analysis Research in Autism group at the University of Leicester, UK, and the former co-program chair and current chair of the Qualitative Research Special Interest Group (AERA). In 2014, Dr. Lester received AERA's Division D's Early Career Award in Measurement and Research Methodology (Qualitative Methodology) and has also won several teaching awards at Indiana University. She has most recently published in journals such as Qualitative Inquiry, Qualitative Research, and Discourse Studies.

Michelle O'Reilly, Ph.D. is a Senior Lecturer at the University of Leicester and a Research Consultant with Leicestershire Partnership NHS Trust. Michelle works in a multi-disciplinary way, working in Media, Communication and Sociology, as well as Neuroscience, Psychology and Behaviour in the university, and in child mental health research in the NHS. Michelle has research interests in child mental health, family therapy and neurodevelopmental disorders. She also contributes to the methodological literature, writing articles on critical issues in methods and on research ethics. She has published over 50 peer-reviewed articles and several books, including two handbooks on mental health with Palgrave. Michelle is currently the Director of the International research group Conversation Analysis Research in Autism (CARA), and works alongside practicing clinical professionals to ensure that the research conducted in child mental health has clinical application in practice.

Context and Planning

1

Introducing
Conversation Analysis

Chapter Focus

In this chapter, you will learn how to:

- Articulate the basic principles of conversation analysis.
- Describe the history of the approach.
- Define and evaluate the differences between mundane and institutional talk.
- Describe the various meanings of applied conversation analysis.
- Recognize the different types of applied conversation analysis.

This chapter introduces you to important assumptions and practices associated with conversation analysis (CA), providing you with the necessary information for making sense of the usefulness of CA to your own areas of interest. Overall, the focus of this book, and this chapter more specifically, is on the nature of applied CA and institutional talk. Closely related to applied CA is the idea of institutional talk, and indeed, there are some important differences between mundane/ordinary conversations and institutional talk. Understanding this distinction is crucial for making sense of the chapters that follow. We thus introduce you to these differences and discuss how they relate to CA generally and applied CA more specifically. We begin the chapter with a brief introduction to the history of CA and introduce you to its key influencers. After this, we provide you with an overview of the key messages of CA, which is followed by a discussion of the nuanced differences between mundane conversations and institutional talk. We conclude the chapter by providing a detailed overview of the meanings of applied CA, offering examples of the various types.

An Overview of Conversation Analysis

CA is a methodological approach to the study of **social interaction**, which attends to the details of **talk-in-interaction** and the sequential order of talk.

Social interaction in sociological terms refers to the changing sequence of actions that occurs between individuals or groups of people—that is, the conversations that occur between people.

Talk-in-interaction refers to the CA claim that language is meaningful within sequences of interactions with others.

Social actions refer to the performative aspects of talk. In other words, the way people *do* things with their talk, such as excusing, inviting, complaining, asking questions, and so on.

Put simply, CA aims to understand how social actors make sense of and respond to one another in their turns of talk. As such, conversation analysts are interested in the interactional organization of everyday and institutional social activities and the way people perform **social actions** with language in the context of social interaction.

For those who employ CA, then, it is central to study how social action is enacted by paying close attention to the organization of talk and examining how turns are designed to perform some action (Antaki, 2011). For instance, when someone says, "Would you like some more iced tea," the talk is not simply about the topic of tea, but, as Schegloff (2007b) noted, the talk might also be about "doing an offer" (pp. 1–3). One speaker, through talk, is offering something to another. Thus, the very social activity can be understood through a focus on interaction. Consider the following example, where a social action of an apology is being performed. Note that CA research uses a specialized transcription system, and this is represented in our data examples. To understand the meanings of the symbols, we advise you to refer to Chapter 6, where this is dealt with in detail.

```
Gordon:  Hey listen I'm sorry about last ni:ght,.hmhh
Dana:    Mm:,
```

(Drew & Hepburn, 2015, p. 7 of online version)

In this example, a specific social action is being undertaken by Gordon, the first speaker, where he issues an apology, "I'm sorry about last ni:ght." Drew and Hepburn (2015) noted that Gordon was apologizing for having called so late the previous night while observing that the transgression was not made explicit by the speaker. While Drew and Hepburn's article provides a much more detailed analysis, our point here is to illustrate what a social action might look like, using a specific example of an apology.

Within the methodological literature, it is generally accepted that CA is a qualitative methodology or approach that aims to investigate social interactions, and through these investigations show how people maintain the intersubjective coherence of such interactions (Drew, 2015). While we recognize that you can do coding or statistical analysis on CA data, which is discussed later in the book (see also Robinson, 2007; Stivers, 2015), CA is usually grouped under qualitative approaches. Further, CA involves the study of "natural" talk-in-interaction, with **naturally occurring data** being favored, and we discuss this in detail in Chapter 5.

> **Naturally occurring data** can be defined as data that exist regardless of the existence or presence of the researcher (Potter, 2002).

The most important point to bear in mind about CA is that it pays close attention to the organization of interaction and thereby inherently assumes that talk can be understood sequentially. CA assumes that people go about "doing" or performing social life through the very way they interact. Sacks (1992) argued that it is through the design of one's conversational turns that the visibility of the "happenings" of social life are made and how such turns set up normative expectations regarding what is to come next in the talk. In the broadest sense, conversation analysts are interested in answering questions such as:

- How do people carry out their everyday business in and through interaction?

- How do people design their turns at talk to perform social action?

- How do individuals then make the next turn and social action relevant in a way to shape the possible responses?

- How do people employ language to conjure up the social worlds of which they are a part? (Adapted from Antaki, 2011, p. 2)

It is important to note that much of the research and ideas of CA are founded on studies conducted in English, especially the early work. Thus, readers should be thoughtful when undertaking applied CA research in other languages and recognize that some of the work that they may be citing in their project may not always be fully translatable to their own work, as social actions pertinent in some cultures may not work in the same way in others. Notably, in more recent years, there have been many studies conducted in languages other than English that have contributed to our understanding of the complexity of talk and its meanings. This is discussed in more detail in Chapter 6 in relation to translation, and again in terms of the critiques of CA in Chapter 9.

(!)

> **CA encompasses both a method and a theoretical approach (McCabe, 2006).**

Theoretical Bases of CA

In terms of its theoretical foundations, CA has a social constructionist epistemology (O'Reilly & Kiyimba, 2015). CA can also be described as an emic approach in that it is one that prioritizes empirical evidence that illuminates the participants' own understandings of an issue (Bolden & Robinson, 2011). Appreciating the influence of the theoretical position of any qualitative methodology is important, as this helps to shape the practice of the analysis and contextualize the analytic claims made.

Social Constructionism

Social constructionism is recognized as a broad assembly of diverse approaches (Burr, 2003), and it does not represent a single position; rather, it can be understood as a rubric for a range of research efforts with similar empirical, theoretical, and methodological foundations (Gubrium & Holstein, 2008). Broadly, however, social constructionism advocates that the human experience, including perceptions, is not fixed or a predetermined aspect of an individual but rather is mediated linguistically, historically, and culturally (Burr, 2003).

The main work on social constructionism was introduced by Berger and Luckmann (1966), who argued that reality was socially constructed. They recognized that social stability happens through social order and noted that people interact within a social system, thus creating concepts and mental representations of their actions. In more recent work, social constructionism has been conceptualized as a movement that has included a recognition of the microlevel processes involved in the construction of knowledge (Gergen, 1985).

The primary premise of social constructionism is a rejection of absolute knowledge, with language itself argued to play a central role in the sharing of knowledge and the development of shared constructs (Zein, 2013). In this sense, experience and perceptions are understood to be mediated culturally, linguistically, and historically, and a critical perspective is offered about the taken-for-granted nature of knowledge. In this sense, knowledge is never understood as being objective but as always situated and tied to human practice (Gergen, 2004).

CA takes up a social constructionist position, as it adopts the view that knowledge is situated. More particularly, many CA scholars tend to take up a ***microsocial constructionism*** stance.

> **Microsocial constructionism** is concerned with the microstructures of language and focuses on talk, situated interactions, local culture, and interactional order (Gubrium & Holstein, 2008).

The relevance of microsocial constructionism can be seen in the underlying premise of the perspective that knowledge is not static but is co-constructed in the detail of mundane interactions in everyday life (Gubrium & Holstein, 2008). Thus, this type of social constructionism views language and interaction as central in the sense that language is viewed as a form of social action. For the sake of balance, we note that microsocial constructionism is typically contrasted with ***macrosocial constructionism***, a position underpinning some of the other language-based approaches, such as some forms of discourse analysis.

Macrosocial constructionism focuses on the constructive power of language and, in that way, orients to language as being shaped by social and material structures and social relations (Burr, 2003). The focus is thus on the notion of power and reflects the view that power is embedded in cultural and historical discourse (Chen, Shek, & Bu, 2011).

> **Macrosocial constructionism** attends to the role that linguistic and social structures play in shaping the social world (Gubrium & Holstein, 2008).

Our Theoretical Position

Our own theoretical position, which is reflected throughout our writing, is microsocial constructionism, which we view as particularly congruent with CA. Specifically, to ground this position, we draw upon the work of Harvey Sacks and other CA scholars, as well as the work of Edwards and Potter (1992), who espoused a discursive psychology approach closely aligned with CA. Our own work has focused predominantly on mental health; therapy; and the social construction of children, childhood, and disability more generally. With such a focus, our collective work has focused on people often positioned as vulnerable, allowing us to also consider how vulnerability is itself a social construct. Across our work, we have drawn upon both CA and discursive psychology. Notably, we take up the position that what we produce is partial and positional, and shaped by our subjectivities.

Emic Approach

There are two broad positions, the etic and the emic, which refer to two different approaches to research. These concepts first were discussed in linguistics and anthropology during the 1950s (Headland, 1990), and coined by Kenneth Pike from the suffixes of *phonetic* and *phonemic* (Harris, 1976). The etic approach is sometimes referred to as the *deductive approach, outsider perspective,* or *top-down position*, and begins from the point of theory or hypothesis. In other words, it argues that constructs such as analyses or accounts are defined in terms of categories constructed as appropriate by scientific scholars (Lett, 1990).

The emic approach is sometimes referred to as the *insider perspective,* the *inductive approach,* or the *bottom-up position*. This approach begins from the perspectives of the participants themselves, and constructs the descriptions and accounts participants express as categories that are perceived as meaningful by members of a culture (Lett, 1990). The focus for the emic approach is on researchers putting aside their own assumptions and focusing on the participants' perspectives (Lett, 1990). For CA, which takes an emic orientation, a priori assumptions are critiqued and questioned as the analysts examine interaction by observing what happens in a given setting. In other words, CA is emic as it explores the social world from the viewpoint of those who participate in the interactions. Thus, in CA terms, researchers work from the frame of reference of the participants—that is, emic—rather than imposing a frame of reference on the data—that is, etic (Taylor, 2001). In CA, an emic position is favored, as it focuses on material that is argued to emerge from participant perspectives engaged in naturally occurring activities (Potter, 2003).

A Summary of Conversation Analysis

We will return to many of the ideas presented in the chapter so far throughout the book, and as you go through the chapters, you will build your knowledge of the core concepts of CA and the ways in which analysis of this kind is built. There are some key ideas about CA that you need to keep in mind as you progress through the book, which we list in Table 1.1. Throughout the chapters, we explore each of these ideas in greater detail.

TABLE 1.1 ● Key messages about conversation analysis

Key Idea/Message	Description
Explores social actions	Conversation analysts are primarily interested in social action (Seedhouse, 2004). In other words, conversation analysts are interested in how language performs actions—that is, how people "do" things with their talk (e.g., excusing, complaining, disagreeing, inviting, apologizing, etc.).
Uses discursive resources	Conversation analysts explore the types of social organizations that are used as resources in interactions. CA investigates the methods utilized by speakers as they organize their social actions through talk (Mazeland, 2006).
Considers talk-in-interaction	Conversation analysis explores ordinary, everyday conversations and institutional talk, and in recent times uses the notion of talk-in-interaction to capture the complex and multifaceted nature of language.
(often) Collects naturally occurring events	Conversation analysts tend to rely on the recordings of naturally occurring talk. For instance, a conversation between a mother and her son at a local market will take place regardless of whether a researcher is audio or video recording the commonplace interaction. This type of data stands in contrast to researcher-generated data, which are data that require the researcher to produce them (e.g., interview data).
Uses the Jefferson transcription method	Conversation analysts are concerned with representing talk with a detailed transcript that captures how things are said (e.g., rising intonation, pauses), as well as what is said.

To summarize, ten Have (2007) highlighted four distinguishing characteristics of CA:

1. CA stays close to the phenomenon of interest by focusing on the detail of an interactional event, attending to the nuances of interaction, and producing a detailed transcript.

2. CA favors naturally occurring data because it conceives of talk as a situated achievement rather than a product of an artificial experiment or a researcher's intentions.

3. CA assumes that talk is orderly.

4. CA studies language as it is used within real-world interactions and focuses on talk-in-use.

What this means: Those who draw upon CA focus on what people actually do and say rather than what people report that they do and say, as well as how, within interaction, people negotiate meanings between themselves on a turn-by-turn basis (McCabe, 2006).

Before you continue further with the chapter, we recommend you pause for reflection and attempt the activity in Box 1.1.

BOX 1.1
ACTIVITY ON TERMINOLOGY

Activity

You likely noticed that conversation analysts tend to use some complex terminology, with many of these terms referring to conversational practices that you probably have an implicit awareness of. There will be many concepts and terms from our discussions of CA generally that are very relevant to the use of applied CA, and it is important that you can describe their meaning(s) in your own words. Therefore, as you work your way through the book, we encourage you to build a personalized glossary, as this will support you in developing your own applied research study.

Now is a good time to begin creating a glossary of core CA concepts and key terms used in applied CA. There are, indeed, many concepts and terms to consider, but we suggest you begin with the following:

- Emic
- Naturally occurring data
- Social action
- Social constructionism
- Talk-in-interaction

A Brief History of Conversation Analysis

To appreciate the value of applied CA, we first take you through a potted history of how the approach developed. CA was pioneered by a group in the United States during the 1960s, with much of this work positioned within the field of sociology. Key figures who developed CA were Harvey Sacks, Emanuel Schegloff, and Gail Jefferson. Sacks, a sociologist by training who eventually worked at UCLA, has generally been credited with the early beginnings of CA. His writing was greatly influenced by several scholars. Maynard and Clayman (2003) noted that these influential scholars included

> (!) Although there were many influences on the development of CA, its origins can be mostly traced back to the work of Goffman and Garfinkel (Schegloff, 2003).

- Garfinkel,

- Goffman,

- Chomsky,

- Wittgenstein, and

- Freud.

The works of these scholars had a great bearing on the way that CA was shaped, and their different ideas about language were important to the very way that CA is understood today.

In the 1960s, Sacks and Schegloff were both graduate students at the University of California at Berkeley, where Erving Goffman was teaching and developing a specific approach to sociological analysis. His approach was grounded in the observation of people interacting with one another, which he described as *the interaction order* (Goffman, 1983). This perspective influenced CA, particularly in relation to considering the value of studying face-to-face interaction.

> ● Goffman (1983) argued that **the interaction order** is enacted through social situations in which two or more people are present in a conversation. He argued that interaction is a "performance" shaped by the environment and audience. Thus, social actors follow conventions and norms within conversation.

Similarly, Garfinkel's (1967) work leading to the development of *ethnomethodology* was a significant influence on CA, with Garfinkel's work also being influenced by Goffman.

Specifically, Garfinkel (1967) described ethnomethodology as a focus on the analysis of "everyday activities" (p. vii), as he argued that ethnomethodology scholars aim to give accounts of social life. To demonstrate that interaction is orderly and that interlocutors orient to social norms within society, he conducted a range of experiments referred to as *breaching experiments* whereby students were encouraged to breach the

> ● **Ethnomethodology** is an approach that studies the methods people use for making descriptions of the social world reasonable and justifiable. In other words, it explores the methods that people use to understand and produce social order and the social norms in the world in which they live.

social norms in their everyday interactions to better understand the standard and normative rules that usually operate unnoticed (Garfinkel, 1967). The focus for ethnomethodology scholars, therefore, was to study how people make and describe the social facts of ordinary society, which are the things of **social order** (Garfinkel, 2002).

> **Social order** refers to the rules and social practices of society adhered to in order to maintain and enforce appropriate ways of behavior.

It is important to note that social order is not so easily defined as we have proffered here, and our definition is one designed for simplicity to just give you a sense of the meaning. Scholars have argued that there are two forms of order: that which refers to the "constitutive nature of face-to-face interaction" and that which refers to the "rule-driven nature of institutional interactions" (Rawls, 1989, p. 147). This reflects some difference between Garfinkel and Goffman, as Goffman was primarily concerned with representations of self whereby meaning and the self are interactional achievements produced in a local context (Goffman, 1959), but Garfinkel's arguments were more theoretical in nature (Rawls, 1989).

Ultimately, CA reflected a fusion of Goffman's and Garfinkel's approaches of devising an empirical method aimed at exploring how people produce order locally and in situated ways—that is, how they coordinate and accomplish activities in real interactions (McCabe, 2006). The very idea of studying participants' methods for producing and interpreting the world rather than applying a priori categories to the data was a rather bold claim. At the time, American sociology heavily favored using quantitatively oriented approaches wherein presumably objective categories were applied to data. However, informed by Goffman, Garfinkel, and others, Sacks and his colleagues argued for something radically different; that is, what people make relevant in their everyday activities was assumed to be worth examining.

While the influences of Garfinkel and Goffman are important in contextualizing the history of CA, it is helpful to consider the cross-pollination of early theories that also influenced Sacks. It is not our intention here to go into detail; rather, we provide a brief summary of the key people to indicate the general relevance of their ideas.

Ludwig Wittgenstein

While in his early work Wittgenstein noted that "the function of language is to represent objects in the world," he later made claims that it is crucial to examine language in practice and observe how social actors employ language in real situations (Maynard & Peräkylä, 2003, p. 237). He argued that philosophy should begin with the inspection of actual uses of language (Potter, 2001). This was particularly influential in CA, as it advocated for the examination of real language and actual talk, and assumed that language was performative; thus, today, CA scholars generally assume that language is always doing something.

Noam Chomsky

Chomsky began working at Massachusetts Institute of Technology in the 1950s and quickly became a prominent scholar in the field of linguistics. His seminal publication focused on syntactic structures, and it was this text (Chomsky, 1957) that began to lay the foundation for the scientific study of language. Notably, Chomsky's linguistic ideas were grounded in biolinguistics, in the sense that he argued that the structure of language is biologically predisposed and that all human beings share fundamental linguistic structures. Chomsky is a globally recognized pioneering theorist on the study of language and was generally influential in CA's focus on the study of language.

Sigmund Freud

Freud viewed language as fundamental to the framework of psychoanalysis (referring to a broad range of theories associated with a perspective on human development and psychotherapeutic techniques). Language was considered important to the therapeutic process, as language was argued to be necessary for consciousness (Freud, 1915). Freud argued that the human mind assimilates perceptual information through language, and because of language, people can make sense of their perceptions. While Freud may seem like an unlikely source of inspiration for Sacks, because of his focus on the hidden recesses of the inner mind, he was an astute observer of human behavior and pointed out things that initially may seem inconsequential to an analyst (Sidnell, 2010). Sidnell argued that indeed the influences on CA were complex and multifaceted, and while not all were direct or profound, theoretical ideas and work by scholars such as Freud were influential to Sacks's thinking.

The Early Years

During his early work in developing CA, Sacks was a fellow at the Center for the Scientific Study of Suicide, where he studied audio recordings of telephone calls to a suicide prevention helpline. This interest shaped the central premises of CA—that is, when people talk, it is not simply descriptive; rather, the conversation itself is the site of social action (Drew, 2015). It was this initial work that allowed Sacks to develop many of the ideas that are foundational to CA.

By studying the interactions produced on the helplines, Sacks examined the levels of social order revealed through the practice of talking and noted that ordinary conversation is both ordered and organized structurally. In other words, through his interest in the interactions, he sought to demonstrate the rules that were demonstrably attended to by the speakers during the telephone calls.

> For example: One observation Sacks noted was that a core rule of conversation is that when one speaker introduces him- or herself, the recipient will do likewise.

Sacks noted that it was common in the calls for this to happen and cited several examples of this in his first lecture (Sacks, 1992, p. 3):

```
A: This is Mr Smith may I help you

B: Yes, this is Mr Brown
```

However, Sacks also noted that when this normative sequence did not occur, there was a display of some trouble, and the usual second part of the sequence did not then occur.

```
A: This is Mr Smith may I help you

B: I can't hear you.

A: This is Mr Smith.

B: Smith.
```

It was this problem that captured Sacks's attention, as it did not follow the usual pattern he had observed in so many of the other telephone calls, and by observing a different form in this example, it also revealed something about the normative calls. He argued that this represented a "procedural rule" where the first speaker chooses his or her form of address and this is responded to (p. 4). Thus, this was a way of requesting a person's name without asking a question.

What is most noticeable is that Sacks's main interest was in the production of talk-in-interaction and the organization of conversation rather than the nature or setting in which talk was produced. Thus, this early work was important in laying the foundation for the study of social interaction.

While Sacks was working on this suicide center data, other important figures in the origins of CA were also working alongside him to facilitate the development of those ideas. Early on, Sacks worked with Gail Jefferson and Emanuel Schegloff (Drew et al., 2015), and they were later joined by Don Zimmerman and Doug Maynard,

> (!) **Sacks's analytic interest was not in suicide or calls about suicidal ideation and how they are presented; rather, he was interested in the organization of the talk (Drew, Heritage, Lerner, & Pomerantz, 2015).**

who offered new insights (Maynard, Clayman, Halkowski, & Kidwell, 2010). The combined interests of these scholars began to generate a new turn in the emphasis on the language-focused work they were undertaking.

Contemporary Conversation Analysis

Over time, CA has developed considerably through increasing publications, CA-focused conferences, growing interest in CA-focused graduate programs and professional training, and international networks of and professional organizations for conversation analysts (e.g., International Society for Conversation Analysis). During the 1980s, a large corpus of work began to illuminate the relationship between talk and the social structural contexts in which the talk is embedded (Maynard et al., 2010). Maynard et al. (2010) noted that this focus continued through the 1990s as there was strong graduate student participation and interest in CA across sociology, education, linguistics, and other disciplines. Contemporary CA has grown further and is now popular across disciplines ranging from sociology to linguistics to psychology to anthropology to education

Interlocutors are those who take part in a conversation (i.e., individuals or speakers participating in the interaction).

and to health, among others. Notably, over the last 50 years, the technical aspects of talk-in-interaction have received greater attention, and more focused studies of how *interlocutors* perform and coordinate their activities through language have been published (Drew, 2015).

Further, conversation analysts have made consistent contributions to understanding talk in workplace settings, offering practical advice to speakers, and to practitioners more specifically (see Stokoe, Hepburn, & Antaki, 2012, for a discussion and examples of how CA has been used in ways directly relevant to practitioners). For instance, Stokoe (2011) developed the conversation analytic role-play method, which uses audio and video recordings of interactions in communication training with professionals across a variety of workplace contexts. CA serves as the basis of this model, which has an explicit focus on making the findings of CA relevant to practitioners.

An Introduction to Mundane Talk and Institutional Talk

To better understand applied CA, it is helpful to develop an understanding of the initial focus that conversation analysts had on mundane or ordinary talk. Initially, much

Mundane or **ordinary conversations** can be defined as those conversations not confined in any way to a specialized setting or to the execution of a specific task (Heritage, 2005).

of the early work by conversation analysts focused on *mundane* or *ordinary conversations,* although it should be recognized that Sacks did study telephone calls to a suicide center but was interested in the structures of conversation rather than institutionality.

For example: An ordinary or mundane conversation could be considered an everyday conversation at a coffee shop between friends or a dinnertime conversation with a partner.

To give you some context, we provide you with an example of some ordinary talk taken from family mealtime conversations that is drawn from the research of Wiggins (2014, p. 11):

```
Mum:     cranberry ↓je:lly Darr↑en::

Darren:  ooh no::

Mum:     not like ↑it

Darren:  I hate cranberries

         (1.4)
```

```
Mum: >it's just like< mint ↓jelly only

     Cranbe(hh)rries heh heh (0.4)
```

A mundane dinnertime conversation like the one represented in Wiggins (2014) can be viewed as mundane talk. In other words, it is talk that occurs between people without an organizational task or focus. This kind of interaction is placed in contrast to what is commonly referred to as ***institutional talk***.

> ● **Institutional talk** is that which not only takes place in an institutional setting but also deals with an institutional task.

Within CA research, the interest in institutional or workplace conversations can be traced back to the publication of *Order in Court* (Atkinson & Drew, 1979), which focused on studying the nature of courtroom conversations. Since this point, there has been a growing interest in talk produced in various institutional settings, including clinics (Silverman, 1997), classrooms (McHoul, 1978; Mehan, 1979), and police emergency services (Walen & Zimmerman, 1987; Zimmerman, 1984), to name a few. Across this body of work, it is assumed that what positions the interaction as institutional is not theories of social structure but the unique speech-exchange system that participants orient to in their talk.

Institutional interactions often have characteristics that set them apart from other everyday interactions, making them distinct and explicitly linked to the space in which they are produced. Interactional events that are considered institutional are those in which the "participants' institutional or professional identities are somehow made relevant to the work activities in which they are engaged," as well as the goals and purposes that may be specific to a particular setting (Drew & Heritage, 1992, p. 4).

> For example: Therapeutic conversations differ from mundane conversations (O'Reilly, 2006), as the members within the therapeutic relationship often take up certain identities (e.g., therapist) and deploy specific rights (e.g., a therapist offers support to a patient).

Take a look at the next example, quoted from O'Reilly, Kiyimba, and Karim (2016, p. 484) and their work on child mental health assessments.

```
Prac: What we've been asked to do is to think about (0.57)
      the time that Simon's been hurting himself with
      (1.12) school because they're really worried about
      that so we the idea was that we would check that out
      (0.79) today (0.97) okay

      ((Mother and Family Support Worker nod))
```

In this example, you can see that the Prac (practitioner) draws attention to the institutionality of the talk by identifying the specific role that she has in the child's (Simon's) self-harm. In this way, the professional identity of the practitioner is made relevant in the talk as she outlines the task in hand, stating, "What we've been asked to do is think about (0.57) the time that Simon's been hurting himself with (1.12) school . . . " Further, the organizational task is also invoked with, "We would check that out (0.79) today."

It is perhaps not surprising, then, that institutional talk is often assumed to be informed and shaped by reference to the goals or explicit purposes of a given setting (Atkinson, 1982). The institutionality of talk is not determined by the setting alone. Rather, the institutionality of talk is related to how the participants orient to their institutional or professional identities as being relevant to the work activities in which they are engaged (Drew & Heritage, 1992).

As another example of institutional talk, we provide two extracts from Levinson's (1992) analysis of the talk produced in an English court of law where a defense lawyer is found cross-examining a rape victim. In this setting, the victim responds to the questions asked as per the normative conversational rule: If a question is asked, an answer should be provided. However, the order and structure of this interaction is shaped by the rules of a court of law.

Extract 1:

Lawyer: Your aim that evening then was to go to the discotheque?

Victim: Yes.

Lawyer: Presumably you had dressed up for that, had you?

Victim: Yes.

Lawyer: And you were wearing make-up?

Victim: Yes.

Lawyer: Eye-shadow?

Victim: Yes.

Lawyer: Lipstick?

Victim: No I was not wearing lipstick.

Lawyer: You weren't wearing lipstick?

Victim: No.

Lawyer: Just eye-shadow, eye make-up?

Victim: Yes.

Lawyer: A powder presumably?

Victim: Foundation cream, yes.

(Adapted from Levinson, 1992, pp. 82–83)

In considering Extract 1, we gain some insight related to the context where this talk was produced. First, the question–answer format is quite unique. Rather than posing questions where the questioner (in this case the lawyer) does not know the answer, the questions produced are all known-answer questions. The lawyer already knows the answer to the posed questions. Levinson (1992) noted that known-answer questions are often most appropriate when constructing an argument, which in this case is sensible given that the lawyer seeks to "form a 'natural' argument for the jury" (p. 84).

Extract 2:

Lawyer: . . . you have had sexual intercourse on a previous occasion haven't you?

Victim: Yes.

Lawyer: On many previous occasions?

Victim: Not many.

Lawyer: Several?

Victim: Yes.

Lawyer: With several men?

Victim: No. Just one. Two.

Lawyer: Two. And you are seventeen and a half?

Victim: Yes.

(Adapted from Levinson, 1992, pp. 82–83)

In considering Extract 2, we see that the questions function to create a certain image of the victim; in this case, a woman with questionable morals. In other words, the very format of the questions makes visible how the participants orient to the courtroom context.

Notably, it is important to remember that the boundaries between institutional talk and mundane talk can be blurred, and that institutional settings can be full of mundane talk.

For example: Two teachers may sit in the staff room of a school talking about a date they went on over the weekend. This is not institutional talk just because it is taking place in an institutional setting.

For the talk to be classified as institutional talk, the conversation must be attending to institutional business in some way, with the speakers often adopting or orienting to some role when interacting.

For example: Two teachers may be discussing a difficult child and working out ways in which they may deal with a child's behavior in the classroom. This is institutional talk, as it has institutional relevance.

For example: A health professional may make a home visit, checking in with a patient in his or her home. Although such an interaction takes place in a noninstitutional environment, an institutional task may still be conducted and, therefore, this may be institutional talk.

Quite often, you will find that the turn-taking organization, overall structural organization, and sequence organization of institutional talk is quite different from what might be found in mundane talk (Heritage, 2015).

What this means: Institutional talk can be thought of as being more restricted than the talk in everyday conversations. Although the organization of talk follows in institutional talk, it is also defined by institutional rules and context.

To understand institutional talk, it is helpful to consider a seminal paper that Sacks, Schegloff, and Jefferson (1974) wrote discussing the range of ways in which ordinary talk might be produced in relation to turn taking. We suggest you access and read this now, as it will help you consider how such turn-taking rules that occur in ordinary conversation also apply in institutional settings:

- Sacks, H., Schegloff, E., & Jefferson, G. (1974). A simplest systematic for the organization of turn-taking for conversation. *Language, 50,* 696–735.

As CA has grown, there has been increasing interest in the study of institutional talk. Much of this work has been tightly connected to understandings of applied CA, which we discuss next. However, before continuing, we recommend that you complete the activity in Box 1.2.

An Overview of Applied CA

Sacks and his colleagues originally developed CA as an effort to produce a "pure science," one wherein the conversation analyst studies how social action is brought about in and through conversation. In fact, Sacks, in the early days of CA, did not deliberately intend for CA to have application (Silverman, 1998). However, many CA researchers sought to apply their findings to areas of practice, and over time, a

BOX 1.2
ACTIVITY ON MUNDANE AND INSTITUTIONAL TALK

Activity

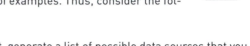

It is often helpful to practice distinguishing between the meaning of mundane talk and institutional talk by generating a "bank" or corpus of examples. Thus, consider the following tasks:

- Considering your substantive area of interest, generate a list of possible data sources that you might classify as mundane talk, and describe why these specific data sources might be useful and informative to your field of study.

- Again, considering your substantive area of interest, generate a list of possible data sources that you might classify as institutional talk, and describe why these data sources might be useful and informative to your field of study.

distinction was made between what is commonly referred to as ***pure CA*** and ***applied CA***.

We would, however, caution the reader to take some care in passively conceptualizing the two forms of CA in this way for several reasons.

- First, while they are conceptualized as two distinctive approaches to CA, there is some overlap between them.

- Second, we recognize that the language used to categorize these different forms of CA might not be entirely appropriate. The notion of "pure" implies that applied CA is secondary or less valuable by virtue of the meaning of "pure."

- Third, it is important to acknowledge that this distinction is less about the structures of conversation and more about the ways in which they reveal social processes.

- Fourth, much mundane talk occurs in institutional settings and thus is analyzed as pure CA but can have implications in applied settings.

Pure CA (sometimes referred to as basic CA) has been described as the analysis of ordinary or mundane conversations to explore the organization and structure of interaction.

In contrast, **applied CA** has been broadly defined as that which investigates talk in institutional settings (McCabe, 2006).

Because of these issues, we argue that it is better to conceptualize these two types of CA as *traditional CA* and *applied CA*.

Nonetheless, in the literature, the distinction is conceptualized as pure and applied. The distinction made is that pure CA examines the institution of interaction as an item in its own right, whereas applied CA examines the management of social institutions in interaction (Heritage, 2004). It is applied CA that is the focus of this book, and while we do draw upon general CA literature throughout, it is important to understand what applied CA is. Ten Have (2001) conceptualized applied CA in two distinct ways.

- First, applied CA can be the application of the findings of pure CA studies to the study of institutional interactions. For instance, one might study the interactions that occur in a school or hospital and look at these interactions through an application of the general work produced in traditional CA, such as looking at how adjacency pairs work in school interactions.

- Second, applied CA can be thought of as including the efforts that are involved in applying CA findings to offer practical advice to organizations or people's practices. For instance, conversation analysts might work directly with clinicians to share their CA findings with them and potentially shape their future practice (see, for instance, the work of Stokoe, 2011).

Notably, applied CA research studies can also focus on mundane settings. For example, you might carry out a study of mundane conversations, such as family mealtimes, and use the findings to inform institutional professionals through training about children's talk. However, while we acknowledge this important caveat to the definition of applied CA, most applied CA research studies are conducted in institutional settings, and thus in this book, as its title suggests, we concentrate on this type of CA.

With a growing focus on applied CA and institutional talk, over time the purposes and intent of applied CA have expanded, resulting in different types of applied CA (Antaki, 2011). We outline the six types or approaches to applied CA as identified by Antaki (2011) in Table 1.2 and return to many of these types throughout the book.

TABLE 1.2 ● Six types of applied CA

Type of Applied CA	Description
Foundational applied CA	This type seeks to reframe or respecify foundational concepts within a discipline, such as psychiatry, as being produced in and through communicative acts. A useful example of foundational applied CA is Edwards and Potter's (1992) work around discursive psychology wherein they sought to respecify psychologized constructs (such as memory) as being fundamentally interactional (rather than internal) and dependent upon the communicational acts that make them real. In many ways, this is similar to how Sacks and his colleagues offered the field of sociology a rather radical alternative to the study of social life.

Type of Applied CA	Description
Social-problem-oriented applied CA	This type is aimed at better understanding social problems and institutions, and addressing macro issues such as class, gender, power, etc. Maynard (1988) suggested that CA has the potential to offer a useful and distinct perspective on "such traditionally-identified social problems" (p. 311), particularly in that many analytic approaches to such macro concerns have not attended to talk-in-interaction in the way that CA does. Kitzinger's (2005, 2008) work around heteronormativity and feminist CA is an important exemplar of social-problem-oriented applied CA.
Communication applied CA	This type attends to disordered talk with the intent of understanding its features. Additionally, in some cases, this work aims to challenge how a disorder and even deficiency has been classed and conceptualized, particularly in that CA explicitly considers how *all* social actors engage in social life. For instance, some work has highlighted the communicational competence of individuals who might otherwise be assumed to be incompetent (Goodwin, 2003). A useful example of this type of applied CA work is Ray Wilkinson's (2015) work on aphasia.
Diagnostic applied CA	This type is perhaps the most controversial, as it attempts to correlate the organization of people's speech with an underlying disorder. This approach to CA theoretically seeks to correlate speech patterns with a given medical diagnosis. A useful example of this type of work is Schwabe, Howell, and Reuber's (2007) research on diagnosing epilepsy.
Institutional applied CA	This type of applied CA typically focuses on studying how an institution carries out institutional work. This approach has not traditionally sought to solve problems or even intervene. Rather, it has traditionally reflected the shift from mundane talk to institutional talk, with studies of the courtroom (Atkinson & Drew, 1979) and classroom (McHoul, 1978) being early examples. A more recent example is O'Reilly, Karim, Stafford, and Hutchby's (2015) work on child mental health assessments.
Interventionist applied CA	This type attends to preexisting problems with the intent to intervene or offer solutions based on CA findings. Specifically, this approach to applied CA assumes that (a) the problem existed prior to the researcher engaging in his or her work; (b) a solution to the problem is likely to emerge based on sequential analysis of the talk; and (c) the research is undertaken collaboratively, with the researcher and practitioner both involved in the process. Several useful examples of interventionist applied CA can be found in Antaki's (2011) edited volume.

Source: Antaki, 2011.

An Interview With Professor Charles Antaki

In this chapter, we have introduced you to some of the distinguishing qualities of applied CA. Notably, Antaki's (2011) book on applied CA has been instrumental in the modern understanding of applied CA research and, more particularly, distinguishing the different types of applied CA. We therefore interviewed him about some of the fundamental aspects of applied CA. His responses are outlined in Box 1.3.

BOX 1.3
INTERVIEW WITH PROFESSOR CHARLES ANTAKI

Charles Antaki is a professor of language and social psychology at Loughborough University. Professor Antaki is well known for his CA work on intellectual disabilities and his contributions to applied CA. Professor Antaki self-classifies as a social psychologist and a conversation analyst. He edited the influential text on applied conversation analysis:

- Antaki, C. (Ed.). (2011). *Applied conversation analysis: Intervention and change in institutional talk.* Hampshire, England: Palgrave Macmillan.

We asked Professor Antaki three questions about applied CA, and his answers to these questions are provided here.

How does applied CA differ from CA?

"Applied CA has some similarities to basic CA. Those practicing applied CA take the findings of basic CA, in other words the rules and structures of conversation, and they examine how they operate in specific settings. In other words, applied CA, like CA, examines the rules and structures of conversation, but applied CA has an interest in these structures in institutional settings. So examples of questions that applied conversation analysts might ask include:

- How do police officers interview suspects?
- How do doctors diagnose symptoms?
- How do customers get their complaints dealt with by a call center?"

Why do you think applied CA is important?

"Applied CA tells the analyst how the rules that we know about talk, gained from our understanding of basic CA, are used in interactions to get specific jobs done. So examples of this include things like the police interview or the doctor's diagnosis, and other such institutional accomplishments. Additionally, applied CA reveals new patterns of talk that are specific to local situations. A good example of this is your next-door neighbor does not talk to you in the same way as your doctor will talk to you. So applied CA is interested in where exactly the differences are. Some of them are obvious and common sense, but applied CA can reveal the subtler ones too."

What initially motivated you to study institutional talk?

"I was involved in a study of how adults with intellectual disabilities were supported by care staff. Some members of the staff were obviously better at providing this support than others, and I wanted to see how exactly they talked (and listened) to their clients. If CA could identify good communication practice, that could be passed on in training and improve the lives of a vulnerable group of people. In other words, applied CA can help to make useful recommendations to improve areas of practice across a range of institutional settings."

Chapter Summary

In this chapter, we provided you with a general overview of the history of CA and introduced you to some of the foundational features of CA. We have also discussed the differences between mundane talk and institutional talk, with the focus on institutional talk bringing to the fore an applied form of CA. Subsequently, we introduced you to the development and various meanings of applied CA, which is the primary focus of this book. The key learning points from the chapter are summarized in the next box.

Learning Points From Chapter 1

- Conversation analysis is a robust and data-driven approach that examines talk-in-interaction from naturally occurring situations.

- There is a distinction drawn between pure/basic CA (the study of mundane conversation) and applied CA (the study of institutional talk).

- Applied CA has the potential to inform practice for those who work in applied settings.

Recommended Readings

There are several key references that are useful for developing background knowledge in basic CA and applied CA. We encourage you to explore the following publications as you further develop your understanding of CA and its relation to your research interests.

- Antaki, C. (2011). Six kinds of applied conversation analysis. In C. Antaki (Ed.), *Applied conversation analysis: Intervention and change in institutional talk* (pp. 1–4). Hampshire, England: Palgrave Macmillan.

In this chapter, Antaki introduces an edited text that contains examples of applied CA work. In so doing, he provides an overview of what applied CA is and examines the different types of applied CA in detail. This chapter serves as a useful introduction to applied CA as it points to other helpful sources of information.

- Drew, P. (2015). Conversation analysis. In J. Smith (Ed.), *Qualitative psychology* (pp. 108–142). London, England: Sage.

(Continued)

(Continued)

In this chapter, Drew provides an in-depth and insightful overview of CA. The discussion is methodological in scope and offers a general introduction to the analytic approach. This chapter also provides some useful references for further study.

- Drew, P., & Heritage, J. (Eds.). (1992). *Talk at work: Interaction in institutional settings*. Cambridge, England: Cambridge University Press.

In this edited book, Drew and Heritage include a variety of CA studies that focus on the study of work settings, all of which are positioned as institutional. The contributing authors focus on a range of institutional contexts, including criminal justice and medical environments.

- Maynard, D., Clayman, S., Halkowski, T., & Kidwell, M. (2010). Toward an interdisciplinary field: Language and social interaction research at the University of California, Santa Barbara. In W. Leeds-Hurwitz (Ed.), *The social history of language and social interaction research* (pp. 313–333). Cresskill, NJ: Humana Press.

In this chapter, Maynard and his colleagues provide a detailed overview of the history of CA. The chapter takes the reader through the key dates in the history of CA and introduces many of its most influential figures.

Examining the Basic Principles of Conversation Analysis

> ## Chapter Focus
>
> In this chapter, you will learn how to:
>
> - Recognize the basic conversational structures central to conversation analysis.
> - Apply the core features or structures of conversation to analysis.
> - Assess the importance of membership categories in analysis.
> - Assess the relevance of embodied action in institutional contexts.

While this book focuses on the practical issues involved in undertaking an applied conversation analysis (CA) research study, it is important to familiarize yourself with the foundational work in CA that informs applied CA research. Thus, in this chapter, we introduce you to the basic building blocks of CA—that is, the core principles that underpin applied CA. Indeed, prior to undertaking any form of analysis, it is important that you have a good working knowledge of these conversational structures. However, we recognize that in this chapter (and more broadly this book) we are only touching the surface and suggest that if you are relatively unfamiliar with CA, you engage in further reading and study to better ground your research practice. In other words, although we give you a general overview of some of the foundational principles central to CA, we recommend that you continue reading, identify useful examples of their use in published studies, and turn to mentors and colleagues for further guidance (if possible).

We begin this chapter by briefly returning to the importance of talk-in-interaction, positioning this as a central assumption within any CA study. We then turn to describing some of the fundamental structures that are central when *doing* CA. Furthermore, we also draw your attention to some other key analytical considerations of CA, including membership categorization devices and embodied interaction. In his early work, Sacks (1972) considered the importance of categorization in talk-in-interaction and demonstrated how particular categories (e.g., mother, teacher, son, woman, etc.) could be utilized rhetorically to perform some social action. We thus provide you with an introduction to this to illustrate the form and function of such categorical devices. Additionally, in contemporary CA, there has been greater attention on embodied action (Heath & Luff, 2013). As such, we conclude by very briefly introducing you to a few considerations related to focusing on embodied action in institutional contexts.

Revisiting the Focus on Talk-in-Interaction

In Chapter 1, we introduced you to the fundamental characteristics of CA, which are centered around talk-in-interaction. We emphasized that talk-in-interaction is defined by those practicing CA as language that is meaningful within sequences of interaction, and that through this sequentially organized language people perform social actions. Thus, talk-in-interaction is understood in terms of what talk is *doing* rather than simply what talk *is about* (Schegloff, 1999). In CA, it is through this focus on talk-in-interaction (as well as text-in-interaction) as *performative* that a systematic investigation of the talk is pursued.

(!) **In a CA study, talk(and/ or text)-in-interaction is the object of study and is more than simply a conversation (Hutchby & Wooffitt, 2008).**

Central to this notion of talk-in-interaction is that social interaction involves meaning making, and every action to some extent is creative in the meaning it creates and conveys (Heritage, 2011). Further, a study of talk-in-interaction involves careful consideration of the fundamental structures of conversation, which we examine next.

Fundamental Structures of Conversation

As noted, this chapter is concerned with the basic principles of CA—that is, the tools used to build or carry out analysis, with these tools being considered the fundamental structures of conversation. In the recent *Handbook of Conversation Analysis* (Sidnell & Stivers, 2013), an entire segment of the book was devoted to the fundamental structures of conversation whereby leading conversation analysts considered the foundational principles of CA. Thus, our purpose in this chapter is to provide you with a general overview to many (but not all) of these foundational structures as a base understanding of how CA works generally. In doing so, our aim is to provide you with the information needed to relate these foundational structures to the work of applied CA. While we present these foundational structures individually, it is critical to note that they are related in important ways.

Sequence Organization and Practices

Conversation analysts argue that the structure and sequencing of conversational turns is important in an interaction. In the literature, this has been evidenced with two of the basic tools of CA.

- The first is the concept of ***sequence organization***, which relates to the core assumption of CA that in any human interaction the current action or talk should be responsive to the conversational turn immediately prior to it (Heritage, 2011).

> **Sequence organization** refers to the orderly nature of talk-in-interaction. In other words, talk tends to occur in sequences through a series of turn taking.

> For example: In many contexts, there is a shared understanding that a speaker's greeting such as "Hello, how are you?" will be followed by the normative or expected response by the recipient, such as "I'm fine" (Heritage, 2011).

> For example: In our own data from mental health assessments, there were many question-and-answer sequences, like the following, where a question was asked and an answer was given, and another question was asked in response to that answer, and so on (O'Reilly, Kiyimba, & Karim, 2016, p. 484).

```
Prac: Yeah so you hit doors anything else?

YP:   No

Prac: Or hurting yourself?

YP:   Yeah

Prac: What d'you do?

YP:   I slit my wrists once

Prac: When was that?

YP:   Erm (1.44) when we went doctors and they referred to
      CAMHS*
```

*CAMHS—Child and Adolescent Mental Health Service (United Kingdom)

So one of CA's primary arguments is that it is through sequence organization that the tasks that are fundamental to talk-in-interaction are managed by interlocutors

(Heritage, 2005). Sequences are therefore made up of a series of turns, with the claim that in interaction, the current action is typically responsive to the turn that is immediately prior to it (Schegloff, 2007b).

- The second basic tool of CA is the notion of ***practices***, which is a concept that refers to the feature of a turn that has

  ○ a distinctive character,
  ○ specific locations within the turn or sequence, and
  ○ unique consequences for the meaning of the action that is implemented by the turn (Sidnell, 2013).

Practices are a component of a speaker's turn that demonstrate the social action that is being performed by the turn.

Heritage (2011) argued that there are three stages when identifying practices using conversation analysis. The first stage is to decide whether a practice is distinctive. He utilized an example from his own work on the practice of the word *oh* (Heritage, 1984). Heritage (2011) noted that initially the practice will emerge as interesting and the researcher will see this as worthy of further investigation. At first, these may be vague (Schegloff, 1997). The second stage is to locate that practice sequentially. In the case of the practice of oh, Heritage (1984) recognized that the production of oh was frequently located at the beginning of a turn. The third stage is to determine the meaning of the practice—that is, its distinctive role. In the case of the practice oh, it was clear that oh-prefaced responses to a question tended to be identified in contexts whereby the question was questioning something either stated or strongly implied, and thus the response was self-evident (Heritage, 2011). Furthermore, Heritage noted that oh in a turn-initial position indicated a change in the local current state of knowledge (Heritage, 1984). Consider the example of this practice, quoted from Heritage (1984, p. 303), where you will see that the oh produced by "J" occurs in the first position and signals a change of knowledge state.

```
V:   Oh I met Jan:ie, eh::m yesterday an' she'd
     had a fo:rm from the Age Concern about that
     jo:b .h=
J:→ = Oh she has?
```

It is important to recognize that practices are not concrete items within an interaction. If a practice is to be effective, the recipient within the interaction needs to be able to recognize what action the speaker means by employing that practice (Sidnell, 2013). As Sidnell noted, "For human interaction to work efficiently, a recipient must be able not only to recognize what action a practice is meant to accomplish, but also to check that his/her understanding of it is correct, or at least sufficient" (p. 78).

Turn Design

At the center of the speaker's conduct within talk-in-interaction is the notion of *turn design*. This notion relates to how speakers construct their turn within the interaction, and how what they select is done in a way that it can be understood as performing a social action (Drew, 2013).

> **Turn design** refers to the way in which speakers construct their turn within a sequence of turns to perform a specific social action.

Drew (2013) suggested that there are three key principles that shape turn design:

1. The location within the sequence where the turn is taken

2. What social action is being performed by the speaker's turn

3. The recipient of the turn—that is, to whom the turn is addressed

Speakers design their turns at talk to be heard by the recipient(s). Thus, the design of a turn is contingent upon the prior turn of the previous speaker, and the turn sets up contingencies for the subsequent turn. This process is termed the *principle of contiguity*, which refers to the fit between the current turn and the turn that preceded it (Sacks, 1987).

> The **principle of contiguity** relates to the close temporal relationship between two turns in an interaction.

Therefore, for conversation analysts, there are contingent connections between a turn and its prior turn, and such contingencies create a need for the next responsive turns and the sequences of connected turns; that is, the progress of the conversational sequence of turns relates to the interlocutors' understanding of what other interlocutors are doing in the prior turns (Drew, 2013). This understanding is considered in CA terms to be *intersubjectivity*, which can be thought of as the shared meanings that are co-constructed in and through the interlocutors' interaction.

> **Intersubjectivity** refers to the shared meanings constructed by speakers in their interactions.

In the context of CA, it is possible to examine how a recipient responds to the prior turn of the original speaker. As such, by focusing on the recipient's orientation to the original speaker's turn, it is possible to frame the analysis as grounded in what the speaker meant by producing a turn; this approach is referred to as the *next turn proof procedure* (Sidnell, 2013).

> The **next turn proof procedure** refers to the understanding of the prior turn as displayed within the interaction, with the recipient's understanding of the prior speaker's turn making relevant the construction of the next turn.

BOX 2.1
ACTIVITY ON ENGAGING IN LISTENING AND LOOKING AT A YOUTUBE VIDEO

Activity

Locate and view a news interview on YouTube. Any video will work. As you view the video, consider the various structures of conversation—specifically, sequence organization and turn design. We encourage you to view the video several times. The first time you view the video, you may just want to "note what you note." The second time you view the video, you may want to attend to sequence organization. Finally, the third time you view the video, you may want to attend to turn design. In other words, look at the relationship between the speaker's turn at talk and see how the recipient treats it; that is, what kind of action does the recipient take this to be?

Now, take a moment to apply what you have learned thus far by completing the activity in Box 2.1.

Turn Construction Units and the Transition Relevance Place

Conversation analysts recognize that conversational turns are produced in real time, and the organizational difficulty faced is in determining when speakers will complete their current turn (Sacks, Schegloff, & Jefferson, 1974). Sacks and colleagues argued that the basis of this system was the ***Turn Construction Unit (TCU)***, which refers to pieces or segments of an interaction that make up a complete turn in the talk.

The following example from a family therapy session shows how a single question from the therapist had a clear beginning and end, which constituted a TCU.

> The **Turn Construction Unit (TCU)** is defined as a unit of talk that makes up a turn in talk and is comprised of sentences, clauses, or even a single word.

> For example:
>
> ```
> FT:   ↑Can I jus' (.) is it ↑alright for us t' >talk about
>       this<
> ```
>
> (O'Reilly & Parker, 2014, p. 299)

Clayman (2013) noted that there are certain indicators that mark or indicate a TCU completion:

- The first is syntax. This is where the syntax indicates an impending completion. Thus, TCUs are organized by syntactic rules that project completion.

- The second is prosody. Syntax may not be sufficient for projecting completion, as some sentences contain more than one syntactic completion point. Thus, utterances are recurrently packaged as coherent syntactic units and as prosodic units (see also Walker, 2013, for a further discussion of this).

- The third is pragmatics. This is where the TCU is understood regarding the action(s) that it projects. So the recipient needs to ascertain the form being produced, which can be used to project completion of the turn.

- The fourth is gaze. Gaze is commonplace in communication and can facilitate sequence-initiating actions as well as turn completion actions.

> (!) **Notably, however, not all TCUs have easily recognizable endings, and not all are completed.**

> (!) **There are some occasions where TCUs are aborted by the speaker (Clayman, 2013).**

This discussion brings us nicely into another element of a conversational turn, which is the ***Transition Relevance Place (TRP)***. Conversation analysts assume that a recipient can project when a speaker is going to finish his or her turn at a point, and refer to this point as the TRP. So in this way, the completion of a TCU establishes a TRP, and it is here that a change of speaker becomes a possibility (Clayman, 2013).

We invite you to consider the following two examples drawn from interactional data:

> ● The **Transition Relevance Place (TRP)** is the place in the turn at talk whereby the conversational floor can be legitimately passed from one speaker to another and tends to occur at the completion of a TCU.

For example:

```
Prac:    ok and when you with a- the problem with ten-year-
         old girls or nine-year-old girls who are nearly ten
         (0.6) is that there's a lot of falling out yeah?

Child:   ((nods head))
```

(Antaki and O'Reilly, 2014, p. 335)

In this example, if you carefully consider the practitioner's (Prac's) turn, you will note that there is a 0.6-second pause in the middle. It could be thought that this is the TRP, but the initial part of the turn sets up a "problem," and thus the suggestion is that the problem is yet to be stated. So although there is sufficient space for the next speaker to come in and take the conversational floor, the TRP has not yet been indicated, and thus the TCU is clearly not complete. Indeed, the completion of the turn is signaled with the questioning "yeah?" and it is here that we see the child come in with a response. Likewise, the end of a turn can be projected by the next speaker as he or she orients to the TRP.

```
Prac:   Kolomban do you know why (0.39) you've come (0.75)
        to[↓day]
Child:     [no ]
```
                                                    (Stafford, Hutchby, Karim, and O'Reilly, 2016, p. 14)

In this example, the child begins the turn in overlap with the practitioner, at the very point in which the practitioner is completing the turn. The ending of the turn is signaled by the falling intonation and the conclusion of a complete question—something projected by the child.

Turn Allocation, Turn Sharing, and Next Speaker Selection

A central concern for CA has been how speakers come to take a turn at talk and how speakers are selected to take the conversational floor. CA research has illustrated that there are methodical procedures used by speakers to express the normative orientation to the achievement of orderly distribution of opportunities to speak (Hayashi, 2013).

(!) **Turn allocation and turn sharing are normatively organized (Hayashi, 2013).**

Turn taking, turn sharing, and turn allocation differ to some extent in institutional settings when compared to ordinary conversations. Although many institutional settings use the same turn-taking organization as mundane talk, there are some specific and systematic transformations in the turn-taking procedures that are important for applied CA research, as they have some potential to alter the speaker's opportunity for action (Heritage, 2005).

(!) **There is an orderly way in which turns are distributed between speakers, and this is often referred to as coherence (Schegloff, 1999).**

In institutional settings, topics and the order of speakership are organized from the outset, and this involves turn-taking procedures different from ordinary conversation. Heritage (2005) argued that these special turn-taking procedures fall into three categories:

1. Preallocation procedures, which tend to be characteristic of courtroom and news interviews;

2. Mediated turn allocation procedures, which tend to be characteristic of chaired and business meetings; and

3. Systems involving both preallocation and mediated turn allocation procedures, which tend to be characteristic of mediation or counseling.

In their early work, Sacks and colleagues (1974) noted that overwhelmingly in inter-action, only one speaker speaks at a time. They recognized that there are therefore conversational rules that apply at the point at which a next speaker becomes relevant, and there are three different ways that this is achieved:

1. The current speaker projects that he or she will choose the next speaker.

Consider the earlier example from Stafford et al. (2016, p. 14) where the speaker selects the recipient (in this case Kolomban, the child):

```
Prac:   Kolomban do you know why (0.39) you've come (0.75)
        to[↓day]

Child:  [no ]

                                                          (p. 14)
```

2. If the current speaker does not select the next speaker, then a recipient may self-select.

Consider the next example in which the practitioner (Prac) directs a question to the young person (YP) who answers, but the "okay" is general and the mother then self-selects to take the floor and provide further information in the next turn.

```
Prac:   So you've got a few local (0.51) policeman who are
        in↓volved

YP:     Yeah

Prac:   Okay

Mother: They're often knocking on my ↓do:or an

                                  (O'Reilly, Kiyimba, and Karim, 2016, p. 485)
```

3. If more than one person self-selects, then whomever began speaking first tends to continue to do so, and other simultaneous speakers end their turn prematurely.

Consider the following example taken from our data (unpublished example). Here you can see that the father finishes his turn and there is a micropause at the completion of that turn. At the next conversational turn, both the mother and father attempt to take the conversational floor at the same time and in overlap. As Sacks et al. (1974) demonstrated, one speaker (in this case the mother) suspends and cuts off her turn, and the other speaker (in this case the father) continues to hold the floor.

```
Father:  = she's always ↓(flicking)(.)

Mother:  [I mean with-]

Father:  [it's like with a book] if you watch her ↓with a
         book she will open the ↓book and ↓do that ((flaps
         hands)) (.) every page
```

Predominantly, the current speaker elects the next person to speak, and there are different ways in which this can be done. A key way in which this is achieved is to select the person through a term of address, such as his or her name. However, the next speakers can also be selected through other means, such as gaze or through tacit addressing—that is, context-tied methods such as the "rules of participation" inherent to a classroom (Hayashi, 2013). On those occasions where the current speaker does not select the next speaker and self-selection occurs, there may be some overlap resulting from competition for the turn space between speakers. Hayashi (2013) acknowledged that there are different types of overlap onset, and we outline these in Table 2.1.

TABLE 2.1 ● Different types of overlap onset

Overlap Onset	Description
Turn-terminal	This is when the self-selecting next speaker begins his or her turn slightly before the completion of the current turn, and thus there is a brief overlap. Typically, these terminal overlaps are fleeting, as the onset is at the point where the speaker's turn completion is imminent.
Turn initial	This is when the two turn beginnings happen simultaneously.
Midturn	Unlike the previous two types, the midturn type is not due to turn-taking miscues. Instead, its onset shows the next speaker's orientation to the current turn's content adequacy and progressivity. In this case, the overlap happens at the middle of the turn before the speaker's turn is complete.

Source: Hayashi, 2013.

Notably, midturn types of overlap can in some cases be interruptive. This is when there are occasions when two people attempt to talk at the same time, or when a second speaker begins his or her turn before the initial speaker has finished speaking (Jefferson, 1986). Interruptions therefore are marked by the interrupted speaker stopping his or her point. Unlike some language-based approaches, conversation analysts do not see interruptions as necessarily a reflection of dominance, but instead attend to the sequential position of the interruption and how it is treated by the different parties. In other words, interruptions become treatable as an interactionally accomplished feature of the production of talk (Sacks et al., 1974), and CA work has demonstrated that children's interruptions are treated differently than adult interruptions and are often ignored by the adults (O'Reilly, 2006, 2008a). The next example shows how the child (Jeff) speaks in overlap with the grandmother (Gran) in the middle of her turn and is interruptive but ignored by the grandmother.

```
Gran:    He (0.2) shouts at ↑Julie he hates her .hh <she's
         lazy> (.) <she neve::r does what ↓he ↓wants> and just

FT:      U↓hum,

Gran:    lays >into< 'er and she'[s ↑had it a::ll we:ek >and<
         so,=

→Jeff:                            [Nan (.) I drawed it Nan

Gran:    =from Julie's >↑point of view< you get that shouting
         at you <every day>
```
                                                    (O'Reilly, 2006, p. 555)

Adjacency Pairs

What we have demonstrated so far in our list is that CA examines sequences as orders of turns and investigates how participants accomplish and coordinate interactional activities (Mazeland, 2006). An important feature of this turn design and turn organization is that talk is typically organized into ***adjacency pairs***, where there is a first-pair-part and the next appropriate action is to deliver the second-pair-part (Sacks, 1992).

We provide an example of a type of adjacency pair that is a question followed by an answer in a child psychiatry setting. Note, however, that there is a whole range of adjacency pair types, including (but not exhaustive)

> **Adjacency pairs** are sequences of turns whereby one speaker provides an utterance (in the form of a first-pair-part) and a recipient provides a response (in the form of the second-pair-part).

- invitation–accept/decline,

- greeting–greeting,

- complaint–excuse/justification,

- request–accept/reject, and

- question–answer.

For example, a question–answer adjacency pair:

```
Prac:    ↑Do you kno:w (0.31)why you've c↑ome here toda↓y?

Child:   Erm because (0.39) I- keep (0.94) doin my- (0.41) I
         thi↑nk it's ↓O- C- D-"
```
                                                    (Stafford et al., 2016, p. 8)

For example, a greeting–greeting:

```
Fortis:  Hello:::,

Jessie:  Hello?
```

(Drew and Hepburn, 2015, p. 2 of online version)

Schegloff and Sacks (1973) demonstrated that adjacency pairs have several characteristics:

- They are composed of two turns.

- They are produced by different speakers.

- They are placed adjacently—that is, one after the other.

- They are relatively ordered so that the first-pair-part precedes the second-pair-part.

- They are pair-part related in that the first-pair-part is paired with a certain type of second-pair-part. For example, a greeting is typically responded to with a greeting, and not something else.

Conversation analysts argue that the production of the second-pair-part in an adjacency pair becomes conditionally relevant (Seedhouse, 2004). That is, the two parts are conventionally paired and the second-pair-part is made relevant, even if it is not produced immediately in the adjacent turn (Hutchby & Wooffitt, 2008).

Repair

An important principle for CA is the notion of **_repair_**, which refers to a set of practices to deal with interruptions to the progress of a conversation.

Repair refers to a speaker's effort to manage the occurrence of trouble in the conversation.

Repair can affect the form of sentences as well as the ordering of the elements within them and thus has consequences for the shape of the sentence (Schegloff, 1979). Schegloff noted, therefore, that repair does not just occur within sentences but can change the shape and composition of them.

CA recognizes that during interaction there is the possibility of trouble occurring during a conversation. _Trouble_ in CA terms refers to anything that the interlocutors consider as impeding the progress of their communication (Seedhouse, 2004). Examples of this phenomenon include

- when speakers misarticulate, or use a word incorrectly;

- the unavailability of a certain word or term when it is needed;

- the failure to hear or trouble in hearing; and

- the failure to understand something said by a speaker (Schegloff, 1987).

Think back to Chapter 1 where we cited an example from Sacks's (1992, p. 3) work on suicide centers.

```
A:  This is Mr Smith may I help you

B:  I can't hear you.

A:  This is Mr Smith.

B:  Smith.
```

This is a good example of repair, as Speaker B demonstrates some failure or trouble hearing as evidenced by "I can't hear you," which interrupts the sequence. Thus, repair is when the speaker interrupts the **progressivity** of the interaction to attend to possible trouble that has occurred (Schegloff, Jefferson, & Sacks, 1977).

Progressivity refers to the continuity of an interaction, in that interaction is made up of flowing sequences as speakers respond to one another and keep the interaction progressing.

Progressivity is important in interaction, and speakers each contribute to the progressivity of the interaction by attending to the next relevant component immediately following the previous turn (Stivers & Robinson, 2006). Repair is used so that the interaction does not stop at the point where the trouble occurs, and therefore the interaction continues (Schegloff, 2007b). Four types of repair action have been noted (Schegloff et al., 1977), which we outline in Table 2.2.

TABLE 2.2 ● Types of repair action

Type	Description
Self-initiated repair	This is when the repair is initiated by the same speaker who was the source of the trouble. Typically, the solution is also offered by this speaker.
Other-initiated self-repair	This is when the repair is initiated by the recipient, but the actual repair is constructed by the speaker who was the source of the trouble.
Self-initiated other-repair	This is when the speaker who was the source of the trouble encourages the recipient to repair the trouble.
Other-initiated other-repair	This is when the recipient of the trouble source also initiates the repair and offers the trouble solution.

Source: Schegloff et al., 1977.

Repairs in conversation also have a range of different components, which were outlined by Kitzinger (2013). We describe these components in Table 2.3.

TABLE 2.3 ● Components of repair	
Component of Repair	**Description**
Frames	This refers to the words and sounds that are reconstructed to "frame" the repair. This generally involves some repetition of some of the talk around the trouble source and may be less or more than the whole word.
Silence and delay	A period of delay or silence may be produced through turn tokens to hold the floor, such as "er" or "uhm." Such hesitation indicates a continued commitment to continue with the turn.
Apologetic terms	These are apologetic-type phrases such as "sorry," and they tend to address the error being repaired.
Repair prefaces	This includes preface items like "well" and "I mean," and these usually occur at a TRP.
Repeats	This is when the trouble source is repeated.
Multiple tries	This is when the first repair solution offered by the speaker is treated also as a trouble source, and thus additional repair attempts are made.
Self-talk	This is when the speaker pauses and turns to him- or herself as if to talk introspectively; thus, the speaker asks him- or herself a question to demonstrate reflecting or thinking about the answer.

Source: Kitzinger, 2013.

(!) **The most common type of repair is a self-initiated repair within the same TCU.**

There is a distinction between self-initiated repair and carrying out the repair in producing a solution. This is a distinction that is important, as a repair may be initiated by one speaker and yet completed by another (Kitzinger, 2013).

There are several different ways of doing a self-initiated repair, and Schegloff (2007b) outlined these as being

- *deleting,* which refers to when a word is cut off so far through the production of it;

- *searching,* which is when the speaker needs to produce an exact term or concept, such as the name of a person, one where there is not an easily substitutable word, and thus the speaker tends to hold the floor while searching for the word;

- *parenthesizing,* which is when the speaker interjects the turn-in-progress, usually with a TCU clausal (i.e., an aside turn to check something out with the recipient) before continuing with the turn;

- *aborting,* which is when the speaker aborts his or her production of the term or phrase; and

- *replacing,* which is a common type of repair in the English language and refers to using a replacement word or similar term (e.g., changing the exact name of someone to his or her role, such as *my teacher*).

So indeed, repairing trouble in interaction is quite a complex accomplishment.

Preference Organization

An important principle of CA is ***preference organization***, which refers to the implicit and explicit principles that speakers follow when interacting.

Sacks (1992) originally proposed the notion of preference in the context of invitations, which he argued have a preferred response of being accepted. Notably, the principles of preference organization are not about the notion of wanting to do something but rather relate to affiliation, disaffiliation, accountability, and sanctions in talk (Seedhouse, 2004).

It is argued that there are two types of preference (Bilmes, 1988):

> **Preference organization** refers to the idea that speakers follow principles in interaction, which are often implicit, and they respond to prior turns based on what is a preferred response.

> (!) **The notion of preference in CA does *not* refer to preference in psychological terms in relation to concerns with what participants are cognitively motivated to say (Bilmes, 1988).**

1. The general rule: This is when one speaker is conversing with another about a topic that the first speaker knows something unusual about, which may be significant for the second speaker, and thus the first speaker should mention it to the second.

> For example: Imagine that you have plans to see a film at the cinema, and your friend knows that the local cinema is undergoing reconstruction work and is thus closed for 2 weeks. The preference is for your friend to give this information to you.

2. Type R preference—that is, relevant absence: This is when certain contexts make relevant some preferred action, and thus when this preferred action is not taken, it is relevantly absent and noticeable.

> For example: If you receive an invitation to come to a friend's house at 6 p.m., you are likely to assume that dinner will be served. Yet when you arrive there is no dinner, and your host shares that they have already eaten dinner. The preference here, however, is that the host shares that no dinner will be served when giving the invitation. In this way, the host would have made relevant this unexpected occurrence, as an invitation for a gathering at dinnertime results in one fairly assuming dinner will be served.

Conversation analysts often note that what is interesting about preference is that preferred actions tend to be delivered quickly and without delay, but dispreferred actions tend to follow a delay and are usually prefaced with markers such as "well" or "um" (Pomerantz, 1984). What is key here is that preferred responses are affiliative (i.e., social actions that build unity or are pleasing), whereas dispreferred responses are disaffiliative.

Consider the following example.

```
A: Can you fix this needle?
B: I'm busy
A: I just wanted to know if you can fix it?
```
(Sacks, 1992, p. 689)

Here, a question is asked by Participant A, which orients to a preferred response of a *yes* answer. However, B responds with "I'm busy," which is dispreferred and does not align with the request. Notably, A repairs the initial question, framing it not as a request to fix the needle but as seeking out knowledge.

Thus far, we have presented quite a lot of information in the chapter. As such, it is important to take a moment to check your understanding of these core features. We recommend you attempt the activity in Box 2.2.

BOX 2.2
ACTIVITY ON THE STRUCTURES OF CONVERSATION

Activity

Locate a published CA study or series of studies focused on a topic that interests you. Carefully review the data extracts that are included in the paper and identify two examples of each of the structures of conversation discussed previously (e.g., preference, repair, adjacency pairs, etc.).

Membership Categorization

In his *Lectures of Conversation*, Sacks (1992) expressed a general interest in the idea of ***membership categorization analysis (MCA)***, and more particularly, membership categorization devices.

Membership categorization analysis (MCA) refers to an approach to analysis that focuses on how people go about categorizing and constructing social identities in talk and text.

Specifically, Sacks (1992) wrote about how when people talk they may use person-based categories as part of a set of categories. That is, speakers categorize others as certain members of society, and those categorizations rely on social categories and how they are organized into collections.

For example: When people talk about "parents," they are often referring to fathers and/or mothers.

For example: When people talk about "religions," they are often referring to Buddhism, Catholicism, Protestantism, Islamism, and the list goes on.

Simply put, MCA refers to an approach to analyzing talk and text that focuses on how people are recognizable as particular members of society, and how this is done through talk-in-interaction, with much of this work highlighting how membership categorization functions to produce social identities and social order. Historically, MCA has frequently been discussed as not being particularly focused on the sequentiality of talk and turn taking. Stokoe (2012) noted that historically, MCA "gives researchers with a primary interest in categorical or 'topical' (e.g., gender, sexuality, ethnicity, identity), rather than sequential, issues an empirically tractable method for studying those issues, as members' rather than analysts' categories" (p. 278).

MCA is a useful analytic approach for studying the ways in which social identities are made evident and accounted for in talk and text.

For example: Hall, Gough, and Seymour-Smith (2012) drew upon MCA to study a young man's YouTube video of a makeup tutorial and the respondents. The researchers specifically focused on how the creator of and respondents to the video managed gender and sexual identities. In their analysis, they found that makeup use by "straight men" was viewed as nonnormative, with respondents associating makeup use with "girls" and "gay men" (p. 222).

For example: Drawing upon MCA, Stokoe (2010) analyzed 120 tape-recorded interviews between police officers and arrested suspects, with an interest in how men's violence toward women was talked about. As such, Stokoe examined segments of talk where gender categories and talk about violence were present. She found that in many cases, men denied "hitting a woman" based on not being that kind of man, which she referred to as a *category-based denial* (e.g., one category being "men who hit" and the other category being "men who don't hit").

It is important to note that categories, or specific identities, are not simply labels but serve to associate various properties or activities with a given category. In other words, categories provide inferences about typical activities of members of the category, and as such, activities are category bound (Sacks, 1992). Sacks (1992) wrote about a classic example found in children's stories where it is often written: "The baby cried. The Mommy picked it up." He suggested that we "hear" mommy is this baby's mommy because there are certain actions (e.g., pick up the baby) or characteristics associated with a certain category. Sacks referred to these types of activities as *category-bound activities*; that is, categories become associated with specific social activities, and this particularity is often made visible in talk and text. In that way, the idea is that we hear the rendering of a certain category of baby as belonging to the broader category of family, and that picking up a baby is a category-bound activity that mothers do. Related to this, being associated with a category is often linked to having rights to speak and responsibilities.

> For example: The category of "school teacher" may justify or be associated with the "right" to speak about how people, and more particularly children, learn.

Within MCA, ***membership categorization devices (MCDs)*** are considered central concepts. An MCD refers to the apparatus in the talk or text that is used to identify categories understood as belonging to a collective category.

> For example: A Canadian and a Norwegian are part of the larger MCD of "nationality."
>
> For example: A mommy and a baby are part of the larger MCD of "family."
>
> For example: A dog, a cat, and a rabbit are part of the larger MCD of "pets."

Schegloff (2007a) suggested that MCDs consist of two parts:

1. one or more collections of categories (e.g., nationality), and

2. rules of application (economy rule and consistency rule—described in Table 2.4).

Stokoe (2012) presented 10 key concepts for membership categorization, which we summarize in Table 2.4.

It is important to highlight that scholars have noted that Sacks's interest or at least writing around MCA became less prominent over time (Schegloff, 2007a; ten Have, 2007). Related to this, there has been an ongoing discussion regarding the place of MCA within CA (see Stokoe, 2012, for a fuller discussion), with some scholars positioning MCA as distinct from (yet related to) CA. In our own work, we have found it useful to consider MCA and MCDs within the context of larger applied CA research. As such, if relevant to your own areas of research interest, we encourage you to read MCA-related literature to gain a better sense of membership categories in talk and text.

> A **membership categorization device (MCD)** is "the apparatus through which categories are understood to 'belong' to collective categories" (Stokoe, 2012, p. 281).

TABLE 2.4 ● Key concepts of membership categorization

Key Concept	Description
Membership categorization device	This refers to the apparatus by which categories are understood to "belong" to a collective category. Generally, it is understood that a category (e.g., baby) can belong to multiple MCDs.
Category-bound activities	This refers to social activities that are linked to certain categories (e.g., children [the category] go to school [the activity]).
Category-tied predicates	This refers to a category's characteristics (e.g., the mother [category] cares [predicate] for the children).
Standardized relational pairs	This refers to pairs of categories that carry duties and moral obligations in relation to the other category (e.g., mother–child, teacher–student, etc.).
Duplicative organization	This refers to categories that work in a unit or as a "team" (e.g., mother, father, grandmother, grandfather, aunt, uncle, and son are in the "family").
Positioned categories	This refers to those collections of categories that occupy a hierarchical relationship (e.g., adult, teenager), such that one category might be accused of acting like another category (e.g., someone says to an adult, "You are acting like a teenager").
Category-activity "puzzles"	This refers to what happens when people perform certain actions by putting together both expected and unexpected combinations (e.g., male nurses).
The economy rule	This refers to one of Sacks's (1992) rules of application wherein a single category may sufficiently describe a person (e.g., a father and daughter had an accident).
The consistency rule	This refers to one of Sacks's (1992) rules of application wherein when two or more categories are used next to each other (e.g., a "father and daughter were in an accident") yet they belong to an MCD (e.g., family).
Categorization maxims	This refers to what Sacks (1992) described as the *hearer's maxim* and the *viewer's maxim*, with these maxims positioned because of the rules of application (i.e., the economy rule and the consistency rule). The hearer's maxim is articulated as, "If two or more categories are used to categorize two or more members of some population, and those categories can be heard as categories from the same collection, then: Hear them that way" (p. 221). The viewer's maxim is specific to category-bound activities and is articulated as, "If a member sees a category-bound activity being done, then if one sees it being done by a member of a category to which the activity is bound, see it that way" (p. 259).

Source: Adapted from Stokoe, 2012.

Embodied Action

CA has often been assumed to be an "exclusively verbal approach" (Pelose, 1987, p. 183). Yet as Nevile (2015) noted, such a view was understood as being "too limited even in the late 1980s" and resulted in what has been termed "the embodied turn" (p. 122). Such a turn refers to the increasing interest in embodiment and, more generally, the interplay between talk, bodily movements, and material and digital resources (Heath & Luff, 2013). It has been argued that isolating language from its environment (e.g., materials, body, etc.) is not analytically useful (Goodwin, 2000). Increasingly, therefore, conversation analysts attend to embodied action, which is particularly relevant for the study of institutional settings wherein materials are often central to the way interaction is sequentially organized.

> For example: A student responds to a teacher's request by writing an answer on a whiteboard.
>
> For example: A therapist engages children by drawing a family tree on a piece of paper and allows them to use their pen to contribute names.

Yet what does it mean to attend to embodied action? In the CA literature, embodiment has often included a focus on gestures (e.g., pointing), gaze, facial expression, body placement, touching or handling objects or technologies, and so forth (see Heath & Luff, 2013, as well as Nevile, 2015, for a fuller discussion on embodiment in CA). Obviously, a focus on embodied action shapes the data collection process, with a researcher typically collecting video data. For instance, Marjorie Goodwin (2007) studied a friendship group of American preadolescent girls on a playground, collecting 60 hours of video-recorded data and 20 hours of audio-recorded data. She was particularly interested in a segment of talk in which the girls engaged in a "gossip assessment" (p. 354) in which the girls evaluated or offered commentary on the captain of a softball game and his girlfriend who had excluded the girls from the game. Goodwin illustrated how both the girls' talk (i.e., what they said) and their body positioning made visible who had the right to participate in the gossiping and offer a negative commentary. To substantiate and illustrate her claims, she included multiple extracts of talk as well as line drawings, such as Figure 2.1, which illustrated the interplay between talk and body placement/positioning. Goodwin suggested the following when describing what such line drawing affords:

> The line drawings . . . allow one to look beyond talk itself to the organization of bodies in social space; through examining the postural configurations of bodies in addition to the sequential analysis of talk, we have access to how participants make visible a local social order of inclusion and exclusion. (p. 359)

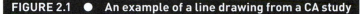

FIGURE 2.1 ● An example of a line drawing from a CA study

Source: Goodwin, 2007.

As Goodwin's (2007) work implicitly points to, an analytic focus on embodied action results in challenges to transcription and representation of the body and other semiotic resources, something which we discuss further in Chapter 6. Regardless, the embodied turn has certainly resulted in a burgeoning area of research in CA, and we thus encourage you to explore the theoretical and methodological discussions related to this further (Nevile, 2015, p. 122).

An Interview With Dr. Trini Stickle

In this chapter, we have introduced you to some of the basic principles of CA and foundational structures of conversation. We acknowledge that learning the nuances of conversation, and CA more generally, requires close study, practice, and effort. Indeed, CA brings with it a unique perspective on language—one which requires time to learn. Recognizing this, we interviewed Dr. Trini Stickle, a scholar who recently completed her PhD, and invited her to share some advice for individuals who may be just learning CA. See Box 2.3.

BOX 2.3
INTERVIEW WITH DR. TRINI STICKLE

Dr. Trini Stickle recently completed her PhD under the guidance of Professor Doug Maynard at University of Wisconsin, Madison. Since completing her studies, Dr. Stickle has taken a position at Western Kentucky University as an assistant professor. Dr. Stickle has undertaken considerable work using CA in the field of autism spectrum disorder (ASD) and recently contributed to a special issue on CA and ASD in the *Journal of Autism and Developmental Disorders*:

- Maynard, D., McDonald, T., & Stickle, T. (2016). Parents as a team: Mother, father, a child with autism spectrum disorder, and a spinning toy. *Journal of Autism and Developmental Disorders*, 46(2), 406–423.

We asked Dr. Stickle three questions about the principles of CA and learning the tools of analysis. Her answers to these questions are provided here.

You have recently completed your CA PhD. What did you find most challenging in the learning process at the beginning?

"The most difficult part of learning CA methodology was suppressing my inclination to try to understand the 'why' a speaker says A or B—that is, my heuristic notion to interpret what the speaker was thinking. While I was simply moving from one who interacts to one who studies interaction, the process was not at all simple. I had to learn how to analyze the 'what' and 'how' of the interaction. This meant learning to pay close attention to the multiple levels of the interaction—the lexical, syntactic, prosodic, and the embodied. And like any other profession, this took practice and discipline."

Can you talk about your process of learning the fundamental principles of CA?

"My process was one of immersion. Once I decided that CA was the methodology that I wanted to apply in a quest to better understand language and society, I was fortunate to be in an environment where I could work with great conversation analysts—Cecilia Ford, Doug Maynard, Junko Mori—as well as numerous other graduate students from linguistics, sociology, and second-language studies. In addition to attending regular and frequent data sessions, I worked as a transcriber on numerous projects. This allowed me to constantly test what I was learning in my readings and coursework on conversation analysis with new data. While transcribing, I would try to apply the terminology and concepts that were foundational to the field. I would also test out my own analytic skills in trying to understand the contribution that syntactic or prosodic variation was having in a turn or interaction."

What advice would you give students who are new to CA?

"My advice to prospective students of CA would be to gain access to or record and transcribe as many interactions as you are possibly able to do. Then, as you learn the terminology of the field, constantly test yourself on how you think the turn is built to make and display sense of the other's turn(s) as the participants make meaning together. Compare your own analyses with those of CA founders and the accepted practices, but also give yourself room to observe interactions offering fresh insights."

Chapter Summary

In this chapter, we introduced you to the basic principles of CA and, more specifically, the fundamental structures of conversation, such as sequence organization, turn design, and so forth. Closely related to this, we provided you with a general introduction to some of the many discursive resources and discursive devices noted across the literature. We also provided you with a brief overview to membership categorization analysis and the various associated concepts. Finally, we highlighted the usefulness of considering embodied action in CA. Our aim in discussing these central concepts is to provide you with the necessary foundation for carrying out an applied CA study; yet we recognize that what we have provided is *only* a general and abbreviated overview and encourage you to continue your study of the basic principles of CA, particularly if you are new to CA. The key learning points from the chapter are thus summarized in the next box.

Learning Points From Chapter 2

- Conversation analysts have studied the microfeatures of conversation, with an interest in fundamental structures, such as sequence organization and turn design (among others).

- Membership categorization analysis and its related concepts are a central way by which conversation analysts study social identities in talk.

- CA has historically been linked to the study of talk, with a focus on the verbal. However, in CA, increasing attention has been given to embodied action.

Recommended Readings

There are several key references that are useful for developing your knowledge of the principles of CA. We encourage you to explore the following publications as you further develop your understanding of CA and the foundational structures of conversation.

- Nevile, M. (2015). The embodied turn in research on language and social interaction. *Research on Language and Social Interaction, 48*(2), 121–151.

This relatively recent article provides an excellent overview of CA literature published from 1987 to 2013 in *Research on Language and Social Interaction*, a leading CA-oriented journal, with an explicit focus on what Nevile terms "the embodied turn" (p. 121).

(Continued)

(Continued)

The article highlights the challenges and practices in CA that have surrounded transcribing and representing the body.

- Sacks, H., Schegloff, E., & Jefferson, G. (1974). A simplest systematic for the organization of turn-taking for conversation. *Language, 50,* 696–735.

This is a seminal article written by the original pioneers of CA. In this paper, the authors take the reader through the key aspects of turn design and sequence organization, outlining the core principles of CA. As an original piece of work, this is essential reading for all those who are new to CA.

- Stokoe, E. (2012). Moving forward with membership categorization analysis: Methods for systematic analysis. *Discourse Studies, 14*(3), 277–303.

In this article, Stokoe examines the relationship between CA and MCA, and critically discusses the role of MCA as an approach. More particularly, she outlines the practical analytic steps and procedures for conducting MCA and provides exemplar analyses to promote MCA as a practice.

Planning Applied Conversation Analysis Research

Chapter Focus

In this chapter, you will learn how to:

- Perform a literature review of applied conversation analysis research.
- Develop a research question for applied conversation analysis research.
- Critically appreciate the iterative nature of applied conversation analysis research.
- Assess the importance of a well-developed research proposal.
- Recognize the value of keeping a research diary.
- Appreciate the value and potential challenges of communicating with gatekeepers.

As you plan to undertake an applied conversation analysis (CA) research study, it is crucial that you make several practical decisions before you begin. The focus for this chapter is on the pertinent decisions you will face when planning your study. CA is an iterative qualitative approach that requires you to revisit your decisions regularly and make changes accordingly. It is thus important to recognize that the plans and decisions you make during the earliest stages of your research are not isolated or invariable. Further, throughout the research process, you should recognize the need to modify and revisit the literature, your research focus and question(s), and research protocol.

Although we draw your attention to the iterative nature of applied CA, this is a pedagogical text and designed to help you learn what is involved in *doing* a project of this kind. Thus, like any other methodological text, our discussion of the research process is presented in a necessarily linear manner; yet in practice, you should move back and forth between the various aspects of the research process (e.g., revisit your data collection process while carrying out data analysis, etc.). It is therefore incumbent that you remain reflexively aware of the need to flexibly move between and within decisions as you develop your research ideas.

When planning your applied CA research study, there will be several things you must consider, including

- conducting a literature review,

- developing and constructing a research focus and research question(s),

- writing a research protocol,

- keeping a reflective research diary,

- preparing for the challenges of recruiting participants, and

- engaging stakeholders and communicating with gatekeepers.

In this chapter, we consider each of these activities in turn while pointing to additional resources that may deepen your understanding of how to design an applied CA research study.

Conducting a Literature Review

It is important to remember that a literature review is not a one-off event that you complete near the beginning of a project and then forget about. Instead, the literature review is something that you will need to revisit at regular intervals as your project unfolds. Indeed, it will be necessary to seek out further literature and evidence to support your arguments as you develop them, both about your topic of interest and the CA literature. There are several different points within the research process where literature reviewing may be needed, for example

- as you shape your ideas, which occurs quite often near the beginning of your project;

- as you refine and reconstruct your research protocol and work toward strengthening your rationale for the need for your research;

- during data collection as the process sparks new ideas and new avenues to pursue;

- as you develop your analysis to help you strengthen some of the analytic claims you make; and

- as you ensure that the literature you are using to build your argument is up to date, which occurs quite often near the end of your project.

Thus, it is important that you do not view your literature review as a product; rather, it is a process of meaning making and decision guiding that informs your theoretical and analytical framework (Ravitch & Riggan, 2012).

Definitions vary regarding what is a literature review, and while there are many similarities and overlap between these definitions, it is necessary to think about what these definitions mean for an applied CA research study. We provide the following three examples of descriptions of the literature review that are summarized from general methodological texts.

> Example 1: A literature review can be thought of as a critical review of the body of knowledge that exists, which includes theoretical, methodological, and empirical works, and is presented as an argument by the author (O'Leary, 2014).
>
> Example 2: A literature review is a critical summary and evaluative assessment of the available literature on any given topic to locate the specific research project within a context (Blaxter, Hughes, & Tight, 2001).
>
> Example 3: A literature review is an explicit systematic method for identifying, evaluating, and synthesizing current and previous evidence produced by both academics and practitioners (Fink, 2005).

If we consider these descriptions together, a literature review can be conceived of as entailing a critical appreciation of the empirical research, methodological literature, and theoretical frameworks as related to your research study. It is important that the literature review is shaped around the topic area that you are investigating, yet it is also important not to lose sight of other important areas such as methods, policies, and so forth. For applied CA research studies, it is perhaps most useful to think about Example 3. In your applied CA research study, you will ultimately need to make clear the practical relevance of your work to the applied field in which you are studying. So, as Fink (2005) pointed out, it is necessary to look at the practical literature produced by those who work in the field. Additionally, CA is a distinctive methodological approach, and thus it is essential that you also engage with the general CA methodological literature, such as this very textbook (among others), to ensure you have a good foundational knowledge of the approach before moving forward. This is particularly important as you engage in data analysis and begin writing up your findings, which we discuss later in the book.

> **You might want to attend conferences that showcase the most up-to-date research in CA and in relation to the topic you are studying.**

Reasons for Carrying Out a Literature Review

There are many reasons that you carry out a literature review and continue to build it throughout the lifetime of your project. Ridley (2012) argued that some of these key reasons include

- to identify the specific context in which you will situate your work, with the earliest stages of the review process often being exploratory in nature;
- to point to what work has already been done in your area of focus and thereby avoid duplicating, which helps to demonstrate the originality of your research; and

TABLE 3.1 • Functions of a literature review	
Function	**Description**
Theoretical foundations	By examining the literature, you will be able to build a greater appreciation of the role that theory plays in CA work.
Gaps in knowledge	By performing a literature review, you will be able to identify what applied CA research, as well as other types of research, has already been done on the topic you are interested in studying. This will help you to think about gaps in knowledge and how an applied CA research study might be positioned as explicitly addressing such a gap.
Research questions	By exploring the existing literature in a certain area, you will be able to develop and refine your research question(s).
Relevance	By examining the literature, you will be able to build a critical argument in relation to your study and demonstrate to a range of different audiences how and why your work is both important and relevant to the field.
Definitions	It is important for any applied CA research study that you are clear in how you are defining concepts, methods, and other aspects of the study. Your literature review can support you in producing necessary definitions of the terminology that are most relevant to your study.
History	The literature on CA spans several decades, and of course the literature base on some substantive topics goes even further back historically. There are likely to be seminal works that are relevant to your project and essential for citation. It is helpful to use your literature review to provide a historical context and an overview of the contemporary position on the specific issue you are researching.
Evidence	The literature review is essential in providing supporting evidence for the problem that your applied CA research study aims to highlight.

- to identify key people/scholars, organizations, and texts that are potentially relevant to your research.

We highlight some additional functions of the literature review in Table 3.1.

Elements of a Literature Review

It is important to note that there are many elements of a literature review. There are different types of resources available, ranging from primary sources to secondary sources to peer-reviewed publications to editorially reviewed publications. While researchers often think about academic journal articles as being the foundation of a literature review, a good literature review should include a range of resources. This is particularly important for applied CA work, as it often aims to offer critical insights that are relevant to both academics and practitioners. We present some of the key elements of a literature review in Table 3.2.

Figure 3.1 provides a useful visual of how to think about building your argument in relation to the different types of sources.

TABLE 3.2 ● Key elements of a literature review

Element	Description
Journal articles	Journal articles are a key aspect of any literature review, as it is essential that you are knowledgeable of both the empirical CA literature on the given topic as well as the empirical literature that employed other methodologies and methods.
Discipline-specific material	There are a range of discipline-specific reference materials, such as key handbooks, encyclopedias, or dictionaries, that may be useful in defining concepts and helping you gather foundational knowledge about the approach or topic.
Books	Books are an important source of information and learning. You may want to start with basic, introductory, and practical texts, and work your way up to more advanced textbooks that deal with the more sophisticated arguments.
Gray literature	A range of available sources, such as policy documents, newspaper/magazine articles, conference papers, and official statistics, are often referred to as *gray literature*. This kind of literature may be particularly important for applied research. Policy documents and media-publicized articles can help you to articulate the relevance of your applied work to practice.

FIGURE 3.1 ● Building a literature review in relation to various sources

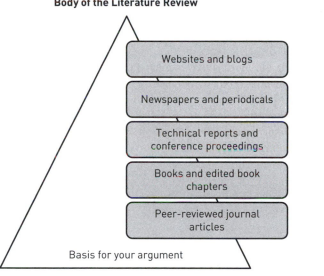

Body of the Literature Review

- Websites and blogs
- Newspapers and periodicals
- Technical reports and conference proceedings
- Books and edited book chapters
- Peer-reviewed journal articles

Basis for your argument

Source: Lochmiller & Lester, 2017. Reproduced with permission.

Practical Aspects of a Literature Review

Indeed, the literature review plays a central role in an applied CA research study and, as we have highlighted, has several functions. When you initially embark on carrying out your literature review, it often feels quite challenging and sometimes overwhelming, leading to several questions: Where do you start? How do you conduct an effective search? Are there key journals and handbooks to consider when pursuing an applied CA research study?

A good starting point for any literature review is with the search engine Google Scholar, as this allows you to start off relatively generally with a free flow of text and then move to more advanced and specific searches using academic databases such as EBSCO, ERIC, Education Full Text, JSTOR, Scopus, Medline, and so forth. Yet even when starting with Google Scholar, your search might feel a bit too general, particularly if you already have a somewhat narrowed focus.

> For example: We searched for *cancer* on Google Scholar, and this rather general search term returned 4,680,000 results (March 2016).

> For example: We searched for *school* on Google Scholar, and this rather general search term returned 4,460,000 results (March 2016).

As such, when searching in Google Scholar and other search engines, it is useful to spend time varying your search terms, combining terms, and being as focused as possible to return relevant resources for your literature review. It is also useful to use academic databases, as these allow you to use Boolean operators such as *and*, *or*, and *not*, and thereby narrow and refine your search (Machi & McEvoy, 2012). Here are some additional tips to keep in mind.

- Identify the key words that you need to search for and write them down so you do not repeat yourself or lose sight of your search process.

- At the start of your literature review, you may want to be overly inclusive, recognizing that you may find as many as 50 articles (or more) that relate to your study.

- At the earliest stages of your review process, it is often first useful to read the abstracts to determine how relevant the article is to your study.

- Try to summarize the articles in your own words and make some critical notes.

There are many practical things to consider while carrying out your literature review and in assessing the evidence you collect. We provide you with some practical tips in Box 3.1 and also offer a list of key CA-related journals and electronic resources in Box 3.2.

(!) **Do not underestimate the value of your local librarian, particularly at institutions such as universities.**

Being Critical of Research Articles

Searching the literature is only part of a literature review. It is crucial that you engage in both *critical reading* and *critical writing*. While both are important, there is a difference between them.

Critical reading: This requires you to identify what the author's arguments and conclusions are in a text, and evaluate the strength of the argument presented by questioning the sufficiency and reliability of the evidence, as well as identifying any assumptions and interpretations made to ascertain the moral, political, and value judgments the author makes (Ridley, 2012).

Critical writing: This requires you to present a logical argument in writing that is clearly linked to the conclusions you draw and provide sound evidence and reasoning that support the argument. A coherent framework that is theoretically sound should be provided (Ridley, 2012).

BOX 3.1
PRACTICAL TIPS IN PERFORMING AN APPLIED CA LITERATURE REVIEW

Practical Tips

✓ While Google Scholar is a useful place to start, it is helpful to also use other readily available databases (e.g., EBSCO) for a more focused and advanced literature search.

✓ Make sure that you keep a record of all full references of any articles, book chapters, or other sources that you read in case you need to return to them at a later point.

✓ It is often useful to use a citation management tool such as RefWorks, Mendeley, Zotero, or Endnote (among others) to catalog your references in a systematic and organized way.

✓ When you are searching through the literature, it is important that you are aware of the copyright and who owns the work. This is likely to mean that there are restrictions on how much of a book or article you can photocopy.

✓ It can be helpful to read other people's literature reviews so that you have a good sense of what one looks like. It is especially important to look at literature reviews written by conversation analysts or those that are focused on a key aspect of CA related to your study (see Paulus, Warren, & Lester, 2016, for an example).

✓ Snowball referencing can help to identify additional sources you may have missed. In other words, the sources that authors are citing within their articles can be identified as relevant to your work and lead you to locate and read the primary source.

✓ For those sources that you deem particularly relevant, it is helpful to take notes as you read. You may want to use the note-taking features within a citation management tool to maintain electronic notes.

✓ Academic professionals such as your supervisor or colleagues can be an important source of help, as experts within a field will have sound knowledge of the literature.

✓ Librarians are typically experts at conducting literature searches. It is thus particularly useful to meet with a librarian to acquire advice and tips for carrying out effective searches.

✓ It can be useful to attend academic-or practitioner-based conferences to gain a sense of the relevant literature.

BOX 3.2
CA-RELATED JOURNALS AND ELECTRONIC RESEARCH

CA-Related Journals and Electronic Research

- While this is not an exhaustive list, the following highlights some of the journals that commonly (or exclusively) publish CA-related research:

    o *American Sociological Review*
    o *British Journal of Social Psychology*
    o *Communication & Medicine*
    o *Discourse & Society*
    o *Discourse Studies*
    o *Issues in Applied Linguistics*
    o *Journal of Communication*
    o *Journal of Pragmatics*
    o *Human Studies*
    o *Language & Communication*
    o *Language in Society*
    o *Linguistics in Education*
    o *Research on Children and Social Interaction*
    o *Research on Language and Social Interaction*
    o *Text & Talk*
    o *Semiotica*
    o *Sociology*
    o *Social Psychology Quarterly*

- The EMCA Wiki (http://emcawiki.net/Main_Page) includes postings related to CA- and ethnomethodology-related jobs, conferences, training, and publications. The bibliography list is quite expansive and is up-dated almost daily to reflect new CA-related publications.

Summarizing what you read is an important step in your literature review process.

When making your notes about an article, book, or book chapter, you need to capture the key information. Key information typically includes making note of the research problem, the focus and purpose of the study, methodological and analytic approaches employed, and key findings and implications (Creswell, 2013). It is helpful to critically read each resource. In practice, this means that you need to make a clear assessment of the argument that the author is making and to recognize any limitations in the argument, as well as any limitations to his or her methodological approach (regardless of whether it is a CA study or not). It is important that you assess whether the design of the study was appropriate (Greenhalgh, 1997). In other words, you should critically question whether CA, for instance, was the appropriate methodological approach for the study in question and the degree to which it was executed well. Your critical approach should also include noting what is positive about the work (Blaxter et al., 2001).

Writing Up Your Literature Review

Before you begin writing up your literature review, it is necessary to assemble and organize the collected information around your topical area, which requires examining, analyzing, and synthesizing the material prior to completing any formal writing (Machi & McEvoy, 2012). There is no uniform structure to the literature review, but generally it presents the current state of knowledge in a field and critiques the empirical evidence (Ridley, 2012). Quite often, people new to the literature review process use a listed style approach where each study is summarized individually in paragraph form. Problematically, this fails to form any kind of argument, fails to identify the core issues at stake for the research, and is not critical in its appraisal of the collected evidence. So this does not give any indication of how or why the included literature may be relevant to your research.

> (!) **Remember that being critical does not mean rejecting the work of the author but means taking a critical position and thinking about how convincing the author was in the presentation of the argument.**

While there are different approaches to writing a literature review, we suggest that a common and useful way is to organize your materials into general themes and then build your argument from the collected (thematized) materials. A more thematic approach to the literature review serves to identify the core issues at stake within an argument, explain how and why the literature is relevant to the question at hand, and facilitate a critical reflection of the evidence in the field.

Developing a Research Focus/Question

In qualitative research, it is necessary to identify a topic of interest, and for applied research consider whether this topic is practical and useful to your field or discipline. The selected topic thus becomes the central idea or focus for your research and may even provide a platform for drafting a title for your study (Creswell, 2013). In some forms of qualitative research, emphasis is given to the importance of developing a research question early in the research process. While it is acknowledged that qualitative research is typically inductive and iterative, and thus a research question is shaped and reshaped during the process of research, it is often argued that a research question should guide a study. The general guidance for many forms of qualitative research is to brainstorm ideas, write down those ideas that seem interesting, and organize these ideas into a question, which then forms the backbone of the project.

Indeed, there are whole textbooks devoted to developing research questions, including the following two books:

(!)
To some extent, developing a research question in a CA study is different in comparison to other approaches to research.

- Andrews, R. (2003). *Research questions*. London, England: Continuum Books.

- White, P. (2009). *Developing research questions: A guide for social scientists*. Basingstoke, England: Palgrave Macmillan.

Although CA is a qualitative methodology, it does function slightly differently than some of the other approaches to qualitative research. CA operates within specific epistemological parameters. Within CA, there is a broader interest in understanding how social actions are achieved through talk-in-interaction, and thus the typical act of designing a research question at the outset of the research is not entirely appropriate, as analysis is driven by ***unmotivated looking*** (Hutchby & Wooffitt, 2008; Sacks, 1992). In other words, those practicing CA seek to understand what happens in certain kinds of interactions without privileging discipline-specific theories or a priori frameworks (Stokoe, 2008).

Unmotivated looking refers to maintaining an openness when engaging with the data set, which stands in contrast to approaching the data with a preestablished theory or a priori ideas regarding what is most important in the data set (Hutchby & Wooffitt, 2008; Potter, 2010).

For applied CA, these interactions often occur within institutions.

For example: These interactions may take place in courts of law (Auburn, Hay, & Wilkinson, 2011), counseling (Hutchby, 2007), family therapy sessions (Parker & O'Reilly, 2012), paranormal accounts (Wooffitt, 1992), and political interviews (Ekström, 2009).

In these applied examples, CA is conceived of as a data-driven strategy, not driven by a specific question or researcher agenda. As such, it is uncommon for a CA researcher to develop finalized research questions prior to engaging in data collection and analysis. Nonetheless, applied CA researchers specifically are working in institutional fields, informing practice and answerable to a variety of individuals including gatekeepers, ethics committees, review boards, stakeholder groups, and other interested parties. Generally, then, applied CA researchers are expected to demonstrate that a particular focus is driving the research.

Pragmatically, some sense of interest in a topic, setting, and overarching question thus does drive the data collection and the subsequent analysis process. It is helpful, though, to ensure that the research question posed is broad and open. We provide examples from our own work to illustrate what we mean by this.

For example: How is a child mental health assessment conducted?

This very general question did not focus in on any aspect of the assessment and instead pointed to an interest in a type of social interaction—that is, the institutional arena of child mental health. In this project, we explored what happens when children are assessed in the United Kingdom for suspected mental health problems as children attend a specialist mental health service.

- See O'Reilly, M., Karim, K., Stafford, V., & Hutchby, I. (2015). Identifying the interactional processes in the first assessments in child mental health. *Child and Adolescent Mental Health, 20*(4), 195–201.

> For example: What happens in family therapy?

Again, this was a very general question that was driven by an interest in a certain institutional social interaction: families in therapy. In this project, we explored the processes that occur in family therapy and examined the interactions that took place between families and the family therapists.

- See O'Reilly, M., & Lester, J. (2016). Building a case for good parenting in a family therapy systemic environment: Resisting blame and accounting for children's behaviour. *Journal of Family Therapy.*

> For example: How do students work up their beliefs and experiences in a computer-mediated communication environment?

Here, too, this question points to a broad and open interest around the way in which students work up or display their beliefs and experiences in the context of a blogging activity. In this project, we were broadly interested in examining the talk of undergraduate nutrition science students asked to make a blog post about what they knew about dietary supplements prior to attending a lecture related to this topic.

- See Lester, J. N., & Paulus, T. (2011). Accountability and public displays of knowing in an undergraduate computer-mediated communication context. *Discourse Studies, 13*(5), 671–686.

As further review, you may want to look back to Chapter 1, Box 1.3, where Professor Antaki provided three examples of broad CA questions:

- How do police officers interview suspects?

- How do doctors diagnose symptoms?

- How do customers get their complaints dealt with by a call center?

At this point, we recommend that you reflect on the points related to research questions in relation to your own area(s) of interest and complete the activity in Box 3.3.

BOX 3.3

ACTIVITY ON RESEARCH QUESTIONS

Activity

Look at your own research question. Is this question sufficiently open to be suitable for an applied CA research study? If not, start to refine the question so that you do not restrict your field of inquiry. Remember that this is simply a starting point for your study, as your question will develop and change as you move through your study and may evolve to include more specific subquestions later in the process.

Writing a Research Proposal

Research planning generally requires developing a ***research proposal***, sometimes referred to as a ***research protocol***. This is a document that provides detail on the theoretical, methodological, and practical aspects of your planned research study. Typically, the proposal is developed during the early stages of planning a project.

> A **research proposal/protocol** is a document that details the theoretical, methodological, and practical aspects of a research study.

Whether you are planning a research study or applying for funding, you will need to develop a clear and easy-to-follow protocol that indicates the core decisions that you will make in your applied CA research study. In developing a research proposal, you must think through your research study in advance of doing anything, which is generally expected by funders, ethics committees, research/dissertation committees, and gatekeepers. This may be quite a complex process for an applied CA researcher because of the evolving process and bottom-up, inductive nature of CA. It can be difficult to isolate the exact processes that will occur in advance of the study. Yet even though some aspects of your research process might change as your study unfolds, we suggest that it is valuable to think carefully through the details of your study long before you carry it out. Thoughtful planning will help you to prepare for the research process as well as avoid unnecessary challenges.

There is a range of different audiences for whom you will potentially write your proposal. How you ultimately write your proposal will depend upon the purpose of your study and the reasons for writing the proposal (e.g., dissertation proposal, funding proposal, ethics board proposal, etc.). We offer several examples of purposes (and the related audiences) that you may write a proposal for.

- If you are a student, it will be necessary that you develop a detailed research proposal for your adviser/supervisor to help you make methodological and practical decisions at all levels of your study. Furthermore, a thesis or dissertation committee may review your proposal prior to approving your study. In such instances, you may use a rather prescribed format for writing— one that requires you to think through all the details of your study and make a strong case for carrying out an applied CA research study.

- You may be developing a proposal for a funding body who may consider granting you an award to help pay for the expenses incurred. Applied CA research can be time consuming, and you may need to apply for funding to cover the verbatim transcription, stipends for participants, costs of traveling to collect data, digital equipment for recording the data, and other miscellaneous costs.

- An important audience who will expect to see a copy of your proposal is the body governing your ethics (e.g., institutional review board/ethics committee). In contemporary research, it is very likely that your research will be judged by an ethics board to determine if your work is ethically viable. Accompanying your application, you quite often need to include a copy of your research proposal.

- Often, research is conducted within a team, and thus you may need to develop a proposal to provide information to your other research team members.

- You may want to write a proposal for yourself to help you organize your thoughts and decisions, and to create a record to check back with as you go through your project. Remember that the process of writing a research proposal will be useful for you. It will help you to clarify and understand the research decisions you plan to make, which ultimately will help you execute your study thoughtfully.

The core purpose of crafting a research proposal is to demonstrate to your intended audience the value of your applied CA research. Applied CA is often intended to examine an area of practice; therefore, one function of your proposal is to outline how your research will be practically relevant. You will thus need to think about how a population, field, and/or practice might benefit from your research and what CA may be able to offer your field of study. So by writing the proposal, you will be able to allow the audience to

- judge the feasibility of your work and the plans you have for implementation,

- assess the quality of your writing and give you some guidance for improving your academic style, and

- appreciate how valuable and relevant your applied CA work is for practice.

How to Write Your Research Proposal

It is important to recognize that there are different ways of writing a proposal; consequently, there is no simple or universal template to follow. How you write your proposal will reflect the purpose of the document as well as institutional requirements in some cases (e.g., dissertation/thesis format specific to your university).

> For example: If you are drafting a proposal to meet your PhD program requirements, such as a dissertation proposal, the institution governing your study may have a template, word count, or structure that they require.

While there are different formats, there are some general items to include:

1. Title page

2. Introduction

3. Literature review

4. Aims and rationale

5. Methodological approach and methods

6. Access and Ethics

7. Expected contribution or significance

8. Timeline

9. Dissemination

We briefly discuss each of these items or sections, recognizing the order often varies based on your personal preference, institutional expectations, and/or audience.

> ① **Remember that your title should be interesting, original, and eye catching, and should reflect the applied CA nature of the work you are proposing.**

Title page

Generally, you should include a separate page at the beginning of your proposal that provides the reader with key information about your study. This should contain your details (e.g., current position, contact details); the institution you are working at or for; and the title of your study. The title of your study will certainly evolve over time, and you may even change the proposed title as you complete your study. Nonetheless, you want your title to include key words that speak directly to the focus of your study.

Introduction

It is important to bear in mind that your introduction is the first thing that your audience will read and thereby make sense of the overall intent of your research. This section of your proposal introduces the reader to the core issues at stake for your research and the seminal research in the field, with the aim of showing how your ideas fit within the broader body of evidence (Punch, 2000). The purpose of the introduction is to outline what the research problem is, demonstrate the importance of your research problem, and highlight key areas that need further attention.

Literature Review

Depending upon your audience (e.g., funding agency versus a dissertation committee), the length and detail of your literature review will vary. Nonetheless, as we noted earlier, the purpose of a literature review is to both summarize and synthesize what is already known about your topic or research area. In doing so, you are aiming to provide the reader with a clear understanding of where your research fits into the broader scholarly landscape. Further, you should envision your literature review as building upon your introduction and further clarifying why your applied CA research study is needed and how it relates (or not) to what has already been published in the literature base. The purpose of this section is to craft an argument that shows the audience why your work is needed and what the gap in knowledge is. This is especially important for applied research, particularly as you must point to the relevance of your work for those who work in your given field. This is thus the section of your proposal where you must set the context for your reader and briefly illuminate the previous research that has been conducted on your topic, both in relation to the broader body of CA research in your area of focus and other relevant substantively focused literature. When developing this section, it is helpful to start with a critical appraisal of the general literature base or relevant evidence and then narrow your discussion further as you build your argument.

Aims and Rationale

All research should be shaped by the aims and goals of the broader project. This is true even of research that is data driven, such as an applied CA research study. In the section of your proposal focused on discussing the aims and rationale of your study, you need to show how your aims or objectives will shape and direct your research, and how you will fill the gap in knowledge you pointed to in your introduction and literature review. It can be difficult to summarize your aims, particularly prior to data collection, but it is important to be as succinct as possible, recognizing that these aims may become clearer as you engage in the research process.

Methodological Approach and Methods

In some ways, your study will be both defined by and driven by your methodology or research approach. Often in qualitative research, the methodological approach and research methods are selected based on the research question developed, with an approach congruent with your research question being utilized (O'Reilly & Kiyimba, 2015). However, it is probable that you have selected an applied CA approach because it is congruent with your worldview. As such, your methodological choices will be determined by the approach itself, with your decisions guided by the parameters of CA. It is important to show your audience the core features of the methodological focus of your study and provide a rationale as to why an applied CA methodology is appropriate. In this section, you should show an awareness of the benefits and limitations of applied CA, particularly in relation to the focus of your work. Furthermore, it is advisable to include a description and rationale for the methods (or procedures) you plan to use, such as your plans for data collection, transcription, and data analysis.

Access and Ethics

As previously noted, in contemporary research you are likely to need ethical approval before you can begin data collection, and you must also complete your data collection and analysis in an ethical manner. Thus, the proposal is an ideal mechanism to outline your ethical strategy and describe your plan for recruiting participants and/or a research site(s). Because an applied CA research study often involves naturally occurring data, unique recruitment and ethical challenges commonly ensue, which you will need to be cognizant of even as you write up your proposal. We discuss key ethical considerations for an applied CA research study in Chapter 4.

Expected Contribution or Significance

As you are planning an applied CA research study, it is useful to introduce your reader to the expected or potential contributions that your research may make. It is important to demonstrate that your research has value to the population and area that you are studying. Considering the applied nature of this type of research, you may also want to highlight your study's potential for informing policy or practice.

Timeline

It is essential that you think about the timeline for the completion of your research. If you are undertaking a thesis/dissertation, the time frame may be dictated by your institution and could conceivably be relatively short. Regardless of your overall time frame, it is critical to ensure that your research aims are realistic, achievable, and sensible, and that you have contingency plans built in, as you may encounter challenges.

> For example: It is important to have a plan in case a research site withdraws from your study.

Dissemination

While it may seem a long way off, it is helpful to think about how and to whom you intend to disseminate your research findings. For instance, you may need to write a report for your participants or those who helped you to access the research site, or perhaps you plan to write solely for academic journals or present your findings at conferences. Regardless, it is useful to include your plans for dissemination in your proposal.

At this point in the chapter, we recommend that you apply these key ideas to your own research and complete the activity in Box 3.4.

A **research diary** serves as a tool for and written record of your ongoing research process, including your decision-making process and assumptions and feelings about the research.

Maintaining a Research Diary

In CA, keeping a ***research diary*** has not always been a priority. As such, it is not commonly

BOX 3.4
ACTIVITY ON DEVELOPING A RESEARCH PROPOSAL

Activity

Take some time to develop a draft outline of your research proposal. As you do so, consider your audience and explore whether there are particular expectations about what should and should not be included in your proposal. After you have created a draft outline of your proposal, share your proposal with colleagues and mentors/advisers, and invite critical feedback.

discussed in CA textbooks or seminars. However, qualitative research more broadly advocates for the use of a research diary or research journal (Watt, 2007). Indeed, many of those practicing CA appreciate the value of being reflexive in the process of research, something which a research diary facilitates.

Maintaining a research diary can be particularly valuable for students or those who are new to CA, as tracking decisions, feelings, and presuppositions can be helpful in writing up the research at a later stage. Practically, keeping a research diary is useful for tracking chronological accounts of events, decisions, and questions that occur throughout your research study (Burgess, 1981). While it may feel like an additional burden in an already time-consuming process, keeping a research diary for your project is important for a range of reasons including, but not limited to, the following:

- to make your reasoning transparent (Silverman, 2009);
- to ensure a clear audit trail (Smith, 1999);
- to facilitate your reflexivity (discussed later in this chapter), both during the process of the research and writing up your research (Nadin & Cassell, 2006);
- to track important appointments or events, particularly during data collection or when engaging with participants (Blaxter et al., 2001); and
- to facilitate your time management skills (Silverman, 2009).

There are many ways in which you can keep your diary, with the most common modalities being:

- Electronic format. You may keep your diary on a password-protected blog (see Paulus, Lester, & Dempster, 2014, for a discussion), or you may simply keep your diary entries on a Word document on your laptop/tablet, tracking your progress using memos or document pages. You can also insert web page links or images to help you organize your ideas and save them for future reference.
- Pen-and-paper method. You may wish to purchase a notebook with inserted divider pages so that you can color code your entries and categorize relevant issues.

- Calendar-style format. You may wish to download or purchase an actual diary with dates. A day-per-view diary would be preferable in most cases so that you can add entries on relevant dates.

We advise that you use your research diary in three main ways (O'Reilly & Parker, 2014), which we discuss in turn:

1. To keep a record of any factual information
2. To track and rationalize your decision making
3. To be reflexive

Factual Reporting

It is useful to record all information in your research diary, some of which will come as you read the literature, engage in discussions with others, communicate with your participants and/or stakeholders, and acquire feedback from advisers/mentors. In this element of your diary keeping, you should track the various appointments and events related to your research study, when you attended them, why you did so, what happened, and what you learned from it.

> For example: A PhD student may attend a general training workshop on CA and be advised that this methodology often favors the use of naturally occurring data, as this is congruent with the epistemological assumptions of the approach. So the student may note in the diary the date of the workshop, who ran it, contact details for the workshop leader for future reference, key things that were learned, and the need to follow up with additional readings.

Decision-Making Processes

In writing up your final research report, you will inevitably spend time describing and justifying the decisions you made. However, remembering the decisions you make throughout a study can be quite challenging, so it is important that you maintain a written record of them. If you make brief notes in your diary about what the decision was, when it was made, why it was made, what evidence and literature you used to make it, who you consulted during the decision-making process, and the outcome of the decision, you will find it much easier to provide answers to questions later.

> For example: Clinical practitioners recording their own psychotherapy sessions with their clients may decide that video recordings would be more appropriate than audio recordings. It will be important that the practitioners note their decision to make video recordings, note the specific date this decision was made, record any literature that informed their decision, and name the people that helped make the decision.

Reflexivity

A core purpose of keeping a research diary in qualitative research is to facilitate the reflexive process, which is important for any applied CA research study. With both the researcher and the researched viewed as active producers of knowledge, it is paramount that we engage in recursive (ongoing) *reflexivity*.

To be reflexive is to intentionally reflect upon our biases and analytical and theoretical assumptions and preferences. Further, reflexivity serves to move researchers outward and thereby expand and complicate their understanding of the phenomenon of focus (Gergen & Gergen, 1991).

Practically, then, a reflexive approach to research is one that aims to account for each decision and works to layer understandings of the data and the theories that inform the design, data collection, and analysis process. The research diary can be useful in clarifying and "unpacking" your thoughts and feelings during the research process (Clarke, 2009), and a useful mechanism for processing your presuppositions and biases.

> **Reflexivity** broadly entails researchers "turning back" on their own identities and presuppositions, taking note of how who they are both limits and privileges what they come to know and understand.

> (!) **We note that reflexivity as a concept and practice is not simplistic.**

> For example: A PhD student studying a sensitive area, such as bereavement counseling, may find listening to the therapist and client talking about these issues upsetting. This may be compounded further if the student had previously lost someone close to him or her. Writing about these feelings in the diary can be a helpful way of managing the emotions but also support the PhD student in thinking about how his or her own experience might impact the analysis process.

Being Reflexive

Reflexivity is "a central and yet confusing topic. In some social theories, it is an essential human capacity, in others it is a system property and in others it is a critical, or self-critical, act" (Lynch, 2000, p. 26). In qualitative research, reflexivity broadly relates to how the type of person you are, your motivations, and your investment in the research will have some impact on how you carry out your project. You will have had reasons for focusing on your topic, and there would be some thought processes to realizing why, and applied CA is the most appropriate way of addressing the questions. All types of qualitative research therefore are argued to benefit from reflexivity, and this includes applied CA.

It can be particularly helpful to the research process if you take a reflective position. We have recommended that you keep a research diary, and this enables you to write down your thoughts and feelings as you collect and analyze your data, reflect on your motivations for doing the research, and think about what you bring to the analysis. Reflexivity refers to examining how you have impacted upon the research process (Finlay, 2003) and how you have influenced that process from the idea formation through to the discussion (Finlay, 2002). In research terms, there are two types of reflexivity. These were outlined by Willig (2008), and we present a description of these in Table 3.3.

TABLE 3.3 ● Types of reflexivity	
Type	**Description**
Personal reflexivity	This refers to the reflection on your personal values, attitudes, political orientation, social identity, belief system, experiences, and the ways in which these have impacted on your research.
Epistemological reflexivity	This requires you to engage with your methodological approach and your research question to consider how the theoretical framework and the question construct contribute to the data production. This type of reflexivity encourages you to reflect on how your theoretical assumptions have shaped the findings.

Source: Willig, 2008.

Reflexivity is important for demonstrating the quality of your project, which is discussed later in the book. It is arguable that the benefit of reflexive research is in gaining a better understanding of your role in the research process, as well as increasing the transparency of the data and the general integrity of the process (Nadin & Cassell, 2006).

However, it has been argued that reflexivity is not simply a deconstructive exercise that locates the author in the world and in the research; rather, there is a diversity of positions on reflexivity. Macbeth (2001) identified three types:

1. Positional reflexivity

2. Textual reflexivity

3. Constitutive reflexivity

First, there is positional reflexivity, whereby reflecting is treated as a self-referential analytic exercise and demonstrates the analysts' uncertain position in the world (Macbeth, 2001). As Macbeth argued, "To my reading of the contemporary literature, this order of reflexivity has nearly become an obliged topic, if not method, for those who would do qualitative research" (p. 39). Second is textual reflexivity, referring to those studies that directly address the work of writing representations (Macbeth, 2001). In that sense, it accounts for a text that considers its own production (Latour, 1988). Third is constitutive reflexivity—that is, reflexivity of accounts in the sense of asking how accounts reflexively constitute the very events that those accounts are constructing (Garfinkel, 1967). Thus, constitutive reflexivity is often not accounted for in general texts on reflexivity but is associated with ethnomethodology and approaches informed by it. This form proposes a different understanding of reflexivity as "both a constitutive organization of everyday life and a practical organization that is available for study and description" (Macbeth, 2001, p. 48). In that sense, therefore, reflexivity in this kind of work recommends a study of ordinary practices, situated practices, and the indexicality of social order. In other words, ethnomethodological reflexivity relates to the organization of ordinary meanings; it attends to how facts and meanings in everyday activities are produced as "practical objectivities" (Macbeth, 2001). Furthermore, it has been argued that the ethnomethodological notion of being reflexive does not privilege a theoretical or methodological position through a contrast with an unreflexive counterpart and, as such, does not position reflexivity as a political, moral, or epistemological virtue in the same way as some qualitative approaches (Lynch, 2000).

Identifying and Acquiring Access to a Research Site

In qualitative research, and applied CA research more specifically, identifying a research site is a critical and often challenging aspect of planning your research study. In applied research, this process often includes identifying an institutional or applied context. Of course, even after you identify a possible research site, you must contact the gatekeepers to determine whether they are willing for you to conduct your research at their site. Thus, you must identify a site where both your phenomenon of interest is likely to exist *and* the gatekeepers at the site are willing for you to carry out your research. Indeed, as you are likely to be recording naturally occurring institutional activities, it is likely that some or all of your gatekeepers will also be participants in the study and will not only facilitate access to those who use the service or practice but also be recorded too.

> For example: If you are video recording medical practices, then the surgery manager and the general practitioners (GPs) will be the gatekeepers to recording patients; however, many of the GPs will also be recorded delivering the health service.
>
> For example: If you are video recording classroom interactions between children and teachers in an educational setting, then your gatekeepers are likely to be the school district administrators (school governors and head teacher), building principal, and the teachers working in the school. However, in the classroom, the teachers and other educational staff such as teaching assistants are also likely to be recorded.
>
> For example: If you are audio recording social workers interviewing families in suspected domestic violence cases, the social-work manager, the local authority representative, and possibly a broader committee are likely to be gatekeepers of the project. Furthermore, the social workers themselves are likely to be participants in the study as they carry out their interviews.

We recommend, therefore, that you treat the process of identifying and accessing a research site as if you are establishing a partnership (Lochmiller & Lester, 2017; O'Reilly & Kiyimba, 2015; Svirydzenka, Aitken, & Dogra, in press). As such, this process inherently demands that you respect the internal policies and expectations of a given research site and recognize that each site brings with it a unique culture and perspective on the notion of research. For instance, many institutional contexts have strict policies regarding the type of research that can be conducted on site and how one might gain access to conducting such research.

> For example: A PhD student wants to study mental health assessment interactions at a local hospital's mental health clinic. She discovers that prior to inviting individual clinicians and patients to participate (which entails her setting up a video-recording device to record their sessions), she must gain permission from the hospital's ethics review committee and management committee. In fact, she is told that prior to

(Continued)

(Continued)

meeting with her face-to-face to learn more about her research idea, the administrators would like to review her research protocol.

Thus, identifying and eventually acquiring access to a research site involves careful forethought about what you hope to study as well as thoughtful consideration of ethical requirements and procedures. There are likely to be layers of gatekeepers involved in deciding whether to allow you access to a site.

The process of gaining access to a research site requires you to communicate with key gatekeepers in thoughtful and respectful ways, recognizing that you may be asking them to give you access as an outsider. In other words, you will need the written informed consent from gatekeepers to access the site and, where necessary, their formal consent to participate in your research. Additionally, in applied CA research, you are typically hoping to audio or video record people's everyday practices, which some people may view as invasive and intimate, and they may feel overly protective of those people in their care. More particularly, within contexts wherein sensitive issues are a focus (e.g., therapy clinic), conducting research often entails some risk; therefore, a gatekeeper at such sites needs to understand the purpose and potential benefits of your intentions. Thus, there is a complexity in securing consent from gatekeepers when attempting to record naturally occurring events; therefore, the way in which you frame your project will be central to managing this.

After identifying a potential research site, you will need to communicate with the gatekeeper(s), who is quite often the primary administrator or director at a given site. There is no one right way to initiate your communication; however, it is paramount that you engage in open and transparent conversation about the goals and aims of your research.

For example: A research team interested in studying interactions between occupational therapists and children with sensory sensitivities hopes to video record therapy sessions. They are interested in the ways in which the body is incorporated into the therapy interaction. As such, the team contacts the clinical director of a local pediatric clinic by first sending an e-mail very briefly stating the overall scope of their project and requesting a short face-to-face meeting. The clinical director responds by indicating that she is willing to meet face-to-face at the clinical site but only has 15 minutes. Once the meeting is scheduled, the lead/coordinating member of the research team meets with the clinical director and provides her with a general overview of the study and invites any questions that she might have.

In Box 3.5, we offer a few practical tips to consider for identifying and accessing a research site for an applied CA research study.

BOX 3.5
PRACTICAL TIPS FOR IDENTIFYING AND SECURING A RESEARCH SITE

Practical Tips

✓ Identify a site wherein your area of research interest indeed exists. For instance, if you are interested in child–school therapist talk, you likely need to identify schools or school districts wherein school therapy is offered to children.

✓ Rather than identifying only one possible research site, consider identifying two or more possibilities, as having a backup plan is always useful.

✓ Determine early on whether you need to secure internal ethical approval to carry out your research.

✓ Request a meeting with the key gatekeepers at your research site to discuss your study and formally invite them to consider participating. It is often helpful to use multiple modes of communication to make your request, including e-mail and phone.

✓ Do your best to adapt your schedule to the needs of a gatekeeper.

✓ Even at the planning stages of your research, it is useful to share potential ways in which you envision your research informing practice. For applied CA studies, gatekeepers will be interested in this as they consider the costs and benefits of participating in your study.

✓ Explain to gatekeepers the nature of your research, the type of data you intend to collect, and why.

✓ Explain to gatekeepers how you plan to recruit participants, recognizing that identifying and gaining access to a research site does not guarantee that individual participants will agree to participate in your study.

An Interview With Professor Doug Maynard

In this chapter, you have likely noted that an applied CA study involves a series of complex decisions, and there are many different things that you need to think about as you go through the process. To build your understanding further, we interviewed Professor Doug Maynard about his applied CA research, asking him three questions about the planning involved in his research. His answers to our questions are in Box 3.6.

BOX 3.6
INTERVIEW WITH PROFESSOR DOUG MAYNARD   (?)

Professor Doug Maynard is a professor of sociology at the University of Wisconsin, Madison. Maynard is well known in the field of CA and has made many important contributions to our

(Continued)

(Continued)

knowledge of this approach. His recent work has been described as applied CA with a focus on medical interactions. He edited the following influential text on CA work in medical settings:

- Heritage, J., & Maynard, D. (Eds.). (2006). *Communication in medical care: Interaction between primary care physicians and patients*. Cambridge, England: Cambridge University Press.

We asked Professor Maynard three questions about how he plans his applied CA research, and answers to those questions are provided as follows.

What do you see as the main challenge of developing a research question in applied CA research?

"Any applied research that I have done has derived from more primary research. For example, I wrote an epilogue to *Bad News, Good News: Conversational Order in Everyday Talk and Clinical Settings* (Maynard, 2003), which was developed after extensive research on the simple question, How do participants, in interaction with one another, deliver and receive 'news'?

Although Jeremy Freese and Nora Cate Schaeffer and I eventually wrote a grant proposal to the National Science Foundation (which was funded), and whose explicit purpose was to improve response rates to survey interviews, it derived from the earlier collaborative research that Schaeffer and I did on the more basic question (following from Manny Schegloff's work on 'ordinary' phone calls) of how the openings to survey interviews are organized:

- Maynard, D. W., & Schaeffer, N. C. (1997). Closing the gate: Declinations of the request to participate in a telephone survey interview. *Sociological Methods & Research, 26*, 34–79.
- Maynard, D. W., & Schaeffer, N. C. (2002). Opening and closing the gate: The work of optimism in recruiting survey respondents. In D. W. Maynard, H. Houtkoop-Steenstra, N. C. Schaeffer, & H. v. d. Zouwen (Eds.), *Standardization and tacit knowledge: Interaction and practice in the survey interview* (pp. 179–205). New York, NY: Wiley Interscience.

So the main challenge, in my experience, has been knowing how a domain of interaction is organized in the first place, such that an applied research question can be well formulated relative to knowledge about that domain."

How do you approach sampling when doing an applied research project?

"I think it's important to remember that *sampling* is a term that has its provenance in large-scale survey research, where the goal is to develop a probability sample that will allow for generalizing to the entire population being studied. That is only one method for being able to generalize. Harvey Sacks taught us that, in studying interaction, the issue of generalization is a different one. We are studying what he called the *construction of the culture*, or what we might also call the *construction of commonsense knowledge*. This sort of knowledge is not organized by way of probabilistic sampling. Rather, as Schegloff has put it, such knowledge and the social actions through which our common sense is implemented are organized on a case-by-case basis. The need is for tools that allow us to capture the order and organization that even a single case will exhibit. So that's why we work with everything from single episodes to 'collections' rather than samples. And collections are opportunistically built. One case will do, if you have the requisite tools for its analysis. More cases will always help, but there is no fixed number, and collections are just another tool. See:

- Sacks, H. (1984). Notes on methodology. In J. M. Atkinson & J. Heritage (Eds.), *Structures of social action* (pp. 21–27). Cambridge, England: Cambridge University Press.

- Schegloff, E. A. (1987). Analyzing single episodes of interaction: An exercise in conversation analysis. *Social Psychology Quarterly*, *50*(2), 101–114.

On the other hand, if you get into studying 'outcomes,' then sampling in a traditional sense becomes very important. So does coding. We can learn about these topics from more traditional methodological resources but with an eye toward the unique challenges of doing CA research by way of sampling, coding, and regression-type techniques."

What is your experience of communicating with institutional gatekeepers for your applied CA research project?

"Every project that I've done in some institution or organization—legal, medical, survey, etc.—has entailed different experiences. We are intruders, and some gatekeepers welcome the intrusion, and some do not. In either case, I think there is an immediate need to speak to what matters most to the gatekeepers about their own enterprise and to raise the issue of whether and how our research might help with their endeavors, or endeavors like theirs, as in other or future settings of the enterprise. This is not only important for getting access, it enhances the research from the get-go because it requires thinking about what the enterprise is in the institution you are studying from the practitioners' point of view. . . . If I were to say more about this question, I would have to write a book.

When starting a project, and seeking permission to video record, my only other caveat is to never take 'no' for an answer."

Chapter Summary

In this chapter, we discussed some of the key considerations for planning your applied CA study. First, we presented the importance and process of conducting a literature review. Second, we highlighted the process of developing a research question within the context of an applied CA research study, emphasizing the iterative nature of an applied CA project. Third, we provided an overview of the common components of a research proposal while also noting that your audience and purpose in writing a proposal shape what is ultimately included. Fourth, we pointed to the value of maintaining a research diary. Finally, we concluded the chapter by describing the sampling process in an applied CA study and offering some practical advice related to identifying and communicating with a research site, participants, and key stakeholders. We summarize the key learning points from the chapter in the next box.

Learning Points From Chapter 3

- Conducting a literature review for an applied CA study includes examining both CA-specific literature and substantively relevant literature.

- Developing a research protocol requires consideration of your audience and specific institutional requirements and expectations.

- Communicating with gatekeepers is a central aspect of pursuing an applied CA study and requires forethought and care.

Recommended Readings

A multitude of general publications highlight critical considerations for planning a qualitative research study. There are relatively few publications that are specifically addressed to those engaged in applied CA research. Nonetheless, we have listed general references that we believe are particularly useful for planning your study.

- Boote, D. N., & Beile, P. (2005). Scholars before researchers: On the centrality of the dissertation literature review in research preparation. *Educational Researcher, 34*(6), 3–15.

While this article was written for an education audience, it offers an important argument about the value of and need for engaging in a careful and sophisticated literature review. The authors provide criteria to use to evaluate the quality of a dissertation literature review, thereby providing readers with a useful heuristic for evaluating their own and others' literature reviews.

- Clarke, K. (2009). Uses of a research diary: Learning reflectively, developing understanding and establishing transparency. *Nurse Researcher, 17*(1), 68–76.

This article deals with research diaries in relation to a phenomenological study, not an applied CA research study. However, it is important that you engage with a broad literature during your project, and what is especially useful about this article is that it is a personal account of an applied student researcher's use of a reflexive research diary. Much of what is written within this article is translatable and useful in the context of an applied CA research study.

- Watt, D. (2007). On becoming a qualitative researcher: The value of reflexivity. *The Qualitative Report, 12*(1), 82–101.

This article provides a useful example of the ways in which a qualitative researcher can engage in reflexivity. The author offers multiple examples from her own research that highlight the value and challenge of engaging in ongoing reflexivity. The value of maintaining a diary is also stressed here, with the central role of reflexivity foregrounded.

Engaging With the Ethics of Doing Research in Institutional Settings

The focus of this chapter is to introduce you to the key principles of research ethics as well as to examine common ethical dilemmas that you are likely to encounter when doing applied conversation analysis (CA) research. Thus, in this chapter, we first provide a general overview of some of the critical considerations related to ethics in research and then discuss core ethical principles. We position our discussion against the backdrop of the contemporary judgment of ethics generated through research panels of ethical experts and laypeople charged with assuring that research teams act ethically within research projects (e.g., ethics committees/institutional review boards).

While we provide a foundational discussion of ethics, the focus of this chapter is on the application of ethical principles to applied CA research studies, and thus we consider some of the specific ethical issues relevant to this kind of research. Many applied CA research studies include participants that may be considered vulnerable and/or include the study of topics that could be viewed as delicate or sensitive; as such, we offer practical advice for dealing ethically with this reality. Furthermore, due to the potentially delicate nature of data collected within many applied CA research studies, and/or some of the potential risks that may be involved in the data collection process, we also consider issues related to researcher safety, providing practical advice for remaining ethically reflexive.

An Overview of Ethics in Research

Ethics, which govern daily moral interactions, are an important part of any research study, with many researchers holding varying views about what constitutes moral behavior.

Whatever ethical views or positions you hold regarding research, it will always be important that you are aware of and remain critically reflexive about the ethical issues that might arise in your applied CA research study. Before reading further, we invite you to reflect on your own ethical position, as this will influence the way you engage with the discussion and ultimately how you approach ethics in your applied CA research study. Consider the activity in Box 4.1.

> In research, **ethics** are the general principles that govern our behavior in everyday life. More specifically, ethics is a branch of knowledge related to moral philosophy.

BOX 4.1
ACTIVITY ON REFLECTING ON ETHICS

Activity

Before you consider the details of the ethical principles relevant to applied CA research studies, it is useful to take time to think about your own moral position in relation to the protection of participants. While one's answers to the following questions are certainly subject to debate, it is useful to consider these questions whenever embarking on an applied CA research study:

- Do you think all participants need to be protected from researchers?

- Do you think researchers typically do enough to protect participants?

- Do you think that as a research community we are overprotective?

- Do you think that some of the ethical concerns that arise in research contradict each other? If so, what might be an example of this?

- To what extent do you think your own moral framework influences the way you do research?

- Do you think applied CA research studies have particularly sensitive ethical concerns in comparison to other approaches to qualitative research? If so, what might these be?

Philosophies of Ethics

Moral philosophy is a complex field with a range of different theoretical perspectives and views of ethics. It is not our intention to provide a philosophical debate here, and neither will we provide comprehensive detail about the different ways in which ethics have been subject to critical rhetoric. Rather, we provide a simplified overview of the more common ethical philosophies that have had an important influence on research practice.

Moral philosophy is a branch of philosophy that concerns itself with various theories of ethics, particularly metaethics (questions of morality), normative ethics (providing moral frameworks to ascertain actions that are right and wrong), and applied ethics (the application of ethical theories to specific cases).

Although there is a broad range of positions in the field of moral philosophy, we suggest that three positions or approaches to ethics have been most influential on research practice.

- Consequentialism: This approach to ethics focuses on the consequences of a researcher's actions and any outcomes of harm that may be caused to participants.

What this means: Although negative outcomes of a research study may not be intended by the researcher, and while a researcher may have followed general ethical rules and principles, the research may still cause harm to the participants.

For applied CA researchers, the general norm is to record naturally occurring events and transcribe them for analysis; a researcher may not consider the consequences of publishing direct quotations from his or her data set. Thus, an applied CA researcher who takes up a consequentialist view of ethics would be particularly focused on outlining potential negative outcomes of his or her research, such as published quotations or transcripts potentially serving to identify a participant unintentionally.

- Deontology: This is an approach which focuses on the creation of moral rules and principles for researchers to follow, and is thus a rules-based approach.

> *What this means:* There is an expectation that ethics is embedded into the research process and therefore something that is considered when planning a study. Also, ethics is considered a universal aspect of research, and general rules are therefore created to guide researchers in their practice.

For the deontologist, what is important is the process of ethics—the actions of the researchers. This approach focuses on the principles that researchers follow in their ethical course. For applied CA researchers, it is necessary to consider the potential benefits and possible harms that may occur by recording naturally occurring events, and taking precautionary steps to maximize benefit and minimize harm, with these steps being based on general ethical principles.

- Virtue ethics: This approach to ethics emphasizes the individual and his or her responsibility as a moral agent, with the researcher viewed as capable of moral reasoning.

> *What this means:* The moral character of the researcher will be highly influential in the way in which the research is conducted.

A virtue-oriented approach to ethics is concerned with the personality, characteristics, and moral reasoning of the researcher. For applied CA researchers, this approach would assume that some researchers will take longer than others to consider possible ethical concerns with the data, whereas others will be more dismissive of potential issues based on their belief that the possibility of harm is minimal.

Ethics Committees and Review Boards

In contemporary research, many researchers utilize a rules-based view of ethics, although some combine this with an assessment of both the risks and benefits of their research. General ethical rules are practically implemented in applied CA projects, with the ethicality of the certain principles or rules being judged in advance by an ***ethics committee*** (i.e., review board).

Ethics committees tend to consist of a group of individuals who volunteer to make ethical judgments about proposed research. Typically, at least one layperson sits on the panel.

These ethical collectives are typically referred to as *research ethics committees* in countries such as the United Kingdom, and as *institutional review boards* in countries such as the United States. Recently, ethical review of proposed research studies (prior to beginning participant recruitment and data collection) has become mandatory in many countries.

To understand the role of ethics committees, it is necessary to have a basic understanding of the history. The broad history of ethics is extensive and lies predominantly in philosophy, but its application to research has been influenced mostly by medical research. This emphasis on research ethics is typically linked to the Nuremburg trials after World War II, although there is evidence that it dates back before this era (Ashcroft, 2003) as there were many ethical transgressions that happened prior to this (European Commission, 2010). However, it was the horrors of the Nazi experiments during World War II, as well as other research scandals, that led to the construction of three influential documents:

- the Belmont Report,

- the Declaration of Helsinki, and

- the Nuremberg Code.

In Table 4.1, we provide a brief description of each of these documents.

TABLE 4.1   ●   Influential ethics documents

Document	Description
The Belmont Report	In 1979, this report was released in the United States in response (in part) to the Tuskegee Syphilis Study. It outlined three research practices for biomedical and behavioral science research: (1) protecting the autonomy of participants by engaging in informed consent, (2) minimizing harm and maximizing benefits to individuals who participate in research, and (3) engaging in nonexploitative research.
The Declaration of Helsinki	This document details the ethical principles developed by the World Medical Association specifically related to engaging in medical research that involves humans.
The Nuremberg Code	This code was developed after the Nuremberg trials where 23 Nazi doctors were tried for their crimes during World War II. This code included the development of 10 ethical principles, with a focus on voluntary consent and the importance of medical research benefiting society.

In the United Kingdom, the first formal health research committees were established in 1991 (Hedgecoe, 2009), and in 2001, social research in health was included in this agenda. Many scholars have noted that institutional review boards have "evolved within a clinical and biomedical framework" that does not always align well with social science research studies (American Association of University Professors, 2000, section I, n.p.). For non-health-based research, it is typically the responsibility of universities or other government-funded bodies to judge ethical credibility.

Large funding bodies have been instrumental in promoting and ensuring this, as well as the pressure applied by journals and the scholarly community to report ethical procedures (Hunter, 2008).

What is notable is that while most Western countries have mandatory ethical reviews, there are some differences in what they view as ethically important and the strategies that they consider necessary for carrying out ethical research. Even within an individual country, different ethics committees take issue with different ethical concerns within projects. Thus, while there may be overarching ethical principles, how these principles are implemented and made relevant to a given project may vary widely across institutions and countries. Consequently, when researchers form collaborative relationships across countries or even institutions within a given country, it is important to explore the ethical complexities that may emerge due to differing requirements.

Ethical Concerns Specific to Qualitative Research

Over the last few decades, there has been a consistent emphasis on ethics in research across methodological approaches. Yet there is a growing body of literature that points to ethical considerations that are unique to qualitative research. Within the field of qualitative research, there is a range of perspectives on its ethicality. Some scholars have suggested that the level of risk is not the same across methodologies, particularly when comparing quantitative and qualitative methodologies (Hedgecoe, 2008). In fact, some have suggested that qualitative research poses far fewer risks to participants (Ensign, 2003). However, others have argued that this may be naïve and highlight an uncritical romanticizing of qualitative research (Kvale, 2008; O'Reilly & Kiyimba, 2015).

We suggest that indeed there are important ethical considerations within a qualitative research project, with many of these being unique given the assumptions inherent to the qualitative research process, and these are relevant to applied CA work. O'Reilly and Kiyimba (2015) pointed to (at a minimum) five unique characteristics of qualitative ethics, which we highlight in Table 4.2.

More generally, O'Reilly and Kiyimba (2015) also presented four markers of ethical qualitative research, which they argued were: (1) acquiring informed consent; (2) maintaining anonymity and confidentiality; (3) attending to issues related to power, coercion, and researcher responsibility; and (4) considering critically the relationship between the researchers and participant(s). As you consider your own research study, take a few moments to complete the activity in Box 4.2.

Ethical Concerns Specific to Applied CA

Applied CA research is likely to invoke many ethical issues that need to be considered in your research project. For example, not unlike other types of data, naturally occurring data can be highly sensitive given that you are recording people going about the "business of their lives." In doing so, people may engage in activities or share details that, if intentionally or accidentally disclosed, could have negative consequences.

TABLE 4.2 ● Characteristics of qualitative ethics	
Uniqueness	**Description**
Depth	Qualitative researchers typically collect in-depth information about people's lives and everyday social activities. This depth may be perceived by participants as intrusive and/or result in the collection of highly sensitive material, which may be particularly evident when including vulnerable populations in a study (Flewitt, 2005). Thus, a focus on depth over breadth can lead to a variety of unexpected ethical considerations and dilemmas.
Researcher involvement	The researcher is inevitably embedded in the research process and is often an integral part of the data collection process. For instance, the qualitative researcher is often described as the "research instrument," as he or she is the "collector" of the data. Often, this requires a researcher to build relationships with gatekeepers and participants at the research site for them to be comfortable with the nature of this in-depth data collection (Duncan, Drew, Hodgson, & Sawyer, 2009).
Iterative process	The qualitative research process is iterative rather than linear, and therefore, the impacts of the research on the participants and researcher are difficult to predict. For instance, changes to research questions may occur as data are simultaneously collected and analyzed. Such changes, of course, should be shared with research participants, with ongoing invitations to consent (or not) to participate in each study.
Visibility	Because in-depth materials are typically collected in qualitative research, there is an increased risk of participant identification. From the actual audio or video recordings to the inclusion of direct quotations in research reports, there are myriad ways in which qualitative research puts a participant at risk of being identified with a certain data set.
Data management	Given that qualitative researchers often collect highly personal information, it is important to consider necessary precautions for securely storing qualitative data.

Source: Adapted from O'Reilly & Kiyimba, 2015.

BOX 4.2

ACTIVITY FOCUSED ON CONSIDERING ETHICAL ISSUES FOR YOUR RESEARCH STUDY

Activity

Your research study will inevitably bring with it ethical concerns that are specific to your research focus, context, and participants. While you cannot predict all of the ethical concerns you may face when carrying out your research study, you can certainly develop a general sense of ethical concerns that may emerge and then develop a tentative plan or process for responding. Indeed, it is particularly important to spend time throughout your research study (including during the planning phases) to consider and plan for ethical issues.

Take a few moments to generate a list of potential ethical concerns or dilemmas that may emerge in your study given its focus and research context. After creating your list, identify the strategies or practices that you might use when working through these ethical concerns.

> For example: A researcher plans to collect data at a counseling center in a local school. Many of the recorded sessions include students/clients sharing negative information about their teachers and peers. This information is highly detailed and personal, and would probably cause distress to the participants if they were to be identified.

Because an applied CA study quite often involves data collection within institutional contexts, the very context of your research study may be inherently sensitive. From schools to medical clinics to mental health centers to law courts, these kinds of research contexts typically involve people sharing sensitive and personal materials. It is therefore important that you remain reflexive about the unique ethical concerns of your study *throughout* your research process.

In the collection of naturally occurring data and using CA to examine the social interaction, there are three broad areas of ethical interest, each of which we consider in turn.

1. General ethical principles
2. Ethics of using video- or audio-recording devices
3. Ethical issues of computer-mediated data

General Ethical Principles of an Applied CA Study

Ethical issues for applied CA work typically relate to the four core principles of ethics, which are

1. respect for autonomy;
2. principle of justice;
3. promotion of beneficence; and
4. ensuring nonmaleficence.

Autonomy refers to the freedom or independence of individuals to govern their own actions. In relation to ethics, autonomy refers to the idea that each participant should be respected and given the opportunity to make his or her own decisions.

Respect for Autonomy

Respect for the ***autonomy*** of your participants is fundamental to ethical practice in applied CA research and is often addressed through the principles of informed consent and right to withdraw.

Informed consent

The concept of autonomy refers to the notion that research participants have the right to make their own choices and that researchers should respect individual liberty. It is this concept that has become central in guiding research ethics. One fundamental way in which this is achieved is through the process of ***informed consent***, which, when collecting data that are naturally occurring, does require some careful attention.

●

Informed consent refers to the participants being fully aware of the necessary facts about a research project upon which to base their decision whether to participate.

Acquiring informed consent is not a straightforward practice, and thus it is important that you think through this aspect carefully. Respecting the autonomy of your participants requires that you do not deceive them and that you provide them with the right to withdraw from your research should they so decide. Acquiring informed consent is particularly important in a project that uses applied CA given that this type of research relies heavily on actual recordings of participants within (typically) institutional settings. Furthermore, this type of research takes a micro approach to the data and investigates the interactions with great scrutiny. It is therefore crucial that the participants understand

1. what the analyst intends to do with the data,

2. how the data will be stored, and

3. how they will be represented in any form of dissemination (e.g., journal publication).

The process of obtaining informed consent may feel like a mere formality, but it is important that it is taken seriously. Certain groups who you invite to participate in your applied CA project may be more vulnerable than others. This may result in you having to explain your study in greater detail or in a different way to ensure that the "informed" aspect of the consent is truly achieved.

For example: If you plan to record visits to sexual health clinics, this is typically viewed as a stigmatized institutional interaction, and the participants could experience some embarrassment. As such, it will be especially important that they understand how the data will be used and recognize they can choose not to participate in the study.

For example: Unaccompanied minors with refugee status who are attending child counseling sessions may find it difficult to fully understand your study due to language and cultural differences. Additionally, prior to including these children in your study, you would need parental consent, which is clearly more complicated in cases in which children are in the care of the state.

What we have demonstrated through these examples is that the process of gaining informed consent can be complicated by the nature of the "applied" setting from which you are seeking to recruit participants. This may be further complicated by the kind of participants you are hoping to recruit (e.g., children versus adults). In addition, the very nature of the institutional interactions you are hoping to record may make some participants more resistant to being recorded for research purposes.

For some groups of individuals, you may need to carefully consider the issue of capacity to make decisions related to a range of vulnerabilities and competencies. In the case of children, for example, their capacity to make informed decisions relates to *Gillick competency*, which has typically been used in relation to medical treatments but is also adopted as a measure of whether someone has the capacity to provide informed consent to participate in research.

> The concept of **Gillick competency** relates to a case in law (the case of Victoria Gillick) that addressed whether doctors could give contraceptives to those under the age of 16 years without parental consent (Taylor, 2007).

In research, the general understanding is that all adults are assumed to have the capacity to decide whether to participate in research unless there is evidence to the contrary. While indeed this is a sensitive consideration, there have been several groups of adults that have historically been positioned as not necessarily having the capacity to make informed decisions for a variety of reasons, including

> (!) **Remember that competence is not a permanent state, and just because someone is competent or incompetent on a given day does not mean he or she will remain in that state.**

- adults with certain mental illnesses,
- adults detained in prisons,
- adults with certain intellectual disabilities,
- adults who are grieving,
- adults who are dying,
- adults in a heightened state of anxiety, and
- older adults with chronic illnesses (e.g., dementia).

Indeed, the issue of capacity and competence is equally important for adults and children. In terms of informed consent and the capacity to provide it, the participant of any age or status must meet certain criteria, as outlined in Table 4.3.

It is important to recognize that it does not necessarily mean the end of your study if your participants do not have the capacity to consent, as you may be able to obtain their *assent* instead, but are likely to also need consent from a legal guardian.

> **Assent** refers to the general (but not necessarily fully informed) agreement by the participant to take part in the research. Typically, assent involves a caretaker first providing consent for an individual to participate (e.g., parent granting consent for a child to participate).

TABLE 4.3 ● Criteria for competence and capacity	
Criteria	**Description**
Comprehension	Must be able to comprehend and retain the information that you give them about your study, including what will happen before, during, and after it.
Risk versus benefit	Must be able to balance the risks and benefits of taking part in your research, including recognizing any potential consequences of their participation.
Communication	Must be able to communicate their preferences to either participate or decline.

It is important to keep in mind that in applied CA research, consent should be iteratively acquired, and it is your responsibility to watch for signals that a participant would prefer to withdraw. Consent is something you acquire in an ongoing way and thus should be checked at various junctures during a research study (Mahon, Glendinning, Clarke, & Craig, 1996; O'Reilly, Parker, & Hutchby, 2011). In applied CA research, this is particularly important, as you are likely to be collecting data in a natural institutional setting and the participants may simply forget they are being recorded and say things that they may not want to be retained. We provide an example of the iterative nature of consent from a research study in Box 4.3.

BOX 4.3

PERSONAL CASE EXAMPLE OF ITERATIVELY INFORMED CONSENT

Personal Case Example

In one of our recent applied CA studies, we video recorded naturally occurring child mental health assessments. For this study, we invited the consent of clinical managers, clinical practitioners (who were also being recorded), the parents (and other adult family members), the child who was being assessed, and siblings (when present).

(Continued)

(Continued)

Because child mental health assessments are often sensitive in nature and may have legal implications, several consent decisions were made:

1. Acute and emergency cases would be excluded (as there may be issues with consent and competency).

2. Clinicians were given the option to exclude certain families based on referral notes before we approached them in any way.

3. Families were sent information about the research study in writing with their appointment letter approximately 2 weeks before the appointment.

4. Families and clinical practitioners gave consent to the researchers in person while they were waiting in the waiting room. All questions were answered at this point.

5. Families gave consent again at the end of the appointment (in case anything came up during the appointment that they did not want included in the research).

6. The right to withdraw was available up to the point of the first publication, and they could still withdraw from subsequent publications.

7. Families were reminded at the end of the appointment how the data would be analyzed and disseminated, and were sent a summary of findings by mail.

Right to Withdraw

In the ethics literature, it is generally understood that participants have the right to withdraw from a research study at any point in the research process, noting that once something is published they generally cannot withdraw their data from it. It is this right to withdraw from the research that provides the participants with some autonomy over the process. A participant's right to withdraw should be made evident in written form. In an applied CA research study, it is not likely that you will be able to step into the middle of a counseling session, a courtroom interaction, a classroom lesson, a wedding, a police interrogation interview, or a child–social work interview (to name just a few examples) to remind participants of their right to withdraw from a study, and thus the timing of the reminder should be carefully managed. Unlike collecting interview data, for instance, where the interviewer may start to see signs of distress or discomfort and then remind the participant that he or she can stop answering questions at any point, a researcher may have less control when collecting naturally occurring data in an institutional setting. Furthermore, it is unlikely (yet possible) that the recording causes the participants distress; rather, the very nature of the institutional interaction may result in distress, which the researcher typically has no control over. Nonetheless, the participants do have the right to withdraw the recordings once the event is complete.

For applied CA research studies, there are several issues that need to be considered in terms of a participant's right to withdraw:

- It is often difficult for participants to exercise their right to withdraw. This is particularly true in applied CA research studies, as the participants may not interact much with the researcher given that most of their interactions are within natural institutional settings.

- It is the responsibility of the researcher to consistently remind participants of their right to withdraw. However, in applied CA research studies this can be difficult, as they are generally not included in the interactions that are being recorded (although some researchers are also the institutional representative—that is, the therapist, teacher, or doctor).

- If one participant does exercise his or her right to withdraw from the research, this may mean that you lose the entire recording, even if all other participants maintain their consent. This would be the case if the interactions of the person who has withdrawn are central to the interactions being analyzed.

Principle of Justice

The principle of *justice* is an important guiding principle in our understanding of our moral obligations to the participants when collecting data that are naturally occurring. This principle is also closely linked to equality and fairness.

> **Justice** in ethics refers to the need to treat your participants fairly and equally, and provide equal opportunities for participation.

The principle of justice relates to providing all people within a specific population equal opportunity to participate in a research study, and when they choose to participate, treating them equitably and justly. Historically, people have not always been treated fairly in research, and for this to be realized in practice means that you need to ensure there is careful consideration of *both* the benefits and risks of your applied CA research study.

> *What this means:* To ensure the principle of justice means that you cannot expose one group of people to any kind of risk solely for the benefit of other groups. As such, when recruiting participants, you need to ensure that you are not treating different types of participants with prejudice or discrimination.

> *For example:* If you are recording classroom reading lessons, you cannot exclude the children who may stutter simply because their speech may be more challenging to transcribe and apply the specialist CA transcription system to.

Freedom From Coercion

In terms of justice, you need to consider the status of your participants and think about whether certain groups of people might be more easily persuaded to allow you to record them in applied settings than others due to a variety of issues, such as fear of authority, eagerness to please, gratitude to the gatekeepers, limited capacity to understand, openness to persuasion through rewards, and so forth.

Generally, there are two main factors that have been identified as potentially affecting participants' willingness to participate, and these include the level of risk that the research may expose participants to and the opportunity for financial inducement (Dunn, Kim, Fellows, & Palmer, 2009). Offering of payment is considered to result in an inducement, and this raises concerns for participants who may be vulnerable, as it may unduly influence their decision. Furthermore, participants are often more likely to respond to a general call to participate in a research study if they stand to gain financially. Thus, it is possible that researchers may even unintentionally coerce people via financial incentives.

> For example: Consider people who may be in a difficult living situation, such as individuals who may be in immediate need of additional financial support. They may be more likely to be coerced to participate in a research study that offers a financial incentive.

Therefore, a risk of coercion confounds the principle of justice, as coercive practices (including those that are unintentional) may encourage certain participants to take risks that they would not otherwise take (McNeill, 1997).

Including Difficult-to-Reach People in Research

A core aspect of ensuring the principle of justice is that vulnerable, hard-to-reach, and otherwise often excluded groups of people are included in research or at least given the opportunity to consider participating in research. You should think critically about strategies that promote the inclusion of vulnerable populations in your research study. To promote such inclusion, you may even need to make special adaptations to your research design and be imaginative in terms of how you recruit vulnerable or hard-to-reach groups in your research.

Beneficence in ethics refers to maintaining the well-being of research participants and is grounded on the idea of maximizing benefits to the participants.

Nonmaleficence in ethics refers to maintaining the well-being of research participants and is grounded on the idea of doing no harm to participants.

Beneficence and Nonmaleficence

The principle of **beneficence** refers to having the best interests of the research participants in mind and acting upon this. In other words, researchers should promote the well-being of the research participants and very carefully assess the benefits of their research study. An applied CA researcher, therefore, should give some thought to what the benefits of the study might be for practice.

The principle of **nonmaleficence** is closely related to beneficence and refers explicitly to doing no harm to participants.

In practice, a researcher is obligated to minimize potential harm, maximize benefits, and reduce risks. The benefits and risks of a study should be assessed in relation to both individual research participants and society at large. Importantly, it is not always possible to *fully* know all the benefits and risks of a given study prior to conducting it.

> *What this means:* To ensure the principle of beneficence and the principle of nonmaleficence means that you must reduce the risk of harm and continually promote the best outcome for your participants. In other words, you should privilege your participants and seek out ways in which your research might benefit them and/or society at large while minimizing any risks.

When considering and promoting the benefits of a given study, it is helpful to think about how the results of your study may impact the well-being of people. For applied CA research studies, this may lead you to examine how studying everyday practices may result in an understanding of how to perform these social practices in a more effective or beneficial way.

> (!) **The risks and benefits of a research study may not be fully evident until after a study has begun.**

> For example: A researcher who is interested in studying medical interactions in an emergency medicine department might focus his or her analysis on the initial interactions between a patient and a clinician. The researcher might position this study as an intervention-oriented study and thus seek to directly impact how the clinicians pose questions and elicit information that may allow them to more meaningfully triage cases and effectively treat a patient. In this case, the researcher may suggest that the benefit of the study is one that might be seen long term—after clinicians begin to implement a more effective questioning sequence that is developed upon careful analysis of the data set.

Quite often, in qualitative research generally and applied CA research specifically, the benefits of a study may occur when giving back to research participants and/or the community in which you conduct your research. Giving back quite often includes a researcher sharing the research findings with the community in such a way that the practical implications of the findings are evidenced.

> For example: A research team studying the social practices of child therapists at a pediatric clinic held community forums in which the research participants were invited to learn about the research findings and discuss the practical implications to their

(Continued)

(Continued)

own work. In these meetings, the research team also invited the participants to speak back to the research findings and offer suggestions for deepening their analysis and furthering the research study.

Beyond considering the benefits, it is critical to examine the risks of your research study. While it might be tempting to assume that no risks are involved in your research, no study is without risk, and indeed, risk comes in many different forms (e.g., physical, psychological, emotional). For instance, in applied CA research, it is important to think through the consequences of a breach in confidentiality. Given that this type of research may entail the collection of highly sensitive and personal data, a breach in confidentiality could result in a participant experiencing negative consequences (e.g., being identifiable to others, damage to reputation, being shamed or embarrassed, etc.). Regardless of the nature of your study, completing a careful risk assessment is important and should be something that you do throughout your study, not simply prior to beginning data collection.

> (!) **Researcher safety is an important consideration when considering the risks of carrying out a certain study, and this includes research using applied CA.**

Closely related to risks to participants, it is paramount that researchers also consider their own safety and well-being, as they too might be placed at risk when conducting research (Parker & O'Reilly, 2013). The methodological literature has highlighted the importance of thinking about researcher safety regarding one's physical safety as well as the emotional impacts of carrying out a research study (Dickson-Swift, James, Kippen, & Liamputtong, 2009) or analyzing sensitive data (Fincham, Scourfield, & Langer, 2008). As such, it is important to consider your own safety when conducting a risk assessment for a given research study.

Ethics of Using Audio or Video Recordings

In many cases, *sensitive* refers to the inclusion of vulnerable groups (e.g., children) and/or data that deal with sensitive topics (e.g., domestic abuse) that may be considered difficult, challenging, embarrassing, or stigmatizing. The nature of such research can be limiting, as some participants may be uncomfortable having naturally occurring (sensitive) activities recorded and thereby represented in semipermanent records. In some of these circumstances, there may be legal ramifications for participants and, therefore, safeguarding issues that the researcher will be obliged to abide by. Regardless, you should remain thoughtful about the potential for ethical issues to arise at any point in the research process, particularly as you begin collecting and analyzing data.

Recording participants in their natural institutional environments does create additional ethical sensitivities. Notably, a digital recording creates a semipermanent record of that interaction (Grimshaw, 1982), and thus there is a longevity to the data that creates additional risks of identification. While we certainly do live in a world of surveillance and people generally are accustomed to being recorded across a range of settings, an often-noted concern is whether what is being said in the natural setting is on or off the record (O'Reilly et al., 2011). Further, video data may create additional concerns given that it creates visual permanence, increasing the chances of participants being easily identified. Given the ethical sensitivity of recorded data, it is important to make thoughtful and reflexive decisions about whether it is essential to collect video data or whether audio will be sufficient for your research purposes (Luff & Heath, 2012).

Related to these ethical issues is the debate regarding the alteration of behavior. As ethical practice requires participants to be informed that they are being recorded, there is the possibility that they may change the way they act because of the presence of a recording device. Some scholars have noted that it is not necessarily true that people will change with the presence of a recording device (Speer & Hutchby, 2003). Generally, people become acclimated to the presence of a recording device and soon continue interacting as they typically do (Bottorff, 1994). Regardless, it is important that you think carefully about the impact of recording devices on the participants' lives and activities, keeping in mind that as a researcher you commit to *doing no harm*.

Ethics of Computer-Mediated Data

Naturally occurring data also raise concerns related to what counts as public versus private, particularly when collecting computer-mediated communication (e.g., grief support group blog discussions). There are ethical concerns that are specific to working with computer-mediated data. The Association of Internet Researchers (https://aoir.org) maintains an Ethics Working Committee that has produced several useful reports delineating critical considerations for engaging in research on and about the Internet. These reports serve as a useful starting point for researchers who plan to collect and analyze computer-mediated data. We discuss this kind of data further in Chapter 6.

Ethical Benefits of Using Naturally Occurring Data

Indeed, there are important ethical concerns related to the collection of naturally occurring data. However, the use of naturally occurring data also brings with it some ethical benefits. For instance, in some ways, collecting naturally occurring data may result in the researcher placing fewer additional demands or burdens on the participants. This is because participants within the institutional setting will be routinely engaging in interactions whether they are recorded or not, and any document will be written regardless of whether research is being conducted. In other words, by collecting naturally occurring activities for research, you may not subject the participants to anything additional that they may find upsetting or embarrassing, as any distress may be attributable to the natural setting and not your research specifically.

An Interview With Professor Tom Strong

Undertaking applied CA research involving data that are potentially sensitive in nature or data that require additional ethical parameters will demand a greater attention to ethics. Professor Tom Strong is experienced in collecting and analyzing data that involve vulnerable participants and potentially sensitive topics. We therefore interviewed him about his work, with his answers listed in Box 4.4.

BOX 4.4
INTERVIEW WITH PROFESSOR TOM STRONG

Tom Strong is a professor with the Educational Studies in Counseling Psychology Program at the University of Calgary and is also a practicing couples and family therapist. He researches and writes widely on the practical potential of discursive approaches to psychotherapy, including conversation analysis. He has also written explicitly on ethical issues in research. A good example of his writing is the following:

- Strong, T., & Sutherland, O. A. (2007). Conversational ethics in psychological dialogues: Discursive and collaborative considerations. *Canadian Psychology*, *48*, 94–105.

We asked Professor Strong four questions about applied CA and ethics, and include his responses to these questions here.

From your perspective, what are the key ethical considerations when designing and carrying out a CA study?

"As someone who has studied Oprah Winfrey's engagement in Lance Armstrong's publicly televised apology, is microanalyzing and further distributing such publicly accessible talk ethical? A related ethical matter comes, I think, with how one could read CA analyses of such talking as imputing intentions to speakers—through the analyses. CA focuses on how social aspects of life are accomplished, while most of society, steeped in the individualist views of psychologists, tends to want to focus on discrete utterances and the psychological intent behind them. Do we know—in the bigger picture—what a speaker intends in moments of conversational interaction? Would you want specific exchanges in your own challenging conversations freeze-framed and dissected? Do we want to have our talking decontextualized for a research audience and traced back to each conversation utterance we make?"

Applied CA uses naturally occurring data. What ethical issues might this specifically invoke?

"Researchers favoring collection and analyses of naturalistic data seek conversations that occur without participants' awareness of their being observed or analyzed. Ethically speaking, how is a researcher to get naturally occurring conversational data, where speakers are having normal conversation, without it being primed by knowledge that their conversational content and turn taking is being studied with their informed consent?"

Drawing upon your CA research, can you share an example of a challenging ethical dilemma?

"In a series of papers, I researched lifestyle consultations where particular therapeutic questioning techniques were used (e.g., use of solution-focused therapy's miracle question). I also invited participants to come back to discuss with me their experiences, retrospectively, of asking or responding to such questioning techniques. One ethical issue for me related to how to regard these retrospective accounts, given that the performances of talk they were ostensibly about were clearly different. Does what a speaker tells you they really meant by what they earlier said trump what they 'actually' said?"

What suggestions might you offer related to engaging in ethical CA research for new scholars?

"I think it is quite important to be clear with one's research intent and questions. There seems to be a questionable genre of CA and discourse analysis that is like 'gotcha' journalism—to draw attention to abuses of social power in discrete encounters, without adequate attention to the broader sequence or context of the talking. For my tastes, there also needs to be some important conceptual work done, explicating the purposes of CA. While Harvey Sacks's early and somewhat mechanical focus on 'architectures of intersubjectivity' seems outdated to me, the most useful aspects of CA are when they orient and sensitize readers of CA studies to more optimally participating in challenging aspects of everyday or institutional aspects of conversation."

Chapter Summary

In this chapter, we first provided a general overview to research ethics, introducing you to philosophies of ethics. Next, we highlighted the role of ethics committees/boards, noting the historical context in which many practices related to research ethics emerged. Then, we offered a general discussion of key ethical principles. Finally, we discussed some of the ethical concerns that are unique to qualitative research generally and applied CA research specifically. We provide an overview of the key learning points from the chapter in the next box.

Learning Points From Chapter 4

- Pursuing ethical research demands that you consider both the risks and benefits of a study, and commit to promoting the well-being of your participants and yourself as the researcher.

(Continued)

(Continued)

- A qualitative research study generally and an applied CA study specifically brings with it unique ethical considerations. For applied CA, much of this relates to the collection of naturally occurring data.

- The use of audio- or video-recording devices creates additional ethical challenges due to the semipermanence of the record and the risk of identifying participants.

Recommended Readings

While there is a relatively large body of literature focused on ethics and qualitative research, far less has been written specific to applied CA research studies. The more general literature base, however, is relevant to CA-focused research, and thus we encourage you to spend time exploring it. We highlight here publications that may be useful starting points.

- Guillemin, M., & Gillam, L. (2004). Ethics, reflexivity, and "ethically important moments" in research. *Qualitative Inquiry, 10*(2), 261–280.

This journal article discusses the relationship between reflexivity and research ethics. Further, the authors distinguish between two types of research ethics: (1) procedural ethics (e.g., acquiring approval from an ethics board) and (2) ethics in practice (i.e., the everyday ethical issues that arise when carrying out a research study). The authors position reflexivity as a meaningful and useful way of understanding the various dimensions of ethics, particularly as researchers commit to pursuing and maintaining ethical practices.

- Israel, M. (2015). *Research ethics and integrity for social scientists: Beyond regulatory compliance* (2nd ed.). London, England: Sage.

This book provides a general overview of ethics and social science research. It thus serves as a foundational text for understanding the importance of ethics in research, the various approaches to ethics, and key codes and principles of ethical practices. It also provides an overview to the history of ethics regulations in research and gives attention to ethical considerations related to international, indigenous, and Internet-based research.

Doing a Project Using Applied Conversation Analysis

PART II

5

Planning and Preparing for Data Collection in Applied Conversation Analysis Research

Chapter Focus

In this chapter, you will learn how to:

- Recognize what constitutes data for applied conversation analysis research.
- Differentiate naturally occurring data from researcher-generated data.
- Critically assess the advantages and disadvantages of using naturally occurring data in an applied conversation analysis research study.
- Recognize the diversity of data sources that might be collected in an applied conversation analysis study.
- Evaluate the strategies for building an appropriate data set.
- Differentiate primary analysis from secondary analysis.
- Evaluate the usefulness of doing secondary analysis in applied conversation analysis.

As you begin planning your applied conversation analysis (CA) research study, a central consideration is the kind of data you will collect and the process of collecting it. As the choice of institutional setting and the relevance of the data corpus are intrinsic to the project, we deal with the issue of planning data collection before carrying out other aspects of the study (e.g., completing transcription). In CA research, naturally occurring data (defined in Chapter 1) are usually utilized, as this is a type of data that represents actual and/or real conversations.

In this chapter, we focus on naturally occurring data and illustrate what constitutes a data source for an applied CA research study. In so doing, though, it is necessary to distinguish naturally occurring data from the more traditional qualitative data type, which is most often referred to as ***researcher-generated data***. This type of data exists only because the researcher provoked or generated it (e.g., interview data).

Researcher-generated data are data that are deliberately and purposefully collected in alignment with a researcher's agenda and are therefore generated for the sole purpose of research.

In this chapter, we provide an overview of both naturally occurring data and researcher-generated data, while also pointing to the benefits and limitations of using naturally occurring data. We also discuss the diverse data sources that may be collected for an applied CA study, including video, audio, and computer-mediated communication (CMC) data. Furthermore, we consider the potential value of using interview data for CA work and some of the tensions that this can create. After providing a general overview of data sources, we present the practical steps for building a data set for an applied CA research study and consider the issue of sampling. In relation to data choices, we also consider the benefits and challenges of using a secondary data set and engaging in secondary data analysis. Finally, we critically examine common concerns related to the amount of data that should be collected and the process of exiting or concluding the data collection process.

An Overview of Data Sources and Data Collection

Before we turn to the specifics of an applied CA data collection process, it is important to think about data more generally. The notion of data is one that is used in a range of different contexts, including in everyday parlance, but its meaning in research terms is not always clear. Thus, an important question is, What constitutes research data?

In general terms, the notion of *datum* is defined as a single piece of information or single fact, and the plural of this is *data* (YourDictionary.com). ***Research data*** are more specific, however, and in the field of qualitative research, data and data collection have quite particular meanings.

Research data are those pieces of information and facts that are collected by a researcher and subjected to analysis.

The very meaning of research data is therefore contingent upon the meanings given to the data by the researchers collecting and analyzing them. In qualitative research, data become research data once they are intentionally assembled to address a research question by the researcher (O'Reilly & Kiyimba, 2015).

For example: Police interviews with suspects are routinely recorded for legal purposes. This is information that is used primarily by the organization and thus constitutes a form of data for them to use in their proceedings. These data would only become research data if, with consent from all relevant parties, they were specifically used for research purposes.

As such, for data to become research data, something needs to happen to ensure their transformation. However, for research data to be useful for an applied CA researcher, they need to be collected through appropriate means. This leads to another pertinent question for the researcher: What is data collection?

In research terms, the collection of data involves a process of gathering information related to the area of interest, which enables the researcher to address a specific research question and to evaluate the possible outcomes and/or processes. The methods of data collection vary depending on the research focus and the theoretical framework(s) that underlie a given methodological approach. The choice of data collection method is aligned closely with the methodological and epistemological framework (Staller, 2013). For instance, CA is a certain methodological approach that is guided by a specific theoretical framework, and it is this position that, as we noted, frames its favored use of naturally occurring data, but note that this does not mean a complete disregard for other types of data.

What this means: Conversation analysts hold the view that knowledge is co-constructed and socially situated. The core premise, therefore, is that a data-driven analysis will elucidate new understandings of social actions, and naturally occurring data provide a mechanism for revealing this (Hutchby & Wooffitt, 2008).

An Overview of Naturally Occurring and Researcher-Generated Data

As noted, naturally occurring data are the usual data source in an applied CA study. Naturally occurring data, in simple terms, are recordings of naturally occurring activities or the use of naturally occurring text-based documents (Kiyimba, Lester, & O'Reilly, in press), although talk-in-interaction is typically utilized as the main source of data, and thus recordings versus documents have been more commonly used.

What this means: Naturally occurring activities or naturally produced documents would still exist even if the researcher did not exist (Potter, 2002).

TABLE 5.1 ● Distinguishing naturally occurring activities from naturally occurring data	
Naturally Occurring Activities	**Naturally Occurring Data**
Naturally occurring activities are defined as interactions that happen in daily life in mundane or institutional settings. These activities occur regardless of the existence of the researcher.	Naturally occurring data represent naturally occurring activities that become data when they are captured by a researcher in audio, video, or text form and are collated for the purpose of research.

Applied CA researchers use the notion of naturally occurring as opposed to natural, as there is a recognition that the activity occurs naturally and would still proceed even if the researcher had not been born (Potter, 1997). Yet the assembling of such activities into research data means that they are not purely natural in the truest sense of the word but do occur naturally. Accordingly, naturally occurring recordings are those that have been intentionally selected by an applied CA researcher with the intent to use them for addressing a certain area of interest or research question. Thus, it is important to distinguish naturally occurring activities from naturally occurring data (Mondada, 2013), which we illustrate in Table 5.1.

You have now been presented with detail about what constitutes naturally occurring data, which we introduced you to in Chapter 1 and have mentioned in other chapters. At this point, it may be useful to check your understanding of naturally occurring data, and thus we suggest you complete the activity in Box 5.1.

BOX 5.1
ACTIVITY ON RECOGNIZING NATURALLY OCCURRING DATA

Activity

Determine which data on the following list are naturally occurring data.

1. Martin finds some letters in a shoebox belonging to his son, which were written to him by his girlfriend, and (with permission) decides to analyze them. Are these letters naturally occurring data?

2. Shaniqua is recording interactions that occur during break times (recess) in schools to examine the construction of teenage identity for her PhD research. Is this naturally occurring data?

3. Priya is interested in telephone complaint lines in a large multinational company and has collected 30 of these recorded phone calls and transcribed them. Is this naturally occurring data?

Hopefully, you have recognized that all three examples are using naturally occurring data, as the letters, child interactions, and telephone complaints are all generated regardless of whether the researcher exists or not, and in all three cases, the researcher intends to use them for research purposes (with the relevant consent).

As we noted, naturally occurring data are typically contrasted with researcher-generated data.

> *What this means:* Researcher-generated data are collected to address a specific research focus or question and are useful in qualitative research for collating the opinions and perspectives of certain populations.

Unlike naturally occurring activities that exist even when they are not recorded or collected, researcher-generated data do not preexist in any other form to be collected. In other words, researcher-generated data are collected to qualitatively examine individuals' or groups' perceptions, opinions, or experiences of an issue or area of interest. In simple terms, researcher-generated data are data generated by the researcher and therefore would *not* exist if the researcher had not actively taken steps to collect them.

Common types of researcher-generated data are interviews and focus groups, and these are frequently collected by qualitative researchers. However, do note that some interviews occur naturally (e.g., job interviews, news interviews). Researcher-generated data collection, and interviewing specifically, has been historically a very popular strategy within the qualitative community. Kiyimba et al. (in press) argued that there are three main reasons for this popularity, and these are presented in Table 5.2.

However, some tension has been noted in using researcher-generated data, as when qualitative researchers interview participants they tend to treat participant responses as a reflection of that person's reality. While there are some critical perspectives on this point of view (see Potter & Hepburn, 2005), and there are different types of interviews with different theoretical underpinnings (O'Reilly & Dogra, 2017; Roulston, 2010), fundamentally, the collection of interviews represents the belief that retrospective accounts usefully reflect the position of the participant. However, CA researchers have argued that any version of reality is socially constructed through interaction, and in an interview or focus group, therefore, the reality is assumed

TABLE 5.2 ● Reasons for the popularity of researcher-generated data

Reason	Description
Accessibility	It has been argued that researcher-generated data are more accessible than naturally occurring data (Silverman, 2006).
Time	As researcher-generated data are perceived to be quite straightforward to collect, it can be quite appealing. It is thought that it is quicker to collect this kind of data and therefore might result in a more efficient data collection process.
Views of participants	It is often assumed that interviews or focus groups are argued to reflect the actual views of the participants. Further, these participant views can directly align with a researcher's area of interest, which may not come up in naturally occurring activities.

Source: Kiyimba et al., in press.

! **Note that in naturally occurring contexts, speakers may be asked what they are thinking by others, and interlocutors within that interaction may express inferences based on the answers from others about what they were thinking.**

to be merely a reflection of that form of data collection (Potter & Hepburn, 2005) and does not mirror what participants "really think." Potter and Hepburn (2005) did not suggest that interviews or focus groups have no place in qualitative research, though, but considered the benefits of naturally occurring data and argued that this minimizes active researcher involvement. It is therefore argued by many CA researchers that naturally occurring data are a more valuable form of data, as examining this kind of data allows a researcher to examine how participants interact within a given situation or context.

We explain these differences between naturally occurring data and researcher-generated data with some caution, however. As researchers ourselves, we have used interview data and focus group data, and while we may privilege naturally occurring data as applied CA researchers, this does not diminish the value of other types of data, as they serve a different function and are used for a different reason. Although researcher-generated data are typically contrasted with naturally occurring data in much of the literature, we would caution against viewing these two types as completely dichotomous. Many studies use different types of data, and the value of researcher-generated data should not be underestimated. Speer (2002) questioned the notion of a dichotomy between naturally occurring or researcher-generated (which she termed *contrived*) data. Speer argued that much of the data defined as naturally occurring could be viewed as prompted by a researcher as a consequence of gaining informed consent, and furthermore, all forms of data could be viewed as natural depending on what the researcher wants to do with them. Indeed, Speer argued we should celebrate the active role of the researchers, a viewpoint shared by much of the qualitative research community. Notably, specific to interview data, the way the analyst treats the interview is important. From a CA perspective, social researchers should analyze any spoken interaction as a "performance," and in that sense, the interview itself is a cultural phenomenon (Atkinson, 2015).

Fundamentally, the favoring of naturally occurring data by CA researchers relates to the epistemological foundations of the methodological approach. Naturally occurring data are characterized as emic (see Chapter 1) and interviews are argued to be etic, and thus as CA is informed by an emic framework, naturally occurring data are congruent with the approach (Taylor, 2001). However, Griffin (2007) challenged the notion that interviews primarily produce material with etic qualities—that is, from the frame of reference of the researcher—and argued that the criticism of interviews reflecting an interaction between researcher and interviewee is too simplistic a view of what those interactions can entail. Indeed, Griffin noted that an interview can be a "researcher inspired conversation" (p. 255), as although there is a schedule of questions for an interview, there is often great flexibility as researchers interact with the participants' agendas. This demonstrates that the interaction could be etic in the sense that it is shaped by the demands of the interview process but also emic in that much of the interview is driven by participant perspectives. Additionally, the interview itself is arguably a form of interaction (Suchman & Jordan, 1990). Ultimately, the issue of using interviews or focus groups as data, and applying CA to those data, is more complex than might immediately be apparent.

Benefits of Using Naturally Occurring Data

No methodological decision should be made without a clear rationale, and it is good practice for researchers to reflect upon and be critical about data collection decisions. Thus, while an applied CA research study typically calls for naturally occurring data, it is important that you understand the benefits that conversation analysts argue are inherent to this argument. As such, in Table 5.3 we offer a general overview of what Kiyimba et al. (in press) described as some of the benefits of naturally occurring data.

We now turn to each of these categories of benefit to consider how they are advantageous, particularly in the context of applied CA work.

Practical and Pragmatic

There are practical reasons that CA researchers prefer using naturally occurring data. It should be noted that while these practical reasons are helpful and relevant, they are not often cited as the primary reasons for its use in general CA textbooks. Nonetheless, using naturally occurring data arguably has the benefit of saving time in the process. This is because there is no need to spend time designing interview schedules, conducting pilot studies in the traditional sense to test the validity of interview schedules, or modifying and constructing the best types of questions to adequately tease out the types of answers wanted by the researcher. Additionally, for some, if not many, types of naturally occurring data, the researcher may not have to spend time being physically present while the data are being collected. Furthermore, because of this, the collection of naturally occurring data may also save money, as costs associated with being present at a research site, for instance, will be eliminated.

TABLE 5.3 ● **The five categories of benefits of naturally occurring data**

Benefit	Description
Practical and pragmatic	There are certain advantages that are practical for the researcher, such as saving time and money.
Transparency	Naturally occurring data spotlight real practices in applied/institutional settings, and thus the process of analysis is grounded in the data. This means that the audience can see how the claims have been made.
Nature of the relationship	The researcher and participants generally have little interaction or communication, and the impact of the researcher is minimized.
Quality and integrity	The use of naturally occurring data ensures that many of the quality markers for qualitative research are satisfied.
Implications for practice	As naturally occurring data represent actual practices, recommendations for good practice and improving practice can be made based on what has been observed.

Source: Kiyimba et al., in press.

Transparency

It is argued that an important benefit of using naturally occurring data, and one that is beneficial for CA research, is that the data produced are authentic and transparent. In other words, the audio/video or textual data are produced for "natural" reasons and become research data when collected for research. This means any distortions of what happens are (at least in theory) avoided. In researcher-generated data collection, there is a risk that what people think and thus report that they do is different from what they *actually* do. Thus, for conversation analysts, it is assumed that by collecting naturally occurring data, the researcher can examine what people actually do and how those around them respond. In this way, it is assumed that the data retain their original context. Thus, transparency is achieved in the data as the turn taking, the language, the content, the context, and so forth, that are available to the analyst are the same as that available to the two speakers. In other words, participants' own understandings of the interaction are actively displayed in the sequence of turns, and this is transparent to the analyst and to an audience of the research.

Nature of the Relationship

Applied CA research does not necessitate face-to-face interaction between the researcher and the participants. Of course, if the institutional professional is also the CA researcher collecting data, this changes the relationship slightly, but often this is not the case. As the participants may spend very little time, if any at all, with the researcher, concerns related to social desirability are minimized. Social desirability, then, is presumed to exist primarily in the context of the relationship with the institutional professionals or other interlocutors, and not because of data being collected. In other words, any analysis undertaken can focus on the intersubjective relationships within the interaction under focus as it unfolds naturally. Thus, the researcher cannot distort the material collected for analysis (Griffin, 2007).

Quality and Integrity

It is the case in applied CA research that the naturally occurring data collection begins with an inductive question or area of interest; therefore, knowledge emerges from the data in ways that are unpredictable and may be unexpected. Thus, for the applied CA project, the research is flexible and is not structured by a schedule or agenda. CA researchers begin from an open perspective and do not have a predetermined agenda of what they are seeking from the data. This approach, therefore, can provide a holistic perspective.

Implications for Practice

By sharing the data and analysis with gatekeepers in the given institution, the very collection of naturally occurring data provides opportunities for training and can be used as a pedagogical resource. The dissemination of findings from an applied CA study affords an opportunity for a range of audiences to learn from the data and, depending upon the focus of your study, may promote the sharing of best practices. It is because of the conversation analytic findings that recommendations for practitioners can be made as best practices highlighted within the data are reported.

Limitations of Using Naturally Occurring Data

While there are many benefits of using naturally occurring data, it is important to recognize the limitations. Some of these can be mitigated by a strategic approach to the data collection, and others are more inherent to the data type. Kiyimba et al. (in press) also considered some of the limitations of using naturally occurring data, and we provide an overview of these in Table 5.4.

We now turn to each of these categories of limitations to consider how they are problematic for the researcher, particularly in the context of applied CA work.

Practical Constraints

One of the main challenges of collecting naturally occurring data for an applied CA project is the time it can take to organize, liaise with key gatekeepers, and collect the data. The consultation process with the key people who may ultimately be pressing the record button on the device is central to the successful acquisition of the data, and this can be time consuming.

> For example: In our data on child mental health assessments, there were occasions where one of the mental health practitioners took the child out to a different room from the parents. While the video continued to record the main room, we relied on practitioners to take the additional audio-recording device with them to capture this split-off section of the session. However, because we had no control over this, there were a few that did not remember to do so, and therefore, that short additional interaction was not captured.

Other elements of the data collection process are also time consuming and will require some organization of the key elements of the process. It can be challenging to access the research site from which you are trying to acquire the data. Therefore, it is wise to allow time to negotiate your relationship with the relevant people and assume that it will take more time than expected.

An important practical constraint you may find in collecting naturally occurring data is the relevance and importance of the recording device. There has been

TABLE 5.4 ● Categories of limitations of naturally occurring data	
Limitation	**Description**
Practical constraints	There are certain practical issues that need to be considered when collecting naturally occurring data, including concerns related to time and resources.
Limited contextual understanding	Although the distance between you as the researcher and the participants can be advantageous within a given study, it can also be a limitation, as there is a challenge in terms of your understanding of the context in which the data are produced. This, of course, can impact your ability to interpret the data and even present practically relevant findings to practitioners.

Source: Kiyimba et al., in press.

scholarly writing around the potential for participants and organizations to respond negatively to the presence of a recording device, despite this being important for quality analysis (Kasper, 2000). Indeed, many applied CA research studies will require data to be recorded. While it may be arguable that participants alter their behavior for the camera, research has indicated that while participants may orient to a camera or audio-recording device as relevant, over time they tend not to influence the participants (O'Reilly, Parker, & Hutchby, 2011; Speer & Hutchby, 2003), as participants typically go back to doing business as usual.

(!)

We now live in a digital age, and many participants (particularly in the Western world) are accustomed to being recorded in a wide range of settings and contexts. Regardless, participants tend to become accustomed to the presence of recording devices over time.

Limited Contextual Understanding

Earlier in the chapter, we noted that in many cases the gatekeepers at a given research site may take responsibility for recording and collecting your data as part of their natural practice, and this can be viewed as an advantage for the project. However, this means that you may not be present while the recording takes place and thus may have a limited understanding of the research context. In some cases, gatekeepers may even insist on acquiring informed consent on your behalf as they know the participants well and/or have concerns about capacity and so forth. This, in turn, may result in limiting your understanding of the participants. Notably, there are different views regarding the extent to which analysts should attend to information beyond the data they have collected—that is, contextual information such as the macrosociological variables of age, race, or gender. As ten Have (2007) noted:

Explanations of what happens in any kind of interaction, institutional or not, that make reference to "fixed" givens such as institutional identities and functions, institutionalized resources or relationships, or whatever, are not acceptable to CA until their local procedural relevance is demonstrated. . . . And even then, what may be said concerning such interactional moments is only that those properties or relationships are "talked into being" then and there. (p. 74)

In other words, CA aims to examine that which other research traditions might position as a given or taken-for-granted reality. What aspects of the context become relevant should be driven by the data analysis process. Notably, some scholars have argued for the importance of engaging in some fieldwork prior to collecting data, particularly when completing applied CA research in institutional settings. Heath (1997), for instance, suggested that it may be useful to engage in nonparticipant observations prior to collecting data. Heath and Hindmarsh (2002) similarly noted that records and documents, as well as manuals and log books, are a central feature of many organizational environments, and therefore, these will play a crucial part in the way in which participants both report and organize their activities and events. Therefore, depending upon your research context, it may be imperative that you gain a sense or deeper understanding of the context. Similarly, Antaki (2011) noted that at times in applied CA work there may be a need for ethnographic-informed understanding:

> The fact that participants will be bringing off some recordable institutional achievement means that the analyst will have to get a grip on what the institution counts as an achievement and as a record. Only ethnographic background—gleaned from documents, interviews and observation of the site—will provide that. (p. 12)

As such, it is important to consider your research design as you reflect upon how you might respond to this limitation of naturally occurring data.

Diverse Data Sources in Applied CA Research

As we have already highlighted, a range of naturally occurring data sources can be used in an applied CA study. In this section, we consider five main data types, which are audio-based data, video-based data, documents, Computer Mediated Communication (CMC) data, and secondary data. In so doing, we provide some research examples to illustrate the value of these data types.

Audio-Based Data

The core concepts of CA were first developed through the study of audio recordings. Like qualitative research broadly, the rise of technology has facilitated the collection of data that allows the analyst to attend to the nuances of hearable speech. Notably, audio recordings have become the default for many researchers, as they tend to be convenient, affordable, and a practical way of recording naturally occurring activities. While there are benefits to collecting audio data, there are obvious limitations to the collection of only audio data, including the omission of gestures, nonvocal interchanges, social activities involving artifacts, etc., which we discuss further in Chapter 8.

In Box 5.2 we provide an example of an applied CA research project conducted by Hepburn and Potter (2011) on helpline telephone data, whereby the participants were in separate locations and audio recordings were inherently sensible.

Video-Based Data

A growing number of scholars have pointed to the incompleteness of audio-based data, particularly when social activities involve the use of objects, the body, artifacts, etc. (Heath, 1997, 2004). Obviously, such activities are not accessible to an analyst when the data are solely audio based. Thus, in terms of naturally occurring data, video enables the analyst to focus on the detail beyond that which is vocal/hearable and, as ten Have (2007) noted, serves to provide "a wealth of contextual information that may be extremely helpful in the analysis of interactional talk-as-such, especially in complex settings with more than a few speakers, like meetings of various sorts" (p. 72). More broadly, in CA, both audio and video recordings have been conceptualized as serving

BOX 5.2
EXAMPLE OF AUDIO DATA

Research Example: Audio Data

In a recent study, Susan Danby and Mike Emmison, in partnership with Alexa Hepburn and Jonathan Potter, audio recorded naturally occurring telephone calls made to helplines for children, including a helpline in the United Kingdom and one in Australia. These helplines offered help and support to children. The broader study examined the impact of technological modalities, and the Australian data consisted of 50 telephone calls. Their research could not have used video to record the naturally occurring data because the telephone calls could come in from anywhere, and thus audio was a sensible way of capturing the interactions. These audio recordings allowed the researchers to examine how the institutional practices of telephone helpline support were enacted in practice.

Example publications from this research project include:

1. Butler, C., Potter, J., Danby, S., Emmison, M., & Hepburn, A. (2010). Advice implicative interrogatives: Building "client centred" support in a children's helpline. *Social Psychology Quarterly, 73*(3), 265–287.

2. Hepburn, A., & Potter, J. (2011). Designing the recipient: Resisting advice resistance in a child protection helpline. *Social Psychology Quarterly, 74*(2), 216–241.

> . . . as a control on the limitations and fallibilities of intuition and recollection; it exposes the observer to a wide range of interactional materials and circumstances and also provides some guarantee that analytic considerations will not arise as artefacts of intuitive idiosyncrasy, selective attention or recollection, or experimental design. (Heritage & Atkinson, 1984, p. 4)

In Box 5.3, we provide an example from one of our applied CA research studies that used video data.

Document Data

Documents or text-based data (e.g., medical records, notes, texts) are not used as frequently in CA—that is, those text-based documents that "live" outside of the Internet, such as paper-based newspapers or magazines—as there is certainly increasing use of Internet-based text documents, such as asynchronous discussion forums, in CA research (Paulus, Warren, & Lester, 2016). However, in CA research, the focus has been on the study of verbal (e.g., doctor–patient interaction) and/ or nonverbal (e.g., gesture, bodily movements, etc.) interactions. Beyond texts produced online, within applied CA there is some important use for text-based documents, with some researchers using them in addition to their audio- or video-recorded data.

BOX 5.3

EXAMPLE OF VIDEO DATA

Research Example: Video Data

In one of our recent research studies, we elected to use video to record naturally occurring child mental health assessments. In the field of mental health, particularly in the United Kingdom, it is common for a child suspected of having a mental health need to first be assessed in a clinical setting. For our project, with ethical approval, we recruited a Child and Adolescent Mental Health Service. The service, practitioners, and 28 families agreed to allow us to record the assessments, which lasted about 90 minutes each. This produced quite a significant amount of data. Video was deliberately selected as adults, and especially children, communicate also through nonverbal means. For instance, in this setting, there was a great deal of shoulder shrugging, head nodding and shaking, pointing, eye gazing, and playing with toys that occurred during the interactions—all of which were important for this research. By using video to capture our data, we could see how speakers were selected (e.g., via a shift in gaze), how children were engaged in the process, and what the practitioners were observing in terms of the child's behavior, which of course is relevant for a mental health assessment.

Example publications from this project include:

1. O'Reilly, M., Lester, J. N., & Muskett, T. (2016). Children's claims to knowledge regarding their mental health experiences and practitioners' negotiation of the problem [Special issue]. *Patient Education and Counseling, 99,* 905–910.

2. O'Reilly, M., Lester, J. N., Muskett, T., & Karim, K. (2017). How parents build a case for autism spectrum disorder during initial assessments: "We're fighting a losing battle." *Discourse Studies, 19*(1), 69–83.

For example: A researcher studying doctor–patient communication decided to include within the data set medical notes.

For example: A researcher who is studying U.S. Supreme Court hearings may also study the court's opinions, which are issued as text-based documents.

As you consider the potential use of documents for your study, it is helpful to consider (1) whether you will use documents *in addition* to other data sources (e.g., video recordings) or as your primary data source, (2) how you will determine whether the documents are relevant within the institutional context of focus, (3) what is required to gain access to the documents, and (4) how your analysis of the documents might be different from the analysis of interactions recorded via audio or video.

Computer Mediated Communication Data

With the rise of new technologies, there is now a growing number of research sites (e.g., the Internet itself) and new data sources (e.g., Facebook). CMC (Herring, 1996) has become a central point of study and has been described using various terms, ranging from computer-mediated discourse (Herring, 2007) to electronic discourse (Meredith & Potter, 2013). This type of communication is also understood as occurring across a range of modalities, from smartphones to websites to YouTube to Facebook to SecondLife. Indeed, the richness of such data has also been promoted with the rise of digital technologies that have enabled researchers to capture the details of people's lives beyond field notes, interviews, focus groups, etc.

In Paulus et al.'s (2016) comprehensive literature review of empirical studies using CA to understand social interaction online, they noted that researchers have been using CA to understand online talk since the 1990s. They also highlighted how researchers have focused on a broad array of institutional forms of talk, drawing upon educational, counseling, and workplace contexts. From online grief support groups (e.g., Varga & Paulus, 2014) to chat counseling (Stommel & Van der Houwen, 2013), there are a variety of contexts and topics that might serve as the focus of your study. Across topics and modalities, it is critical to consider the unique ethical challenges that are common to CMC data. For instance, whether you position online data sources as private or public shapes your research process and brings with it many ethical considerations (see Paulus, Lester, & Dempster, 2014, for further discussion). Moreover, there are also important methodological considerations, such as whether the core principles of CA are fully applicable to these new data types (see Giles, Stommel, Paulus, Lester, & Reed, 2015, for a further discussion of digital CA).

In Box 5.4 we provide an example of CA research conducted by Stommel and Koole (2010) whereby the participants posted discussions about eating disorders online.

BOX 5.4
EXAMPLE OF CMC DATA

Research Example: CMC Data

In a recent study, Wyke Stommel and her colleagues (2010, 2011) examined the contribution to an online support group for people experiencing eating disorders. Using CA as well as membership categorization analysis (MCA), they examined how members of the online community interacted with other members of the group. Using CA, they could investigate how groups operate as a "community of practice" and how those members constructed their illness. In their work, they looked at pro-anorexia as a membership category and the thresholds for help seeking in this group.

Example publications from this project include:

1. Stommel, W., & Koole, T. (2010). The online support group as a community: A micro-analysis of the interaction with a new member. *Discourse Studies*, *12*(3), 357–378.

2. Stommel, W., & Meijman, F. (2011). The use of conversation analysis to study social accessibility of an online support group on eating disorders. *Global Health Promotion*, *18*(2), 1–9.

BOX 5.5
ACTIVITY ON DATA COLLECTION

Activity

As you think about your own research interests and plan for an applied CA study, discuss the following with a colleague, mentor, or adviser:

- Describe the kind of data you plan to collect.

- Considering the data source(s) you intend to collect, what are some of the advantages and disadvantages you anticipate?

- What unique ethical constraints might you need to consider in regard to the data you intend to collect?

Take a few moments to apply some of your new understandings of data sources in an applied CA study to your own areas of interest by completing the activity in Box 5.5.

Secondary Data

There have been ongoing discussions in the literature around the benefits and challenges of using secondary data sets in qualitative work (e.g., Hammersley, 1997; Parry & Mauthner, 2004). Many of these discussions have centered around concerns and potential problems related to reusing data in qualitative research, such as not having access to the original context in which the data were collected (e.g., Gillies & Edwards, 2005). However, Moore (2006, 2007) suggested that perhaps these concerns are not as severe as originally thought. Mason (2007) argued that one of the outcomes of such debates around data reuse in qualitative research has been a general suspicion regarding the ethical and epistemological problems with secondary data, and this suspicion is likely unjustified. Notably, Mason suggested "that good qualitative research" is "about energetically and creatively seeking out a range of data sources to answer pressing research questions in quite distinctive ways, as well as about using those sources critically and reflexively" (n.p.). In other words, whether you are analyzing primary or secondary data in your project, you will need to engage with your data in thoughtful, creative, and reflexive ways.

Additionally, an issue relevant for applied CA researchers is the nature of the data when considering whether it is primary or secondary. Conversation analysts generally use data which are naturally occurring rather than researcher generated, which raises different kinds of arguments regarding the status of those data as being primary data or secondary data. To address this issue, O'Reilly and Kiyimba (2015) differentiated publicly available naturally occurring data from privately solicited naturally occurring research data.

For example: News interviews broadcast on television between newsreaders and politicians are publicly available naturally occurring data.

> For example: Telephone calls to a crisis service and recorded for research purposes are privately solicited naturally occurring research data.

O'Reilly and Kiyimba (2015) noted that in the case of privately solicited data, there are the necessary consultations with gatekeepers, securing consent, use of recording devices, and so forth, and thus they are private data recorded for research purposes. Therefore, any further analysis of those data by other researchers beyond the original team (with the necessary permissions) becomes secondary data analysis. However, some naturally occurring data are publicly available, like documentaries or news interviews, and can be subjected to analysis by a range of different researchers at different points. To all involved, the data are their primary data corpus, and thus they are each doing primary data analysis. Therefore, the privately solicited data are only available to the researcher collecting them, and he or she may allow others to conduct secondary analysis upon them, but the public data are available to many researchers to analyze at different time points, and consequently, they are primary data for all.

As Hammersley (2010a) and others have noted, conversation analysts commonly analyze data collected by others. This is perhaps unsurprising given that conversation analysts are interested broadly in everyday and institutional social interaction. Whether they were the individual collecting the data is not necessarily a primary concern, although there is certainly room for debate on this point. A key criticism of secondary data analysis has related to the specific contextual detail of the original project (Hammersley, 2010b), as it is claimed that the situated nature of the data collection has an impact on the way in which the data are analyzed (Bishop, 2007). However, traditional notions of context are of less concern for conversation analysts than some other qualitative research. Of course, context itself can be defined in varying ways, and the degree to which you need to be familiar with the contextual norms of an interaction is dependent upon the focus of your project. Regardless, generally what is of most interest to a conversation analyst is not whether the data are classified as primary or secondary but rather whether they can be described and oriented to as interactional.

Nonetheless, while arguments around secondary data and secondary data analysis differ slightly in CA because of the status of the data as naturally occurring, we do encourage you to think carefully about the ethics of any secondary analysis you might undertake when using the data provided by others. Arguably, it is advantageous from an ethical perspective to perform secondary analysis, as you are not recruiting additional participants and thus exposing them to further risks or burdens (Heaton, 1998). However, if future use of the data has not been written into the original consent procedures and permissions to share transcripts or the raw data themselves have not been secured, there are issues with allowing other researchers to access them (O'Reilly & Kiyimba, 2015). Thus, if consent for sharing or archiving was not secured, then judgments about the ethicality of secondary analysis must be considered (Bishop, 2007).

Building a Data Set for Your Applied CA Project

Pure or basic CA (or as we prefer, *traditional CA*) has typically focused on building a large collection of data, often from as many sites as possible, to allow for comparison across sites. Schegloff (1999), for instance, argued that researchers should "take the observations" they make in one context "and ask how that serves to confirm and specify what has seemed to be the case with that phenomenon in other data, or how it mandates a change in our understanding of the phenomenon" (p. 146). In Sacks's (1992) lectures, he emphasized that if we assume people organize their language-in-use in an orderly way, it does not matter where we collect interactional data. From coffee shops to telephone conversations to online dialogue, the possibilities are endless. Data collection from this perspective, then, may be centered on collecting data in relation to a phenomenon or specific interactional event (e.g., storytelling) with the hope of acquiring "new variants" (Heritage, 1988, p. 131) as you move across multiple settings.

However, for an applied CA research study, the approach is typically more focused, as you aim to attend to interactions produced in specific *institutional* contexts (e.g., teacher–student interactions in a classroom, police officer–suspect in an interrogation room). Consequently, building a data set for an applied CA research study will obviously be closely aligned with the aims or focus of a given project as it relates to a given institutional concern. That is, you are not simply interested in interaction broadly; rather, your researcher lens is attuned to a certain institutional context(s) and the social interactions produced therein.

> For example: A researcher interested in studying child–therapist interactions in a child mental health therapeutic context must secure data produced within this context.

As such, during the earliest stages of your research process, your data collection process will be grounded in your desire to study a certain type of interactional phenomenon, which will arguably take place within a specific setting(s). Therefore, you will design your data collection process around this context/setting. Yet as ten Have (2007) noted, even when you are interested in a certain setting, you should still consider collecting (a) data produced within that setting and (b) (potentially) "data from other settings for comparative purposes" (p. 71). Indeed, your choices related to collecting data at one or multiple sites need to be made considering your research goals and are central to your overall research design. Further, it is important to keep in mind that like qualitative research more generally, the data collection process is often informed by your analysis of the data. As you begin analyzing your data, it is quite possible that you will identify a need to collect additional data at your primary research site and/or identify additional sites. In other words, the data collection process and data analysis process are iteratively connected.

Practical Considerations for Building a Data Set

There are indeed a multitude of practical considerations for building a data set, with many of these centered on technical issues related to recording, storing, and downloading data. Beyond technical considerations, an important starting point is related to gaining access to your research site. Indeed, there are many ethical considerations related to gaining access to your research site as well as practical considerations. As you plan to collect data, it is important to think about both *gaining access* to a research site and the process of *exiting* the research site.

- First, it is critical to recognize that gaining access is a process; that is, it is important to recognize that gatekeepers and/or participants shape your access throughout the research process. In other words, gaining access is never a given, nor should it be conceptualized as a one-time event. Rather, you should plan to manage your access throughout the research process.

- Second, once you have completed your data collection, it is important to be thoughtful about the way you exit or conclude the data collection process. Generally, it is wise to leave open the possibility that you may return for further data collection. As noted previously, the analysis process informs your data collection process; thus, within qualitative work generally and applied CA research specifically, it is possible that through your analysis you will conclude that additional data collection is needed.

Additionally, in applied CA work, it may also be valuable to invite insiders to offer perspective and critiques of your emergent analysis. In fact, many participants may request to see what you did with the data you collected and may even request that your findings serve to shape discussions of their daily practices (particularly in intervention-oriented projects). Thus, when you exit a site, it is important to be explicit about your intentions, including disclosing your next research steps and the role (if any) that participants may play beyond data collection.

Sampling in CA

Beyond concerns related to gaining access and exiting your research site, it is also critical to consider your approach to **sampling**, which relates closely to the size of your data set. Note, however, that the very notion of a "sample" for an emic approach to research is somewhat contentious, but like qualitative research broadly, it is important to think about the approach you take to including and/or excluding participants, research sites, interactional events, materials, etc., when building your data set.

In qualitative research, there are a variety of approaches to sampling, which have been discussed extensively in the general methodological literature (see Patton, 2002, for further discussion). And as Sandelowski (1995) noted,

Sampling refers to the process of defining the boundaries of your research, including how you will identify a research site and participants, and mull through your corpus of interactional data—that is, the individuals, research contexts/sites, or materials (e.g., computer-mediated discourse data) that will be included in your study.

Adequacy of sample size in qualitative research is relative, a matter of judging a sample neither small nor large per se, but rather too small or too large for the intended purposes of sampling and for the intended qualitative product. (p. 179)

Most generally, qualitative researchers, including applied CA scholars, tend to use purposive or purposeful sampling to some extent; that is, the site and/or participants are selected based on specific criteria.

> For example: An academic is interested in studying the interactions that take place in local council meetings. Therefore, that academic needs to select local events where politicians meet to make decisions and discuss local issues.

However, it is important to keep in mind that in CA research, a maximum variation strategy is also quite common—that is, an approach to sampling where as much variation as possible is generated when identifying research sites and sampling or narrowing your data corpus. This approach to sampling relates to a core assumption of CA in which the analyst seeks to

build up large collections of data from as many natural sites as possible . . . these growing data bases contain many variations of particular types of interactional events whose features can be systematically compared. Analysts constantly seek for new variants and may focus their searches on particular settings in the expectation of finding them. (Heritage, 1988, p. 70)

A maximum variation strategy highlights the assumption that an interactional feature, such as question formulations, may unfold differently in a pediatrician's office versus an elementary (primary school) classroom. The maximum variation strategy is quite common to a traditional (pure) CA study, while an applied CA study may call for a more restricted or purposeful approach to sampling (ten Have, 2007).

> For example: A PhD student is interested in studying the talk of teachers participating in a professional learning community focused on how to teach students learning English. This student is particularly interested in studying teacher talk around student identities. She recognizes that she must first identify a research site wherein this type of talk is occurring and thus uses a purposive or purposeful sampling strategy to identify her research site. Once she commences her study and begins the data collection and analysis process, she recognizes that she needs to engage in sampling her data set, mulling her data for instances wherein teachers engage in talk about students.

Your choices around sampling involve multiple considerations, ranging from where you will collect your data to how you will collect your data to what episodes or cases of talk you will select to analyze from your larger corpus of data. In other words, your interest is the language used rather than the individual who uses the language or the texts

> ⓘ In an applied CA research study, it is important to recognize that your "sample" is most often conceived of in relation to the social interaction itself rather than the number of participants.

in which the language is represented (Potter & Wetherell, 1987). This perspective stands in contrast to some of the other approaches to qualitative research in which you might be asked, "How many people did you interview for your study?" In these studies, there is a reliance on the notion of saturation, which argues that a researcher will stop sampling when no new ideas are emerging during data collection (Francis et al., 2010). However, this marker of sampling adequacy is not appropriate for all approaches, including CA (O'Reilly & Parker, 2013). While saturation can be thought of as being when it makes no sense to collect more instances unless they stimulate new ideas, provide additional information, or serve a purpose to promote generality, for applied CA work, the analytic purpose is generally different from other approaches, and therefore the scope of your analysis can be intentionally more limited to a specific setting or interaction type (ten Have, 1999). In applied CA research, you are focusing on the language-in-use, and therefore the number of people is typically not a primary concern. In fact, there are myriad published examples in which CA researchers may have recordings with only two or three speakers, as the focus is on the interaction itself. Thus, in your applied CA research study, you can think about your sample as being your conversational and/or textual material.

Sampling for your applied CA study is therefore a particularly important consideration, as it also helps you to reflect on the critical question of "How much data is enough data?" This is a difficult question to answer and perhaps is most accurately answered with: It depends. In published CA research, there are many examples of what some might describe as small data sets—involving only a few hours of conversational data. Indeed, some CA scholars focus their analysis on a single case or episode (Mazeland, 2006), something which we consider in greater detail when discussing strategies for analyzing your data.

In contrast, there are many published studies that could be described as involving large data sets—involving 20, 50, or more hours of conversational data. Indeed, Sacks himself tended to collect large numbers of cases so that he could account for those cases that did not fit the pattern and thus make the findings more robust. Further, CA studies that use CMC data often involve a range of data set sizes (see Paulus et al., 2016, for further discussion). Communication scholars have suggested that the sample size should be dictated by the research focus and emergent research questions, with "the success of a study … not in the least bit dependent on sample size" (Potter & Wetherell, 1987, p. 161). Generally, then, when thinking about whether you have enough data, it is important to keep in mind that there are no set standards related to how much data you should collect. Rather, your decision should be grounded theoretically, methodologically, and directly related to your research goals/aims. Ultimately, your choices around sampling shape what you can say about your data, as well as the degree to which others view your findings as grounded in your data set. In applied CA research, it is important to keep in mind that sampling entails both considerations related to identifying a research site and recruiting participants, *and* developing a strategy for sampling your larger corpus of naturally occurring data.

An Interview With Dr. Tim Auburn

Indeed, many applied CA researchers utilize naturally occurring data to examine an area of interest. One good example of this is the work on courtroom interactions led by Dr. Tim Auburn, and thus we interviewed him to ask some key questions about his preference for using naturally occurring data in his work. His responses are outlined in Box 5.6.

BOX 5.6
INTERVIEW WITH DR. TIM AUBURN

Dr. Tim Auburn is a senior lecturer with the School of Psychology at Plymouth University. His work has examined how applied CA might inform and facilitate approaches to professional practice in law courts in England. Dr. Auburn has particularly undertaken useful work considering the merits of using naturally occurring data to examine courtroom interactions, and such an example is provided here:

- Auburn, T., Hay, W., & Wilkinson, T. (2011). The place of an advice and support service in a magistrates' court. *Probation Journal, 58*(2), 112–125.

We asked Dr. Auburn three questions about applied CA, and his answers to these questions are provided as follows.

Why do applied conversation analysts favor using naturally occurring data for their work?

"Perhaps the most straightforward answer to this question is that applied conversation analysts favor using naturally occurring data largely because the discipline of conversation analysis is their overarching analytic framework. That answer may seem a bit of a tautology, so let me explain my understanding of conversation analysis. Conversation analysis is based upon understanding the organization of the interaction order; this focus in turn entails drawing data from that realm and putting it under close analytic scrutiny. To 'apply' their findings or undertake 'applied' projects, the analysis has to have derived from data which have originated in this realm; it is difficult to see how conversation analysts could say anything of relevance without first having examined and developed an understanding of a particular lived sector of the naturally occurring interaction order. More broadly, I would suggest that it is not just applied conversation analysts who favor naturally occurring data. I think any social psychologist who has been influenced by the discursive turn, or the *turn to language*, would regard it as problematic not to use naturally occurring data in their work.

The term *data*, though, can, I think, be cast quite widely. Data can include a range of discursive phenomena arising from the interaction order. Thus, the term *naturally occurring data* can cover a range

(Continued)

(Continued)

of sources from informal face-to-face interaction; more formal institutional interaction (for example, courtroom interactions, telephone helplines); mediated communication (chat shows, political interviews); written texts such as newspaper articles or institutional mission statements; and even qualitative interviews insofar as advocates of this method would argue that they allow the interviewees to express themselves in their own terms. Normally, however, the sort of data with which conversation analysts normally work concerns talk and the nonverbal behavior which accompanies it.

I would also argue that the term *natural* needs some exegesis. What are the grounds for claiming particular data is natural over artificial; indeed, is any data artificial? One answer was provided by Jonathan Potter, who proposed the 'dead social scientist' test. In this test, data can be regarded as natural if it would have occurred without the intervention of the social scientist. Thus, a problem-solving meeting with an offender as part of a community justice initiative would have occurred with or without the presence of the researcher; it so happens that the researcher has made arrangements to 'capture' this particular encounter. In contrast, a qualitative interview with a woman who has experienced a traumatic birth would not count as natural, as the interview has been proposed, arranged, and conducted by the researcher for the researcher's own ends. This distinction seems practical and clear.

However, could we treat the qualitative interview or indeed a psychological laboratory experiment on the effects of noise on performance as natural? Although they have been arranged and conducted by the researchers, they nevertheless are an accepted practice for carrying out the business of an institution concerned with education and research, in the same way that a problem-solving interview is a practice for carrying out the business of a community court. It is through examining these ostensibly unnatural methods as institutional practices that gives the conversation analyst the rationale for investigating them; the distinction here is between 'using' and 'examining.' Whereas the researchers in the former cases have an epistemological commitment to the practice as yielding something over and above the practice itself (e.g., the insides of the interviewee's mind, or information-processing decrements occasioned by loud noise), the conversation analyst has a different orientation. The conversation analyst has no such epistemological commitment and is only interested in these activities as institutional practices and how they are accomplished by the participants themselves. Whereas the researchers have a 'window-on-the-mind' epistemology, that certain phenomena (talk, scores on a performance task) can point to entities in the mind of the research participant, the conversation analyst has a 'discourse-as-topic' epistemology, that discourse is organized in and of itself in order to accomplish certain sorts of business. By taking the epistemological stance of the conversation analyst, then, it is possible to treat these practices as 'natural,' as constituting a sector of the interaction order, and therefore legitimate arenas of research for the applied conversation analyst. The sorts of research questions which would be asked are very different. The qualitative researcher might ask: 'What are the key factors which influence attachment following a traumatic birth experience?' In contrast, the applied conversation analyst might ask: 'How [are] cooperation and empathy displayed in the interview?'

So the boundaries of the dead social scientist test are flexible and seem to depend on whether the conversation analyst is an 'insider' with the same commitments as the authentic insider or an outsider viewing these as practices, which can be understood as complex accomplishments by the participants. In short, what counts as natural or not, in large part depends on the stance of the researcher. Conversation analysts have a unique stance, which differs from the standardly accepted one in the sciences."

When have you used naturally occurring data in your research?

"A lot of the research in which I have been involved has examined talk-in-interaction within the English criminal justice system. One of my first projects, with Susan Lea, focused on prison-based sex offender treatment groups. It was concerned with a key therapeutic concept in sex offender treatment; namely, *cognitive distortions*. An example of a cognitive distortion is minimization. We were interested in the sorts of discursive practices which the group participants oriented to as displaying cognitive distortions as well as how the participants used the term itself as a way of formulating the meaning of offenders' narratives of their offenses. At the time when we ran this study, we were able to gain permission from the prison to access the recordings that the prison itself made of the group sessions. Audio copies of these were made and subsequently transcribed to aid with the analysis.

More recently, I have been involved in an Economic and Social Research Council-funded project (ES/J010235/1) that has examined the operation of a community justice court. One unique way in which this court operated was to conduct problem-solving meetings with low-risk offenders. One aspect of the project was to examine how these meetings were conducted: how problems were identified and formulated, how help and support were described, how advice was worked up and delivered, and whether offenders accepted or rejected this advice. We were given the opportunity to sit in on these meetings and audio record them. We then had a corpus of audio recordings, which we examined for recurring practices which could be heard to constitute these meetings."

What were the advantages and limitations of using naturally occurring data for your research?

"Clearly, one of the main advantages of naturally occurring data is that it captures more or less veridically what actually happened in the sector of the interaction order in which you, as a researcher, are interested. What are the limitations of using this sort of data? Often, especially with institutional data and perhaps even more so in relation to the criminal justice system, there are a lot of constraints on what and where recording can be undertaken. For example, it is a criminal offense to make recordings of the proceedings of the courts themselves. Even taking recording devices into a court building requires bespoke permission. To gain permission for recording, there is often a lengthy and intensive ethics procedure to undergo. This procedure also involves developing positive professional relationships with the main stakeholders. However, a positive consequence of going through these procedures and building such relationships is that the stakeholders at all levels develop a close interest in the research project and its outcomes. One follow-on advantage, then, of having collected naturally occurring data is that in feedback meetings with stakeholders, it is possible to use their actual talk to illustrate the particular phenomena and practices identified in the research. Elizabeth Stokoe of Loughborough University has developed a systematic methodology which fully exploits the opportunities of using the 'real' data for education and training of stakeholders.

A difficult issue around the use of naturally occurring data in research is the openness of the research data. There is an increasing emphasis across all sciences for researchers, and especially those conducting publicly funded research, to make their data sets available to other bona fide researchers. This requirement is built into the funding procedures for the U.K. Research Councils. For qualitative research, the research councils and those who manage data archives recognize that qualitative researchers who have used interviews or recordings of naturally occurring data have a duty to protect their participants. This protection usually takes the form of anonymizing the data. However, a concern is then how and to what extent should the data be anonymized. At a minimum, names and other explicit identifying references need to be redacted, but there can be other features which on their own do not allow identification but when put together with other information in other parts of the data corpus can lead to identification. The U.K. Data Archive, which stores data sets and makes them available to other researchers, is developing guidelines on these matters. But it is often the case that it is a long and time-consuming process to search the corpus and ensure that the identity of the participants is not compromised."

An Interview With Professor Kathryn Roulston

Some applied CA researchers utilize interview data to examine an area of interest. A premier example of this is the work of Professor Kathryn Roulston, and thus we interviewed her to ask some key questions about her use of interview data in CA. Her responses are outlined in Box 5.7.

BOX 5.7
INTERVIEW WITH PROFESSOR KATHRYN ROULSTON

Kathryn Roulston is a professor at the University of Georgia, United States. Professor Roulston is a leading scholar in the area of qualitative interviewing and has also written extensively in relation to interviews and CA.

She has published in the area of interviewing and CA, with one particularly useful article being the following:

- Roulston, K. (2006). Close encounters of the "CA" kind: A review of literature analysing talk in research interviews. *Qualitative Research*, *6*(4), 515–534.

We asked Professor Roulston three questions about applied CA and interview-based data, and her answers to these questions are provided here.

How do you conceptualize/theorize interview data in CA research?

"Harvey Sacks, in *Lectures on Conversation* (Sacks, 1995, Vol. 1), indicated that he was more interested in examining phenomena in naturally occurring settings than via interview data. Using the example of anthropologists, whose work he said that he 'would recommend very much' (p. 27), he rejected the use of interviews to examine research topics as part of his own research agenda. Following this tradition, conversation analysts typically do not use interviews as a primary source of data. Nevertheless, there has been a range of studies since the early 1980s in which researchers have examined research interviews with a view to unpacking what gets done in the co-construction of research interviews. This work encompasses standardized surveys, focus groups, and qualitative interviews (for reviews, see Roulston, 2006, 2017). When researchers use CA to examine research interviews, they are typically examining the conversational resources used by speakers to do interview talk and asking questions about how research data are generated. Analysts also make use of MCA to examine speakers' descriptions. This work is typically framed using ethnomethodology while incorporating CA (Baker, 2002)."

From your perspective, what is the role of interview data in applied CA research?

"When researchers use applied CA to examine interview data, the focus of the analysis shifts from examining the *topics* of talk to *how* the topics of talk emerge in research contexts. This work takes a constructionist view of interview data and frequently responds to methodological questions about how interviews get done. For one recent example, Irvine, Drew, and Sainsbury (2013) compared the conduct of interviews via telephone with interviews conducted face-to-face. Applied linguist Steven Talmy (2010) described this move as viewing the research interview as a *social practice* rather than the typical view of it as a *research instrument*."

What are some critical considerations for researchers collecting interview data for an applied CA study?

"Researchers would not typically collect interview data for an applied CA study. Rather, analyses using CA to examine *how* research data are constructed are typically led by the particular phenomena that are observed by researchers both during and after interviews are conducted on particular topics (i.e., the interview as a research instrument). Work is typically focused on methodological issues and is conducted as a secondary or supplementary analysis complementing findings speaking to the research questions posed in the initial study. Researchers using this approach with interview talk argue that it can be used as an approach in helping novice researchers learn about interview practice, and can explore methodological issues that occur in interview settings (e.g., failed interviews, difficult interactions, the accomplishment of rapport, etc.). Scholars (Prior, 2016; Rapley, 2012) have argued that analyses of research interviews made possible by the tools of CA have only scratched the surface of the potential topics yet to be examined."

Chapter Summary

In this chapter, we introduced you to the preferred data sources in an applied CA research study— specifically, naturally occurring data. In doing so, we have distinguished between naturally occurring data and researcher-generated data, highlighting both the advantages/benefits and limitations of using naturally occurring data. We also introduced you to a variety of data sources that can be used in an applied CA research study, which include audio data, video data, documents, CMC data, and/ or secondary data. We concluded by offering some key considerations for building a data set, collecting "enough" data, and entering/exiting your research site. We summarize the key learning points from the chapter in the next box.

Learning Points From Chapter 5

- Building a data set for your applied CA research study is an iterative and inductive process.

- Naturally occurring data are often favored in an applied CA research study.

- There are a variety of data sources that might be included in an applied CA study, including audio, video, documents, or CMC.

Recommended Readings

We highlight three resources that provide a variety of perspectives on collecting naturally occurring data for research purposes, with two specifically focused on discourse analysis or CA-related projects.

- Kiyimba, N., Lester, J., & O'Reilly, M. (in press). *Collecting naturally-occurring data*. London, England: Springer.

The focus of this book is on naturally occurring data. This book is a simple and practical guide designed to provide accessible advice on using naturally occurring data for research. The book illustrates what does and does not constitute naturally occurring data, the benefits and limitations of such data, and provides examples of this kind of data in use.

- Potter, J. (2002). Two kinds of natural. *Discourse Studies, 4*(4), 539–542.

This paper was part of a special issue in *Discourse Studies* that discussed the benefits of using naturally occurring data in research. The paper makes a case for how the use of naturally occurring data is essential for research that uses discourse approaches (including CA). We recommend that you look at all papers in that special issue, as the authors develop an argument about the use of naturally occurring data and what kinds of data can be classified as such.

- Potter, J., & Hepburn, A. (2005). Qualitative interviews in psychology: Problems and possibilities. *Qualitative Research in Psychology, 2*(4), 281–307.

This paper is considered a seminal paper focused on key critiques related to researcher-generated data, specifically open-ended and conversational qualitative interviews. Further, the authors point to the ways in which interview data can result in a researcher's agenda being emphasized rather than what the participants actually do in their everyday lives. The publication of this paper included multiple counter-critiques and responses, and we encourage you to read across this scholarly dialogue as you establish your own perspectives on this ongoing debate.

6

Completing Transcription in Applied Conversation Analysis Research

Chapter Focus

In this chapter, you will learn how to:

- Distinguish between the different types of transcription.
- Define and apply the Jefferson method of transcription.
- Recognize the symbols used in the Jefferson transcription system.
- Recognize the process of transcribing multimodal interaction.
- Evaluate the complexities of translating other languages into English.

If you are planning to undertake an applied conversation analysis (CA) research study, then the type of data you collect will be important. As we have noted earlier, applied CA researchers typically rely on naturally occurring data, such as recordings of events in institutional settings or online talk. Further, a great deal of applied CA research has relied on audio or video recordings of naturally occurring settings. For qualitative research more generally, it is common and typical for researchers to create a transcript that represents the data.

In this chapter, we consider the transcription process within a CA project while also highlighting some of the debates around the practice of transcription and the level of detail that may or may not be required in creating a transcript. Specifically, we introduce the *Jefferson system*, outline the key symbols, and provide some examples from our own work to show you what it looks like.

> The **Jefferson system** of transcription is a specialist transcription system that utilizes a range of different symbols to represent the verbal and paralinguistic features of talk-in-interaction.

A central decision researchers must make is whether to undertake the transcription themselves or pay a professional transcriptionist. Although conversation analysts tend to do transcription themselves as it is part of the analytic process, paying a transcriptionist to produce the verbatim version first can be helpful. However, be cautious as some applied CA research can be sensitive in nature. This may have an emotional effect on any professional transcriptionist that you need to take care to mitigate (see Kiyimba and O'Reilly, 2016b). In carrying out your own transcription, it is important to consider the varying ways that transcripts are produced to represent multimodal recordings, and we discuss this. A related complexity for some applied CA researchers is that their data may be collected in a language other than English and therefore require translation for international dissemination activities. This translation process is not a straightforward one, as there are linguistic, transcription, and practical issues. We thus conclude the chapter by considering critical issues related to translation.

Transcription: An Active and Interpretative Process

The transcription process is not straightforward, nor is it a neutral process. Rather, it is interpretative and positional (Ochs, 1979), and demands a reflexive stance. Transcripts should represent a detailed and accessible version of the data. Indeed, transcripts are also central for disseminating and sharing findings from research (Peräkylä, 1997), as they are an important source of evidence for audiences to assess the analytic claims that are made (Roberts & Robinson, 2004).

It is perhaps tempting to think that transcribing data is simply a technical and mundane process, or a process that results in an unproblematic representation of the words that people say. However, now it is widely understood that a neutral transcription process is not possible, nor that a transcript is simply a transformation of an audio or video file into a written representation (Psathas & Anderson, 1990). As Brun-Cottan (1990) noted, transcriptions (specifically referring to video data) are "partial flat copies" that "reduce the ecological complexity of the original interactions" (p. 294). In this way, a transcript is inevitably selective and partial, and, as some scholars have argued, "most alive, most useful, and most beautiful when used with the audio or video recordings" that it serves to represent (Hopper, 1990, p. 169).

> ⓘ For those who practice CA, transcription is thought of as a situated practice (Mondada, 2007).

Further, a transcript is understood as only being possible because a researcher makes choices informed by a certain theoretical position (Lapadat & Lindsay,

1999) as well as the conventions common to a specific perspective or discipline (Green, Franquiz, & Dixon, 1997). In the methodological literature, it is commonly argued that researchers have an obligation to disclose the rationale for their transcription decisions (Skukauskaite, 2012). For applied CA researchers, decisions about transcription are tied to the epistemological and practical concerns of the methodology (Hepburn & Bolden, 2013). In other words, a transcript is understood to be a representation of a recording that is shaped by the researcher's theoretical position. As we have noted, in CA research generally and applied CA research specifically, the transcription system that has traditionally been used is referred to as the Jefferson system, with the use of this transcription system closely connected to the assumptions of CA.

Just to remind you, **social constructionism** is a theoretical position that claims that reality—that is, the human experience—is not fixed but rather mediated historically, linguistically, and culturally (Burr, 2003). In other words, it argues that understandings of the world are the platform for shared assumptions about reality, and this reality is co-constructed. See Chapter 1 for further discussion of this.

What this means: Applied CA researchers adopt the theoretical position that underpins the methodological approach as we outlined in Chapter 1, and this is reflected in the transcription preference for detail. In other words, the *social constructionism* epistemology of the CA approach means that to examine the co-construction of reality through talk-in-interaction often requires a transcription system that accurately reflects *how* things are said and not simply *what* is said.

Approaches to Transcription

What we have emphasized thus far is that it is necessary for you to reflect upon how your methodological approach influences the nature of your transcripts and the level of detail you include. There are a variety of transcription types in general qualitative work, including

1. verbatim (i.e., word-for-word transcript),

2. gisted (i.e., captures the overall sense of the interaction),

3. visual (i.e., broad-stroke description and images that represent the participants' actions), and

4. Jefferson (i.e., includes details of what is said and how it is said).

(Paulus, Lester, & Dempster, 2014)

It is important to remember that different qualitative researchers collect different types of data for different purposes, and the transcription system should reflect the aims of a given approach (Lapadat, 2000). Because of this, there has been some (ongoing) debate about the most appropriate transcription conventions.

- One side of this debate has argued that a high level of detail within a transcript is distracting and makes the representation of data inaccessible; therefore, researchers need a transcription method that is readable by multiple audiences.

- The other side of the debate has argued that the transcript should represent the data as closely as possible to promote transparency and minimize misrepresentation.

Regardless of the position one takes, there are several decisions that you need to think about when providing a rationale for the detail included in your transcript. Hammersley (2010a) outlined nine such considerations in relation to qualitative transcription generally, which we present in Table 6.1. Alongside Hammersley's nine considerations, we provide responses to his queries in relation to applied CA, as CA research has some specific guidance about doing transcription that relates to Jefferson conventions.

TABLE 6.1 ● Nine decisions in transcription

Decision as Noted by Hammersley	A CA Informed Response
How much data?	An important decision to make is whether to transcribe your whole data set or just selections of it. This depends on the approach taken. For applied CA research, it is often helpful to produce a transcript of the whole data set, as at that stage you will not know what is going to be relevant. Further, transcribing your entire data set is one way to become familiar with your data set. It is an important part of the analytic process. You might not need to include the full level of Jefferson detail for your entire data set, however.
How much representation?	Different approaches require different decisions regarding how to represent the talk, including pitch, intonation, dialect, nonverbal, etc. For applied CA research, the decision is to some extent inherent in the approach, as CA advocates that a high level of detail is necessary. The Jefferson system requires that pitch, intonation, emphasis, dialect, and so on, are all represented in the transcript, as *how* things are said is viewed as equally important as *what* is said.
Who is addressed?	Decisions about who is being addressed in the talk need to be made. Speakers talk to one another in interaction, and in applied CA research there can be some level of description of who the participants are in the transcription.

Source: Hammersley, 2010a.

Decision as Noted by Hammersley	A CA Informed Response
Should paralinguistic features be included?	It is necessary to decide from the outset whether paralinguistic features, such as laughter, intakes of breath, coughing, sneezing, crying, and so forth, should be transcribed. For applied CA researchers, the answer to this question is yes. Paralinguistic features of the interaction are analyzable and interactionally relevant, and therefore should be represented in the transcript. These paralinguistic features can be difficult to transcribe precisely. Active noises (e.g., onomatopoeia) are especially difficult to reproduce in a transcript (O'Reilly, 2005).
Should pauses and gaps be included?	General qualitative researchers make decisions regarding whether to include periods of silence and pauses, and if so, whether to time them or simply give an indication of length (i.e., long pause, short pause). For applied CA researchers, the Jefferson transcription system advocates for the precise timing of pauses and silences, and while a micropause is represented as (.), any pause of length (0.2 seconds or more) should be timed. This can be facilitated using computer software.
Should gestures and fine motor movements be included?	An important decision to make is whether to include gestures and fine motor movements. Of course, the modality of your recording may make this impossible (e.g., audio recordings), although field notes may be helpful in this regard. Applied CA researchers typically prefer multimodal communication to be transcribed whenever possible.
How should the talk be laid out on the page?	When transcribing your data, it is necessary to make decisions regarding how to physically lay out interactions on the page, and this includes decisions about how to represent talk that overlaps or is interruptive. For applied CA researchers, there are certain conventions for layout of transcriptions on the page. First, transition relevance places are identified. Second, talk is represented as it was produced. Third, a font that allows the alignment of overlapping talk is applied (typically Courier New; Hepburn & Bolden, 2013). Fourth, line numbers are used to help the analyst refer to specific aspects of the transcript when sharing his or her line-by-line analysis with others.
How should speakers be represented?	You must decide how you are going to represent each of the interlocutors in interaction in terms of using numbers, names, roles, etc. It is important to remember that the way you represent the speakers in your transcript has implications and is not a neutral decision. For example, "Mrs. Brown," "Doctor," "Woman 1," "Participant 1," "Mother," "Mum," and so on, all imply something about a participant. It is important to remember that CA examines next speaker selection in terms of address in its analysis, and therefore, this is an important issue for transcription.
How to define an extract?	When selecting segments of a transcript for dissemination purposes (e.g., publication), you need to consider how to represent your transcripts, which includes considering where to start and finish a certain extract of data. Applied CA researchers typically make these kinds of decisions in relation to the units of talk; that is, the units of talk represented in a transcribed extract need to represent clear turn construction units, have transition relevance places, and include enough of the interaction for the analyst to make the analytic claims.

It should be evident that the process of transforming verbal data into written text is challenging, particularly if background noise, multiple speakers, overlapping speech, incomplete speech, a poor-quality recording, or a general lack of clarity exists (McLellan, MacQueen, & Neidig, 2003). In addition to this, some qualitative researchers might tidy up their transcripts, correcting grammar, pronunciation, and so on. Of course, in an applied CA study, you would *never* do such tidying in the transcription process, as your focus is on what was *actually* said, attending to both the *what* and the *how*.

A Closer Look at the Jefferson Method

If you are going to do an applied CA research study, it is important that you have a good understanding of what the Jefferson method of transcription is and the process of using it. The aim of the Jefferson transcript is to attend to as much of the vocal, verbal, and multimodal detail of the interaction as possible (Jefferson, 2004a). This system has developed and evolved since its inception, and incorporates a range of different symbols to represent the recorded social activities and capture the characteristics of speech delivery (Atkinson & Heritage, 1999). The high level of detail included within such a transcript is argued to be essential for promoting quality in the analysis process (Potter, 1996a). Therefore, those who practice CA generally use a wide range of orthographic and typographic conventions to represent the phonetic, prosodic, and other vocalic details of recorded talk, including the ***temporal features*** and ***suprasemental properties*** (Roberts & Robinson, 2004).

Temporal features are those time domain features of talk, including silences or pauses in talk.

Suprasemental properties (or spectral features) are those features that are based on frequencies and include, thus, features of the talk such as speech rate, rhythm of the talk, pitch, and so on.

Before we go into detail about the different symbols and their respective meanings, we first want you to reflect on and think about what different levels of transcription look like in practice to show you why a Jefferson transcript is so important for those practicing applied CA. To help you do this, we provide three different versions of an extract of data taken from one of our studies focused on child mental health, which was positioned as an applied CA research study that sought to examine children's epistemic rights (O'Reilly, Lester, & Muskett, 2016).

In the first extract, we deliberately tidy up the talk, correcting grammar and pronunciation, and therefore provide no details at all except the talk itself. You will see how this loses much of the relevant detail. In the second example, we include some detail related to pronunciation as well as the relevant pauses, but this fails to demonstrate the nuances of the interaction. In the third example, we include a full Jefferson version, which was the version we included in our publication.

Example 1: Verbatim and tidied-up version:

```
1   Prac:   So when you said that you were going to take a
2           knife to yourself yes? What were you hoping
3           would happen?
4   Child:  For me to actually kill myself.
5   Prac:   Mummy would?
6   Child:  No me to kill myself.
7   Prac:   Say that again mummy would?
8   Mum:    No for her to kill herself.
9   Prac:   Right you are smiling as you say that which
10          makes me think that was that really something
11          that you wanted to do was kill yourself?
12  Child:  When I am angry I do
```

Example 2: Some level of detail:

```
1   Prac:   so when you ↓said that you were going to take a
2           knife to yourself
3           (1.0)
4           yeah?
5           (1.1)
6   Prac:   What were you ↓hoping would happen?
7   Child:  Erm
8           (2.4)
9           for me to actually kill myself.
10  Prac:   Mummy would?
11  Child:  No me to kill myself
12  Prac:   Say that again mummy would?
13  Mum:    No for her to kill herself.
14  Prac:   Right you're smiling as you say that which
15          makes me think that (.) was that really some-
```

(Continued)

(Continued)

```
16              what you wanted to do was kill yourself
17  Child:  When I'm angry
18          (1.7)
19          I do
```

Example 3: Jefferson, taken from page 907 of the published paper:

```
 1  Prac:   so when you ↓said that you were going to take a
 2          ↓knife to yourself
 3          (1.0)
 4          yeah?
 5          (1.1)
 6  Prac:   What were you ↓hoping would happen?
 7  Child:  Erm
 8          (2.4)
 9          f::or me to ↓actually kill my↓self.
10  Prac:   Mummy w↑ould?
11  Child:  No me ↓to kill ↓myself ((smiling))
12  Prac:   Say that ↓again mummy would?
13  Mum:    ↓No for her to kill her↓self.
14  Prac:   Ri:ght you're ↑smiling as you ↓say that which
15          makes me ↓think that (.) was that really some-
16          ↓what you wanted to ↓do was kill yours↓elf
17  Child:  When I'm ang↓ry
18          (1.7)
19  Child:  I ↓do (.)
```

In the third example, the full Jefferson representation was used, which included a set of symbols to represent *how* things were said, not simply *what* was said. For those who are unfamiliar with these conventions, the symbols might appear confusing at first, but with time and practice you will become familiar with the way these symbols serve to represent the microdetails of the talk.

We next provide you with a brief overview of the main and common symbols used in Jefferson transcription so that you might begin to practice this approach to transcription. The overview of these different symbols is based on Jefferson (2004a) and Hepburn and Bolden (2013, 2017), and we strongly recommend you consult these sources for more detail on what we provide. For each of the symbols, we provide an example from our own data—either our child mental health assessments data set or our family therapy data set—for illustrative purposes. These two data sets are considered naturally occurring, with the initial child mental health assessments including 28 families and family therapy sessions with four families across multiple therapy sessions. Some of the examples are from published data (and this is shown), and some are from unpublished data.

Sequential Positions-Related Symbols

There are certain symbols in the system that denote the sequential relationship of talk, and these illustrate where in the talk they occur.

Latching (=)

There are occasions in talk when one speaker's turn latches to the next speaker's turn, or two turns of one speaker are latched together with no discernible space between them. In other words, latching can occur between two different speakers' turns or within a single speaker's turn as they rush through to the next point (Hepburn & Bolden, 2013), which Jefferson marked with an equal sign.

```
Doctor: still a bit sc<u>ary</u> isn't it=

Child:  =it's not

                        (Example taken from family 2 assessment data)
```

In this example, which is drawn from our child mental health assessment data, as the doctor completes his turn, the child latches his or her turn to it immediately, without any pause or gap. This shows that the child's turn immediately comes in as the doctor closes the final word of his.

Overlapping Talk ([ ])

Talk can occur in overlap or as an interruption to another speaker, and it is important to represent this in the transcript. Why is this important? Transcribing the overlap highlights something about the turn-taking structure, showing that speakers project possible completions of turns and therefore may interrupt (Hepburn & Bolden, 2013). For Jefferson, this is marked by an opening and closing of a square bracket. This marks the exact point when the overlap begins with a left square bracket and closes with a right square bracket.

```
CPN: and he's quite (0.34) big and str↓ong for a fourteen
     yea[r ↓old isn't he?]
Mum:    [↓yeah (.) he is ] ↓yeah
```

(Example taken from family 7 assessment data)

As you can see in this example, the mum/mother starts to respond to the assessment of the community psychiatric nurse (CPN) before the nurse has fully completed his or her turn, and thus the mother comes into the conversation with overlap toward the end of the turn. As this comes toward the end of the turn, it suggests that the mother has projected the transition relevance place and come in with a response rather than interrupting the turn.

```
Mrs Niles:  >I mean< I did, suggest when I [went to se:e that
            doc↓tor]
FT:                                         [>Can I ↑just< say
            as well ], sorry (.) <sorry to interrupt> (.) i-
            if this is <about Steve>
```

(O'Reilly, 2008a, p. 512)

Notably, in this example the square brackets are once again used to denote interruptions as a form of overlapping talk. This example is slightly different, as the second speaker, in this case the family therapist (FT), starts his or her turn at a point when the first speaker is still holding the conversational floor and shows no sign of a turn completion. In this case, the second speaker recognized the turn as interruptive and issued an apology for taking the floor.

Pauses or Gaps in Talk (.)

It is common in CA for the researcher to measure pauses to the nearest tenth of a second, with these measured pauses included in the transcript. Additionally, those pauses that are less than one tenth of a second, that is, a micropause, is also represented by a full stop (period) inside parentheses (.). In CA, there is a distinction made between those silences that occur *between* turn construction units and those silences that occur *within* them (Sacks, Schegloff, & Jefferson, 1974). The following example includes two timed pauses that occur at transition relevance places but are treated in different ways.

```
Child:    I smoke weed ↓near enough every day
          (0.5)
Child:    about ten pound* worth a ↓day
```

```
Therapist: ten pounds worth a ↓day

           (0.7)

Child:     ((child nods head))

*pound in this context is English pounds value (£), not
pounds in weight
```

(Example taken from family 2 assessment data)

This short extract has two timed pauses that are different in nature. The first pause of 0.5 seconds occurs at a transition relevance place whereby the child offers up some information about his smoking weed. The turn is ostensibly complete, and the gap provides a space where another speaker could take the floor. However, in the absence of such uptake, the child continues and provides further information. The second timed pause occurs at the end of the reflection of the therapist, as he repeats the child's turn. The pause provides space for the child to come back in and confirm or disconfirm the therapist's clarification, which results in the child providing a nonverbal response (e.g., represented by a description placed within double parentheses).

Intonation- and Pronunciation-Related Symbols

There are certain symbols that illustrate how words sound in terms of volume and speed.

Volume

During interaction, there are various ways in which speakers change the volume of their talk, and this can be captured in the transcription system as it has different meanings for the interaction, and therefore for the analysis. Volume shifts tend to be represented in three different ways (see Hepburn & Bolden, 2013, for full description):

1. Underlining the emphasized word or part of the word

2. Including capital letters to represent when speakers raise their voice or shout

3. Using single degree signs for a quiet voice and double degree signs for a whisper

```
Child:     [where]

Mum:         [I'll get ↓some]

       I'll take you in a [↓minute]

Child:                    [where] from [↓mum]

Mum:                                   [wait till Erin] comes
```

```
            ↓back coz Erin's on the ↓toilet at the minute
Child: MUM whERE FROM

Mum:    from the shop
```

(Example taken from family 8 assessment data)

In this extract, two types of volume can be seen. If you look at where the extract starts, you can see that at this point there is an interruptive sequence as the child and mother speak in overlap. The mother is speaking to the child's sibling, not the child, while the child is interjecting with a question designed for the mother. With no response, we can see that toward the end of this extract the child raises his or her voice and shouts out the question, "MUM whERE FROM," which elicits a response.

```
FT:     ↑Do you think you're a na::ughty boy?

Steve: ◦Yeah◦

FT:    Yeah?
```

(O'Reilly, 2007, p. 237)

This extract shows that Steve's response was audibly quieter than his usual volume, which is marked by the Jefferson symbols of degree symbols on both sides of the word that was spoken more quietly (i.e., ◦Yeah◦).

Changes in Pitch

Like volume change is that of pitch, which is subtler in presentation but nonetheless should be transcribed using Jefferson symbols. In speech, shifts in intonation are marked by arrows when the pitch is raised or lowered, and by colons when the sound is stretched. A speaker's intonation may rise and fall within one spoken word, and this can also be represented with upward and downward arrows. This is an important consideration, as conversation analysts often note that even slight variations in pitch can be interactionally significant (Hepburn & Bolden, 2013). Hepburn and Bolden (2013) suggested that for a sharp rise or fall in intonation, a double use of arrows should be used to symbolize this in the transcript.

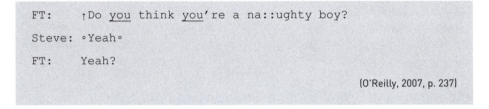

```
Clin Psy:    at the end of the er: the hour we might (0.49)
             not necessarily come to a con↓clu:sion (0.56)
             and if we need to meet a↓gain then we'll try
             and arrange ◦another meeting◦
```

(Example taken from family 10 assessment data)

This extract includes a couple of different examples of pitch (and one of volume). Two of the words spoken have downward arrows (↓), which represent a fall in intonation at that point in the word. Also, the word *conclusion* held a stretched sound in the middle of it, with the "us" being stretched. This is represented by a single colon to show a short stretch (u:s). Multiple colons would illustrate a longer holding of the sound (e.g., u:::s).

Unit-Final Intonation (Hepburn & Bolden, 2013)

Hepburn and Bolden (2013) described using punctuation marks in the Jefferson system to mark the final intonation of a turn construction unit, while also cautioning that this is not meant to be understood as grammatical punctuation. We list these symbols next, as outlined in Hepburn and Bolden (2013):

- A full stop (period) "." shows that the intonation fell when the word was spoken.

- A question mark "?" indicates a strongly rising intonation, which can be questioning but is not necessarily the case.

- A comma "," represents a slight rise in intonation; this does not necessarily mark the continuation of a speaker.

- An inverted question mark "¿" can demonstrate a pitch that is raised in a stronger way than a comma represents but weaker than a full question mark.

- An underscore "_" represents a level intonation when it occurs at the ending of a turn.

```
Dad:    'cause a few years >ag↓o I probably< would 'ave (.)
        killed 'im by ↓now

FT:     Right.

Dad:    >To be< 'onest

FT:     What ↑literally?
```

(O'Reilly, 2008b, p. 282)

This extract illustrates a unit-final intonation marked by a question mark, which in this case demonstrates a strongly raised intonation on the word *literally* as an interrogative. The upward arrow at its start illustrates a slight raise at the beginning of the word, and the question mark represents a strong raise at the end.

Speed of Speech

It may also be relevant to represent the speed at which speech is spoken, which is typically represented with the *more than* and *less than* symbols. Slowed down speech is represented <like this>, and faster speech is represented >like this<.

```
Dad:    'cause a few years >ag↓o I probably< would 'ave (.)
        killed 'im by ↓now
```
(O'Reilly, 2008b, p. 282)

This extract represents the speed at which the Dad spoke ">ago I probably<," representing that this segment of his talk was spoken more quickly than the surrounding speech.

Paralinguistic Features of Talk

Aside from talk itself, there are several other sounds people may make when interacting, such as laughing, crying, coughing, sneezing, drawing in breath, outtakes of breath, active noises, etc. These features of talk have drawn a great deal of attention in the CA transcription literature, and there are different ways of transcribing them.

Aspiration

There are occasions in talk where the breathing of the speaker is more apparent through an intake or outtake of breath that can be short or elongated. In the Jefferson method, this is demonstrated with the letter "h," with inhalation being marked with a full stop (period) preceding the "h" and exhalation being "h" alone. In practice, this looks like .hhhh or hhhh, with the number of "h"s representing the time taken. The number of letters represents the length of the breath.

```
Doctor: and I meant to ↓ask you a really important question
        ↓at the beginning an' I for↑got how ↑old are ↓you

Child:  .hhh em (0.60) I'm nine and I'm ↓ten next m↑onth
```
(Example taken from family 6 assessment data)

In this extract, the child took an intake of breath before answering the doctor's question, and this is marked with the full stop (period) and the repeated letter h.

Laughter

Laughter occurs with different pitch, sound, and volume. The function of laughter has been examined extensively in the CA literature (see, for example, Jefferson, 1984). Hepburn and Bolden (2013) noted that in transcripts, laughter can be represented in different ways, which include:

- Huh

- Hah

- Heh

- Hih

They further argued that these laughter particles may have a raised volume or pitch and may contain aspiration within it. Additionally, speakers may demonstrate laughter particles within words rather than as separate entities, and this is represented by the letter "h" in parentheses as (h).

```
Psychiatrist:  Right o↓kay all right did you just have that (.)
               one (.) °↓meeting with her or°

Mum:           um I had ↓one I turned up on me own heh[heh heh
               he↑h]

Psychiatrist:                                        [(h) oh
               right ↑okay]
```

(Example taken from family 9 assessment data)

In this extract, the phonetic "heh" is sounded by the mother, and we can see here that she laughs at the end of her turn, treating her response as in some way troublesome rather than humorous. In other words, the reporting of turning up to a family meeting by herself is noted as in some way problematic through the occurrence of the laughter. In terms of the transcription, the length that the laughter lasts in the turn is represented by the four "heh" sounds.

Active Noising

Active noising refers to when speakers attempt to recreate noises and sounds in some way (O'Reilly, 2005). Onomatopoeic sounds are generally easier to transcribe than representations of noises, as these can be phonetically reproduced in the transcript.

For example: When recreating onomatopoeia, speakers tend to sound out the noise, saying words such as "bang," "whoosh," and so on.

Representations of noises are more challenging, and therefore along with the effort to transcribe the noise, it is also useful to provide a brief description of the sound in single parentheses.

```
Dad:   >I said to him< (.) I said (.) if you want to
       be treated like a baby (.) ↑I'll get you
```

(Continued)

```
(Continued)
some nappies and some baby clothes
     to wear, (0.2) >and then he jus- went<
  →  kkwwwp ((makes ripping sound)) ripped it like the
     incredible hulk and threw it (.) threw it stamped
     his feet
```
(O'Reilly, 2008b, p. 759)

In this extract, the transcript includes a representation of the sound that the father imitated in his describing of a shirt ripping. The father here is describing the actions of his son, Steve, as he ripped up some clothes. The sound here is important to capture, as it authenticates his version of the account, showing the therapist what the sound was like at the time. However, transcribing a ripping sound is challenging, and here is represented phonetically. This alone is probably insufficient to truly capture the noise that was made by the father, and thus the addition of a transcription comment helps to illustrate this more accurately.

Crying

In certain applied settings, participants may cry. In therapy, courtrooms, child helplines, and so on, one or more of the participants may show signs of distress, and this should be transcribed too. In her earlier work, Hepburn (2004) provided some instruction for how to represent crying in a Jefferson transcript. This included a reduced volume in speech, sniffing, wiping eyes, increased aspiration, or pitch. Additionally, transcriptionist comments can be added to provide detail.

```
Doctor: you can [↓stay here ↑with me ]

FSW:            [want me to wait with you ↓mate]

Child:  ↑no.hhh ↑fuck ~off~ hhh ((crying))

FSW:    al↓right ((walks over to child and kneels down to
        talk to him))

        ((mum shakes head at doctor while comforting
        child))

Doctor: °o↓k°
```
(Example taken from family 8 assessment data)

In this extract, the child's crying is difficult to capture in the transcription but is indicated in several ways. First, it is represented through the raised intonation and emphasis on the "no," which suggests a negative response to the doctor's request. Second, it is represented with the intake and outtake of breath, which shows some trouble in speaking. Third, it is represented in the swear word directed to the family support worker (FSW). Fourth, and probably the most helpful, it is represented by the transcriptionist's note that the child at this point in the interaction is crying, as well as that the FSW kneels and the mother offers comfort.

We do, however, acknowledge that the transcription of crying can be more detailed than we have shown here, and it is possible to capture more detail. Hepburn (2004) provided some symbols to use in transcription to represent the different kinds of sounds made when crying:

- .shih—to denote a wet sniff

- .skuh—to denote a snorty sniff

- (hhh)—aspiration inside parentheses to indicate a sharper sound than without the brackets

- Huhh.hhih—to denote sobbing (combinations of "hhs" can indicate inhaling of breath with many voiced vowels)

- ~—used on either side of a ~word~ indicates a wobble in the voice

Symbol Summary

We have now provided you many Jefferson symbols, and in doing so, we recognize that it will take time to learn these symbols and recognize their meaning when applying them to your own transcription process (as well as when reading Jefferson transcripts produced by others). To help you, we provide you with a simple summary in Table 6.2.

TABLE 6.2 ● Summary of Jefferson symbols

Symbol	Description
=	Represents latched speech
[ ]	Square brackets are used to represent overlapping speech (including interruptions)
(.)	Micropause
(0.2)	Timed pause in seconds
Underlined	Represents emphasis on the word
SHOUT	Raised voice, typically shouting
° °	Degree symbols demonstrate words spoken more quietly
°° °°	Double degree symbols demonstrate a whisper

(Continued)

(Continued)

Symbol	Description
↑	Upward arrow represents raised intonation
↓	Downward arrow represents falling intonation
::	Colons represent a stretched sound
.	A full stop (period) is used when the intonation falls at the end of a turn
,	A comma is a slight raise in intonation
?	A question mark shows a strong rise in intonation and can be interrogative but not necessarily so
_	An underscore represents a level intonation at the end of a turn
><	Shows the speeding up of speech
<>	Shows the slowing down of speech
((comment))	A description in double parentheses shows a comment on the data
(word)	A word or words in single parentheses shows that the transcriptionist has some uncertainty as to the accuracy of the hearing of that word or words
~	A wavy line on either side of the word indicates a wobble in the delivery

Source: Jefferson, 2004a.

Transcribing Multimodal Interactions

The Jefferson method was originally designed to focus on the transcription of verbal language—or that which is hearable. Yet as Nevile (2015) noted in his literature review of 400 articles published in *Research on Language and Social Interaction* from 1987 to 2013, CA researchers are increasingly using video data and focusing on interactional aspects related to the body (e.g., facial expressions, pointing, gaze, manipulating physical objects, driving, etc.). For as Hepburn and Bolden (2013) noted, "In face-to-face interactions, participants' visible conduct is instrumental to how social actions are accomplished and coordinated, which means that it has to be represented on transcript" (pp. 69–70). Thus, within interaction, parties may carry out courses of action together using talk as well as embodied actions, and in so doing attend to each other and phenomena in the world that are the focus of their activities (Streeck, Goodwin, & LeBaron, 2011). As such, Streeck and colleagues noted that this provides a basis for the systematic investigation of phenomena central "to the organization of human language, social organization, culture, and cognition" (p. 3).

To date, however, there is not a common or shared transcription system used for producing transcripts that represent visible conduct/behaviors. Nonetheless, it is widely understood that transcribing visible conduct is interpretive and necessarily selective. There is no possible way for a researcher to represent *everything* that is seen, and indeed, they must focus their transcription around certain visible characteristics (e.g., the way documents are part of the interactional order). This is particularly notable when working with video data in which there are endless potential ways to focus your transcription, ranging from attending to gaze to the physical layout of a space to pointing to shaking heads.

Broadly, when transcribing visible conduct, conversation analysts have relied upon a variety of transcription systems, often combining one or more of such systems with the Jefferson method, three of which we discuss next (Hepburn & Bolden, 2013).

Comments Made by the Transcriptionist

One of the simplest ways to represent visible conduct is to include a brief description within double parentheses. For instance, consider the following extract.

```
FT:   Bob (0.2) can you get out from >under the chair< (.)
      please

((Bob throws a small wooden block at his mother))

Mum: Shall ↑I throw it back?
```

(O'Reilly, 2008b, p. 281)

The family therapy data was video, and therefore the visual as well as audio was available. This meant that the transcripts could capture actions as well as words within the therapeutic interactions. In this extract, the child, Bob, threw a wooden block at his mother while the therapist tried to coax him out from under a chair. While much of this can be ascertained from the talk, the visual representation in the transcript gives the audience more information, which is also relevant for the analysis.

Visual Representations of the Interactions

It is becoming increasingly common to include visual representations alongside or embedded within a detailed Jefferson transcript. There are a variety of technologies that support the creation of such transcripts, which we discuss in Chapter 8. This approach to transcribing visual conduct is often one that is easily accessible to and understood by readers. Such a transcript might be in the form of a sketch or drawing, such as in the following example.

Example of a pictorial representation of gaze between two speakers:

```
(A)   Tim:    ↑why'zit ↑sto
```

(Continued)

(Continued)

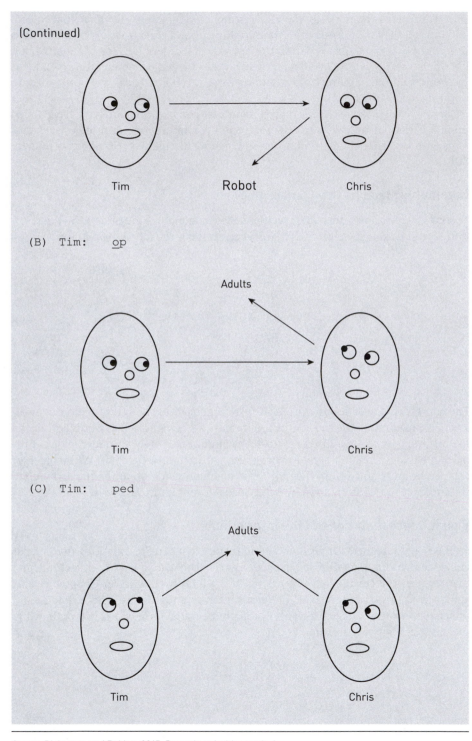

(B) Tim: op

(C) Tim: ped

Source: Dickerson and Robins, 2015. Reproduced with permission.

In this extract, shift in gaze is represented with the arrows and the positioning of the eyes. Note also that a Jefferson transcript is embedded as well, being placed above the corresponding drawings.

Another common approach is to embed screenshots from the actual video data into the transcript, such as seen in the next example.

Example of a transcript with embedded video images:

```
"+                          ↓((C gazes at K))

1    B   You-you You'll decide what you want you want him
         happy or sad

2    B   Look at (it)

         ↓((All gaze at control pad, CP))

3        - - - - - - - - (0.8)
```

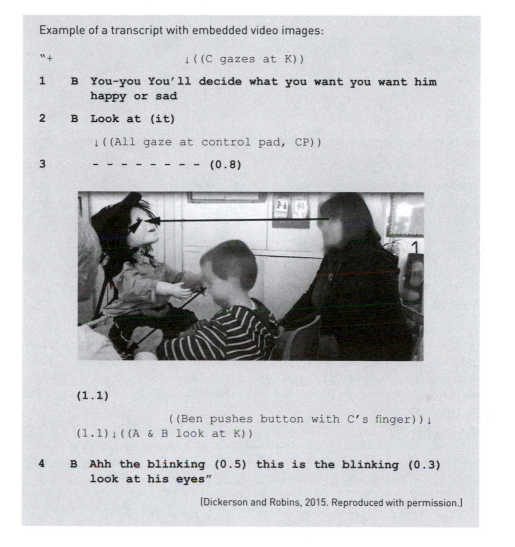

```
     (1.1)

                   ((Ben pushes button with C's finger))↓
     (1.1)↓((A & B look at K))

4    B   Ahh the blinking (0.5) this is the blinking (0.3)
         look at his eyes"
```

[Dickerson and Robins, 2015. Reproduced with permission.]

In this extract, an interaction between a child with autism ("C"), an adult ("A"), and a robot ("KASPAR") used in the context of therapy is represented. In addition to Jefferson's symbols, the researchers include + to represent when the child independently presses a button on the robot's control pad and X to represent the specific locations of the child's gaze apart from the control pad. Arrows are also included on the video frame grabs to represent gaze. Notably, both the child's and adult's faces are distorted to protect their identities.

TABLE 6.3 ● Multimodal conventions

Symbol	Description
* * + + Δ Δ	Gestures and descriptions of embodied actions are delimited between two identical symbols (one symbol per participant) and are synchronized with the correspondent stretches of talk.
*---> *--->	The action described continues across subsequent lines until the same symbol is reached.
>>	The action described begins before the excerpt's beginning.
--->>	The action described continues after the excerpt's end.
.....	Action's preparation.
----	Action's apex is reached and maintained.
,,,,,	Action's retraction.
ric	Participant doing the embodied action is identified when (s)he is not the speaker.
fig #	The exact moment at which a screen shot has been taken is indicated with a specific sign showing its position within turn at talk.

Source: Mondada, 2007.

Specialized Transcription Systems (e.g., Mondada's System)

There are also a variety of specialized transcription systems that can be used to generate a transcript that attends to visible conduct (e.g., Goodwin, 2007; Heath & Luff, 2013; Mondada, 2007). As just one example, Lorenza Mondada has developed a system for transcribing multimodal practices used in interactions. Some of these multimodal conventions are shown in Table 6.3. Refer to Mondada (2007) for a complete description of the multimodal conventions.

Translation

Producing transcripts in a language other than English can be challenging for a variety of reasons and may require a researcher to determine how to

1. represent languages that do not use the Roman alphabet,

2. transcribe tonal language (e.g., Thai), and

3. present data in languages other than English to English-speaking audiences (Hepburn & Bolden, 2013).

Additionally, ten Have (2007) noted that when researchers produce transcripts for publication in a language different than the publication outlet, there are a variety of approaches that might be taken. He suggested, however, that some of the more common and acceptable approaches include

- producing a translated transcript in the body of the text, with the original transcript given immediately below it as a separate block of text;

- producing a transcript in the original language, with a translation into the language of the publication immediately below; or

- producing a transcript in the original language with first a morpheme-by-morpheme gloss and then a translation into the language of the publication immediately below it, line by line.

Regardless of the approach you might take, we encourage you to familiarize yourself with the literature related to translation in CA (for further discussion, see Hepburn & Bolden, 2013, 2017; ten Have, 2007) as well as published CA studies that include translated transcripts. A really useful resource for those who are planning to work with languages other than English is Hepburn and Bolden (2017) as well as Egbert, Yufu, and Hirataka (2016).

Practical Steps for Creating Your Transcript

The Jefferson method aims to preserve the microdetails of the interaction (Jefferson, 2004a), with no detail in the interaction dismissed as irrelevant (Hepburn & Bolden, 2013). In practice, the process of including such detail in a transcript is time consuming and requires significant amounts of energy and focus; thus, the extent and detail of the Jefferson system you include in your research will to some degree depend on the time frame you have available for your project.

> For example: In general, a qualitative researcher who transcribes a 30-minute interview will likely take anywhere from 2 to 6 hours to transcribe, depending on the level of detail the analyst wishes to include (Lucas, 2010).

> For example: For conversation analysis, the level of detail required for a Jefferson transcript takes much longer, and typically requires about 1 hour for every 1 minute of audio recording (Roberts & Robinson, 2004), and this can be even longer for video recordings.

You will therefore need to think about how much time you devote to your transcription process and how much detail you provide within the constraints of the time you have available for your project. It is therefore helpful to think about producing your Jefferson transcript in rounds (Paulus et al., 2014). Specifically, we highlight next six practical considerations for producing a Jefferson transcript.

Step 1: Familiarizing

Before you even begin the process of transcribing your data with detail, you first need to make sure you are familiar with the data set in its entirety. To achieve this, you need to engage in a process of repeated listening/viewing. Indeed, you will need to be prepared for the number of hours you will need to spend with your data. It can be helpful during this initial step to focus on certain aspects of the data that seem interesting to you, and listen to them many times to ensure that you come to know your data well. Creating initial memos at this stage is useful, as this serves to record your unfolding responses to the data. During this step, you can listen/view for overall sequences and for specific aspects of those turns. This will help you to identify different speakers, listen to accents and colloquialisms, and so forth.

Step 2: Transcription Decisions

Before you begin the transcription process, it is important that you consider some of the nine decisions that we outlined earlier in Table 6.1. We suggest you go through all nine, but bear in mind that some decisions are inherent to the methodological perspective you are taking up, and others you have more control over. In this step of the process, you need to think about how you will lay out your transcription on the page, such as margin size and font; how you will represent your participants; whether and how you will attend to and represent visible conduct (e.g., facial expressions, gaze shifts, etc.); how much paralinguistic detail you will include in the overall transcript; and whether translation is needed and at what point you will complete it.

Step 3: Transcribe the Verbal

It is helpful to transcribe the basic interaction as it is spoken prior to layering your transcript with Jefferson symbols. Thus, you will first produce a rough verbatim transcript as a baseline for adding in the additional detail. Make sure that in this version of your transcript you identify who is speaking and transcribe exactly what was said by the participants and in what order.

Step 4: Time the Pauses/Gaps

The next useful step is to go through your transcript, which hopefully is synchronized with your data files, and time the gaps, pauses, and periods of silence. This will then allow you to populate your transcript with this level of detail. The gaps and pauses may be interactionally relevant and should be as accurate as possible. There are digital tools that can help with this, and we discuss this in Chapter 8.

Step 5: Add the Jefferson Symbols

At this point, you will have listened to your data many times and will be familiar with it. Now is a good time to start the Jefferson process. It is important to take your time in adding in all the relevant symbols to represent *how* the words have been spoken. During this phase, you can also add in any paralinguistic features, transcription comments, and other features of the transcript such as the line numbers and footnotes that illustrate the timings (i.e., minutes and seconds into the data that the transcript is at the bottom of each page).

Step 6: Finalize the Level of Detail

Given the time-intensive nature of producing Jefferson transcription, it may be the case that when you are engaged in Step 5 you only generate a rough or simplified Jefferson transcript rather than a fully detailed one. Thus, in Step 6 you need to make a decision about the level of detail you are going to apply to build on the previous step. If you have many hours of data, you may decide not to generate a detailed Jefferson transcript across your whole data set, but you may feel it is necessary for the whole corpus to have that level of detail. In other words, the final step, Step 6, is to do analysis and finalize which segments of data need the full level of attention and representation.

An Interview With Professor Alexa Hepburn and Dr. Galina Bolden

What we have demonstrated in this chapter is how important it is to have a detailed transcript—something that is congruent with the applied CA approach. To do so, we have drawn upon the work of Hepburn and Bolden, as they have advanced the CA community's understanding of the Jefferson transcription process and have contributed heavily to the literature. We therefore asked them some questions about transcription, and we provide their responses in Box 6.1.

BOX 6.1
INTERVIEW WITH PROFESSOR ALEXA HEPBURN AND DR. GALINA BOLDEN

Alexa Hepburn is a professor of communication, and Galina Bolden is an associate professor at Rutgers University, United States. Professor Hepburn and Dr. Bolden have contributed to the growing debates and pedagogical literature on transcription, and have provided empirical work from a CA perspective on this issue.

Most recently, they have published a useful book focused on transcribing that describes in greater detail many of the points we discuss in this chapter:

- Hepburn, A., & Bolden, G. B. (2017). *Transcribing for social research*. London, England: Sage.

We asked Hepburn and Bolden three questions about applied CA and transcription, and their answers to these questions are provided as follows.

Why do you think the level of detail in transcription is necessary for applied CA studies?

"Many qualitative social scientists see data transcription as a straightforward job of reproducing what was said in a standard orthography. However, in the last 50 years, research using conversation

(Continued)

(Continued)

analytic transcriptions has begun to facilitate an understanding of human conduct in various complex institutional situations that is distinct from conceptions offered by methods such as experiments and surveys. If we take seriously the basic conversation analytic insight that talk is a medium of action, then whatever data we are analyzing, whether it involves sentencing someone in a court of law, taking important details about child abuse on a helpline, or breaking bad news in a medical interaction, these activities will all be realized through talk-in-interaction in orderly and reproducible ways. Conversation analysts argue that the specific features of delivery—the trailing off; the pauses; the stretched, emphasized, and cut-off sounds; the changes in pitch and volume; and the nonverbal actions that accompany these elements—are not simply insignificant distractions from the main business of talk; rather, they are highly consequential to understanding the actions that talk is performing. The practice of transcribing in more detail gives us a way of slowing down the talk and capturing these relevant interactional features on the page. An accurate transcript is an investment of time that supports much more robust analytic claims, and as such provides other researchers with a useful resource to interrogate those claims."

How has using the Jefferson approach for transcription in your own applied CA work been helpful?

"Speakers routinely incorporate and orient to both verbal and nonverbal elements of talk. Various applied studies in conversation analysis and related fields have shown that when we share our examples and analysis from everyday materials, they can facilitate sophisticated discussions with practitioners about their own practices for managing the everyday interactional challenges that they might be facing.

In my (Hepburn's) applied work on child protection helpline interaction, I focused on things that call takers said they found difficult or problematic, mainly delivering advice, overcoming advice resistance, and managing heightened affect such as upset, anger, and conflict (see Hepburn, Wilkinson, & Butler, 2014). This involved exploring specific sequences of talk in which these activities take place, and following analysis, translating research findings into training materials, with the aim of codifying good practice and turning it into a set of controlled strategic possibilities. For this, detailed transcription is essential.

To take *upset* as an example, to understand it from an interactional perspective, I developed a body of research that focuses not simply on the categories or formulations of upset, but also on the specifics of its interactional display (Hepburn, 2004). This research showed that pitch, timing, volume, and other specifics of delivery play a key role in how something is hearable as, and responded to as, upset. Displays included increased aspiration, elevated pitch, tremulous delivery, sniffing, and sobbing. Careful transcription of these features and different ways of responding to them facilitated identification of some core interactional features. For example, analysis showed that crying is something that can inflect and replace talk, so can interfere with as well as dramatize or underscore talk. This can make its uptake complex and tricky—it involves orientating to something that is displayed rather than to an action, claim, or proposition. Also, criers may be reluctant for their emotional state to become part of the interaction, which creates further difficulties in acknowledging and affiliating. Building on initial work, Hepburn and Potter (2007) and Potter and Hepburn (2010) showed the value of setting out a procedural definition of uptake, such as sympathy and empathy.

One challenge is then how to feed these extensive findings back to call takers at the helpline. We begin by using our analytic insights to generate 'choice points' where different types of upshot can be delivered—leave more silence, offer a sympathetically inflected continuer, start to build back toward advice, and so on. In a workshop, we play a recording of the call, stop the recording at key points of choice, and ask call takers to consider what their next turn would be—not just the wording but *how* they would deliver it. The intensity of group engagement in such exercises is palpable. The exercise offers a platform for demonstrating skills and commenting on those of others. We ask call takers to explain why they might make this choice and then compare their responses with other call takers. For many parties, this is the first time they have had a focused conversation of this intensity about their strategic choices. As Hepburn et al. (2014) noted, call takers are highly skilled at managing callers, yet they lack expertise in articulating those practices, which are typically organized at a level of detail that is hard to remember or reproduce. An accurate transcript is a crucial element in capturing those specifics."

What do you think are the limitations of using the Jefferson method for applied research?

"Many conversation analytic researchers at the beginning of a new project will collect large amounts of recordings, which would require significant resources of time/money to transcribe in detail. While standard orthographic transcripts are fairly cheap and easy to produce, Jefferson transcription is much more labor intensive, both to learn and to produce. As we have noted elsewhere (Hepburn & Bolden, 2017), a solution for this is to work carefully with the data until you have identified which sequences to single out for detailed examination. Given the key role the transcription process plays in the analysis, the development of transcription skills is a fundamental step in research training. While transcribing is very time consuming, the analytic and educational payoffs are hard to overemphasize."

Chapter Summary

In this chapter, we introduced you to the typical approach for producing transcripts in an applied CA research study. We focused on the Jefferson method, which is the method used in CA to generate detailed transcripts. In doing so, we positioned the act of transcription as inevitably selective and interpretative. Indeed, transcription is a process that involves several critical decisions that are central to your analysis. In addition, we provided you with a brief overview of some of the key ways that researchers represent visible conduct, noting also some of the challenges you may face if working with data in a language other than English. The key learning points are summarized in the next box.

Learning Points From Chapter 6

- Transcription is an interpretative and theoretically driven activity.
- The Jefferson system is the preferred transcription approach for an applied CA study.
- Specialized transcription systems are useful when transcribing multimodal interactions.

Recommended Readings

We highlight two resources that point to seminal writings around transcription in CA research. We encourage you to review these two chapters and use them as key guiding resources when you engage in the transcription process.

- Hepburn, A., & Bolden, G. (2013). The conversation analytic approach to transcription. In J. Sidnell & T. Stivers (Eds.), *The Blackwell handbook of conversation analysis* (pp. 57–76). Oxford, England: Blackwell.

This chapter, written by Hepburn and Bolden, provides an accessible contribution to the literature on the Jefferson transcription method. The focus of this chapter is on the symbols used in the Jefferson system along with critical discussions of other aspects of transcription, such as multimodal communication and critiques of the detailed transcription methods.

- Jefferson, G. (2004a). Glossary of transcript symbols with an introduction. In G. H. Lerner (Ed.), *Conversation analysis: Studies from the first generation* (pp. 13–31). Amsterdam, Netherlands: John Benjamins.

This is an essential reading for anyone doing applied CA research, as it was written by the pioneer of the transcription process preferred in CA research, Gail Jefferson. It outlines the full transcription system as it was created for CA. It is important that you familiarize yourself with the notation system common to Jefferson's method, and this chapter is certainly a good starting place.

7

Analyzing Data in Applied Conversation Analysis Research

> ## Chapter Focus
>
> In this chapter, you will learn how to:
>
> - Describe the different stages of engaging in an applied conversation analysis.
> - Recognize the importance of planning and preparing for analysis.
> - Recognize the stages of undertaking an analysis.
> - Appreciate the importance of data sessions.
> - Consider the place of coding in conversation analysis research.

In Chapter 2, we outlined some of the key principles of doing conversation analysis (CA) and provided an overview of why these are important for carrying out this type of research. It is important to revisit these principles in learning about how to complete the practical steps of analysis, as they are central to this process. Indeed, the foundational principles of CA underpin the framework for doing analysis; therefore, we encourage you to become familiar with these prior to moving forward with this chapter.

The aim of this chapter is to introduce you to the iterative process of undertaking what can be quite a complex and layered analytic process. To move you through the analytic process, we provide you with a step-by-step guide for doing applied CA and give examples from institutional data sets to illuminate the practical stages of completing such an analysis. To help clarify this analytic process, we methodically go through each analytic stage and illustrate some of the complexities.

Institutional Talk and the Process
of Doing Conversation Analysis

In Chapter 1, we introduced you to the meaning of institutional talk as well as applied CA. In that chapter, we outlined why institutional settings were of interest to applied conversation analysts and contextualized that against the historical backdrop of CA. Before we offer you a practical guide for carrying out your analysis, we provide context for this discussion by considering institutional interactions as a focus of analysis.

Throughout the book, we have noted that it is necessary that you understand the core principles of CA, as this is a critical foundation for analyzing talk-in-interaction within institutional settings (Seedhouse, 2004). Broadly, the main aim of CA is to interrogate the social organization of activities that are produced through talk within interaction (Hutchby & Wooffitt, 2008). In using CA, analysts can examine the kinds of social organizations that are used as resources in interaction (Mazeland, 2006) as well as focus on how participants negotiate meaning on a turn-by-turn basis (McCabe, 2006). Further, given that our focus here is on applied CA, it is helpful to consider some of the distinct features of institutional talk before you begin the analytical process. Notably, Heritage (2005) and others have suggested that the distinctions between institutional and mundane talk are not "fixed and demarcated" yet still "useful and empirically sound" (p. 108). Heritage outlined some of the core distinct features of institutional interactions as follows.

Turn Taking

The turn-taking organization of interaction within institutional settings is typically different from turn-taking procedures that occur in mundane settings. In other words, the interactions that take place in institutional settings tend to involve specific and systematic transformations of interactional procedures. For example, the interactions that occur in a courtroom or classroom have distinct turn-taking systems (e.g., a teacher asks a question, a student responds to this question, and the teacher then evaluates the student's response), with this very orientation making visible the participants' orientations to the institutional norms. Note also that some scholars have highlighted the differences in computer-mediated communication (e.g., social media) talk as well (Paulus, Warren, & Lester, 2016).

Structural Organization

The overall structural organization of interactions within institutional settings is generally distinct from mundane settings. This is important, as conversation analysts claim that it is through sequence organization that the tasks central to the unfolding interaction are locally managed. So in institutional settings, they are often marked by a range of question–answer sequences, but these are less commonly found in mundane interactions. For instance, conversation analysts who studied 911 emergency calls found that the opening sequences of the calls included specific details that functioned to establish the identities of the 911 caller and 911 dispatcher (Wakin &

Zimmerman, 1999; Zimmerman, 1992a, 1992b). In this particular example, the structural organization marked the talk as institutional.

Critical Analytic Practices: Sensitizing Practices

There are several core activities or ways of thinking-being that we encourage you to pursue as you begin analysis; these sensitizing practices are particularly important to keep in mind during the earliest stages of your analysis. First, some of your earliest encounters with your data are likely to take place as you engage in transcribing your data. While we do not discuss transcription in this chapter (as that is discussed in Chapter 6), it is helpful to keep in mind that for conversation analysts, transcription is positioned as an analytic act. In other words, it is part of your analysis process. Second, we position unmotivated looking as a core practice when engaging with and orienting to your interactional data (something we introduced and defined in Chapter 4). Third, gaining general familiarity with your data is critical, particularly as you prepare to engage in a more thorough analysis. Finally, planning for analysis often requires that you return to the literature. We therefore next discuss (1) engaging in unmotivated looking, (2) familiarizing yourself with your data set, and (3) reexamining the literature in more detail.

Engaging in Unmotivated Looking

From the start, you should plan to approach your data through the lens of unmotivated looking. Unmotivated looking means that the analyst is open to the discovery of patterns or phenomena (Seedhouse, 2004). As such, unmotivated looking demands that you go into your analysis with an open mind, avoid imposing any type of research agenda onto your data, and allow yourself to be immersed in the data set. This analytic commitment ensures that your understandings and interpretations of the data remain grounded in the data, with your categories of interest not being imposed upon the data within the analysis process (Schegloff, 1996). In other words, your pet theories should not dictate how you make sense of the interactions. It can be difficult to suspend some of your a priori beliefs and ideas when looking through the data, but it is important that you allow the data, and not your preconceived ideas about them, to drive your analysis. As an applied researcher, you might have some desire for social change or improving things; thus, pushing for the data to confirm those ideas might be tempting. However, it is essential that you engage in a data-driven technique and use the technique of unmotivated looking to ensure this.

The specifics of the notion of unmotivated looking have been challenged by some who argue that it is not possible to be completely unmotivated, as simply looking at the data originates from the researcher being motivated to investigate it (Psathas, 1990). Psathas argued, therefore, that in CA terms, unmotivated looking is when analysts are unmotivated in a way as being open to discovering phenomena and suspending their beliefs as they investigate the data in an open way. In other words, for the conversation analyst, they remain as unmotivated as possible by not having preconceived ideas about what they might find in the data and having an open and unspecified question to open the project. So for unmotivated looking in CA, the analysis is "not prompted by prespecified analytic goals" and thus notices a practice or something interesting and pursues that further (Schegloff, 1996, p. 172).

Familiarizing Yourself With the Data Set

Across all approaches to qualitative data analysis, familiarizing yourself with your data set is an important early step in the analytic process. This is indeed true of applied CA, which relies heavily on the actual recordings of the events or the texts that are to be subjected to analysis. As we noted in the previous chapter, before you can truly begin the process of doing CA, you need to be completely familiar with the data and ensure that your transcripts reflect the data adequately. The more you view/listen to your data and read through your transcripts (or read your texts), the more tuned in to the interactions you will become, and this will ultimately facilitate the analytic process. Furthermore, this familiarity will facilitate the unmotivated looking part of the process. At this early stage, we encourage you to make ***memos*** that document your increasing familiarity with the data set.

> **Memos** are written reflections of our ideas, hunches, questions, etc., about our data (Lochmiller & Lester, 2017). It is helpful to keep in mind that memos need to be "conclusive" but can be positioned as a "creative" and "suggestive" activity (Dey, 1993, p. 89).

Reexamining the Literature

In Chapter 3, we discussed the importance of planning your research project. As part of that discussion, we noted the importance of reviewing the literature, with this process positioned as iterative and multidimensional. In other words, reviewing the literature is not simply something that you do at the beginning of your study and then put to one side. This is especially important for an applied CA project, as the research question(s) is often broad and open, and thus the specificity of your literature review develops and evolves as the project evolves.

> **At this stage, your revisiting of the literature will remain fairly broad, as until you engage with the data more fully and in more depth, you may be unable to refine this further.**

During the analysis planning and preparation, there is another opportunity to revisit the literature. The empirical evidence base in the general area of interest as well as the methodology literature will be helpful for you. The methodological literature related to CA is particularly useful to review as you reflect on how CA is done and the core principles of the approach. Furthermore, the broad topic that you are investigating will be central to any analysis that you do; therefore, an understanding of the general empirical evidence in that area will help you to incorporate that.

The Practical Stages of Doing Applied Conversation Analysis

Engaging in CA analysis can be quite complicated and is certainly something that requires time, practice, and training. While analysis is an iterative process and should not be thought of as linear (i.e., as occurring in a stepwise fashion), when learning CA, it can be helpful to think about the various stages common to the analytic process. We organize our discussion of the practical steps of doing an applied CA but note that the steps overlap and turn back on each other, and cannot be thought of as linear. Nonetheless, we find it helpful to think about analysis in this more concrete, systematic way and thus share eight steps proposed by Drew (2015):

1. Examine the interaction for social activity.

2. Attend to the turn-taking sequences.

3. Examine the details.

4. Explore recipient responses.

5. Identify the shared features of language.

6. Collect several cases of the phenomenon.

7. Provide an account for the pattern.

8. Write up the findings.

Using Drew's framework for practical steps to doing CA, we take each of these in turn and introduce you to each in more detail.

Step 1: Examine the Interaction for Social Activity

There is some variation in how you can take your first step toward analyzing your data, with CA scholars voicing slightly different opinions in terms of where to begin. Indeed, it can feel quite overwhelming, particularly if you are faced with hour after hour of recorded data or page after page of naturally occurring text. The preparation stages we described previously will certainly help you in becoming familiar with your data corpus; yet even after engaging in unmotivated looking, a far more detailed analysis is needed.

Drew (2015) proposed that the first step for CA is to examine the interaction for *social activity* (sometimes referred to as a social action). We introduced you to the notion of a social action in Chapters 1 and 2, noting that this is a particularly central concept to the study of talk-in-interaction.

> In CA, a **social activity** refers to the action that a person is doing/performing with their talk. When people interact, it is assumed that they "do" things with talk, which is considered a social action or social activity.

Thus, in this step of your analytic journey, you should note these activities and see how they are managed in and through the talk. As an analyst, you should be frequently asking yourself this question: What is the participant doing here?

> For example: There are many social activities or social actions people can perform in interaction, such as complaining, arguing, assessing, inviting, questioning, moaning, criticizing, excusing, and so forth.

Your first step, therefore, is to look through all your data, noting that when participants are interacting they are doing more than merely talking to one another as they are engaging in social activities (Drew, 2015). In fact, we would suggest that you produce multiple memos across your data that record your responses to this question, linking your memo to the actual data.

Drew (2015) reminded us that these activities/actions have a social character, as it is assumed that engaging with the social world means performing and responding to such activities. He noted that when researchers study conversation, it is not an idle study of language but the study of how language is used in doing things in the social world.

While this first step is important in the process of doing CA, analyzing across your entire data corpus can be a lot of work, particularly if you are new to CA. Some CA scholars have suggested that narrowing down your focus is thus perhaps a first important step. This of course links to the preparation stage of unmotivated looking, which is a process that should have helped you note some of the more interesting aspects of your data. Indeed, "what analysts find interesting or noticeable depends upon, and plays off of, their own tacit knowledge, expectations and interests" (Pomerantz & Fehr, 1997, p. 71). Pomerantz and Fehr (1997) argued that in this initial stage of analysis, it is helpful to select a few interesting sequences just to start you off.

> *What this means*: When you listen to your recordings or read through your textual data, it is helpful to select a place to begin. Through unmotivated looking, it is useful to identify several sequences of interaction that you find interesting.

Identifying a sequence can be challenging, as often it can be difficult to ascertain the beginning and end of a sequence:

- *Start of the sequence*—To locate the beginning of a sequence, you need to identify the turn whereby one of the speakers initiated an action or topic and was responded to by the other interlocutors.

- *End of the sequence*—To locate the end of your sequence, you will need to look through the interaction until you can find the place whereby the speakers are no longer specifically responding to the prior action or topic (Pomerantz & Fehr, 1997).

When you have identified a single sequence or just a few of these sequences, you can then examine the social activities that are taking place within this sequence(s) and then apply that method to the rest of your data as your confidence grows. Your aim is to characterize the social action or actions that you see being performed. Sometimes, a speaker will perform more than one social action in his or her turn, so certainly be open to this and take note.

To illustrate this, we offer an example of a sequence from our own data (O'Reilly & Lester, 2016, p. 503) and consider the social action that is being performed.

```
FT:   >I wuz gonna ask< (.) >you know< what kind of
      explanations you 'ave, fo::r (.) >you know< why it is
      that 'e's (.) he's ↑started doin' these (.) <the:se
      things>

Mum:  <I don't know> (.) I say it t' scho:ol (.) and >you
      know< there's this theory is it in the g::enes
```

We provide this example of a sequence to show how social actions can be identified. This sequence begins with a topic shift from the family therapist (FT) through his question and explanation-seeking of the child's behavior. The social actions in this sequence can be identified as *account-seeking* and *accounting*, as the therapist seeks an account from the parents for the child's behavior (previously described), and the mother provides an account with, "There's this theory is it in the g::enes." The sequence continues with more detail as the therapist moves on to more specific questions. Our intent here is to merely illustrate how social activities can be seen in a short sequence of data, and indeed, we encourage you to begin identifying sequences and social activities within your own data sets. It certainly requires practice to recognize all social activities, but the more you engage with talk or text and ask yourself the question "What is the participant doing here?" the more you will begin to see and make sense of the performative nature of talk. Before moving further, we suggest that you complete the activity in Box 7.1, which invites you to think about social activities/actions with your own data set.

BOX 7.1
ACTIVITY ON IDENTIFYING SOCIAL ACTIVITIES

Activity

Go through your data corpus (just the first few minutes or so) and identify all of the social activities that you can see, such as invitations, asking questions, justifying something, excusing a behavior, accounting for an action, blaming, complaining, and so forth. Keep the following question in mind: What is/are the participant(s) doing here? Notably, this can be a challenging activity, and thus we certainly encourage you to work with colleagues to identify social activities in your data.

Step 2: Attend to the Turn-Taking Sequences

The second step to doing CA is to pay attention to the sequences of turns by looking at the turn that preceded the initiated action so that you can explore how the identified social activity arose from that sequence. In other words, there will be a sequence of turns that leads up to the initiation of the action you note in a sequence, and thus you can examine how the activity may have arisen from that (Drew, 2015). You will need to do this for all the key sequences you identify in Step 1.

During this step of analysis, it is necessary to pay attention to how the timing and taking of turns allow for understandings of the social actions. In other words, for each of the turns in the sequence, it can be useful to describe how the speaker obtained the turn, the timing of the turn initiation and termination, and whether the speaker was selected or if there was an open conversational floor (Pomerantz & Fehr, 1997).

In institutional settings, there is often an orientation to the institutional business at hand, and this can be examined by looking at the sequences of turns within your sequence and those just before it. It is helpful to look at what precedes your sequence to see what came before it. Let's return to our earlier example and consider how the turn-taking occurred.

```
FT:    >I wuz gonna ask< (.) >you know< what kind of
       explanations you 'ave, fo::r (.) >you know< why it is
       that 'e's (.) he's ↑started doin' these (.) <the:se
       things>

Mum:   <I don't know> (.) I say it t' scho:ol (.) and >you
       know< there's this theory is it in the g::enes
```

(O'Reilly & Lester, 2016, p. 503)

In this extract, it is noted that there is a clear question–answer sequence, and the response to the question is in the form of self-selection from the mother. What we mean by this is that the mother elects herself to respond to the therapist's question. Question–answer sequences are the fundamental body of a therapeutic interaction, so this in itself is not surprising, but what matters here is how the turns are treated by the interlocutors. So if we take a closer look, we can see that the therapist is asking his question in response to something said prior by the parents.

Indeed, the parents spent some time prior to this question providing a description of the child's behavior, as seen in the following (unpublished) extract.

```
Dad:   even with Joan ((social worker)) and what 'ave ya an'
       and saying well "look something's not right" >you know
       what I mean<

FT:    ↑Yeah

Dad:   and eventually (.) he's (.) he'll 'ave t' go away for
       'is own protection

FT:    Hu::m

Mum:   He goes out there

Dad:   O::r he's gonna be one of these that end up
       in a prison (1.4)
       jus' basically because there's no other facility for him
```

The extreme nature of the child's behavior is described here by the father who proposes that due to the child's behavior he is likely to end up "in a prison." It is not our intention here to analyze these turns in detail; rather, we aim to show how it was the parents' joint description of their son that occurred prior to the therapist asking a question that sought out an explanation for that behavior. So while the question did not occur as a distinct topic shift as it was tied to the previous set of turns, it does take a subtle topic shift in the sense that the question begins to seek an explanation for the behavior, something that was not considered previously.

> *What this means:* Each turn in interaction is intrinsically tied to the preceding turn in the conversation. The subsequent turn—in this case a question from the therapist—was in response to the extreme description presented of the child's behavior.

Step 3: Examine the Details

At this point in the analytic process, you will begin to examine the detail in the design of each of the turns in your sequences, particularly whereby the action was initiated in the talk. In our previous example, this was where the account seeking was initiated through the question design of the therapist. It is at this point in the analytic process where you start to look at the specific words or phrases that have been used by the speaker, as well as the intonation or any other paralinguistic features that the turn contains.

If we again turn to our example, we can see that the initiating turn is in the form of a question, and through its intonation and style is designed to seek an account from the parents for the child's behavior. This is done through the use of words, which position the parents as understanding the reasons their child is behaving in a particular way.

```
what kind of explanations you 'ave, fo::r (.) >you know<
why it is that 'e's (.) he's "started doin' these (.)
<the:se things>
```

If we examine the detail in this question, we can see that there is a lot going on here. Primarily, two main issues are being dealt with. First, there is an assumption that there should be an explanation for the child's behavior and that the parents will be able to provide some understanding of those explanations. Second, the focus is on the reasons that the child *started* engaging in those behaviors, identifying the initial cause of the time when the behaviors began.

Step 4: Explore Recipient Responses

In identifying the detail in the initiating turn, it is equally important to examine how the recipient responded to that turn. In so doing, you are bringing together Steps 1 and 3 in examining the next turn (Drew, 2015). If we turn to our example, you will see that the mother's response to the question treats this question as account seeking, and thus an account is provided.

```
Mum:  <I don't know> (.) I say it t' scho:ol (.) and >you
      know< there's this theory is it in the g::enes
```

Notably, the account provided by the mother is cautiously presented as a theory as opposed to a fact. The detail in the recipient's response is relevant and linked to the question asked by the therapist, and offers up a plausible explanation for the child's behavior. In other words, the idea that a child's inappropriate behavior can be caused by genetics is offered up as a possible explanation—that is, as a possible account. In so doing, the mother here is accounting, albeit cautiously, for the child's behavior in a way that mitigates any possible blame that it is their parental discipline that is the problem.

Step 5: Identify the Shared Features of Language

Drew (2015) noted that the fifth stage is a more implicit stage of the analysis. It is at this point in your analytic process that you begin to identify any shared features of the language. In other words, you should examine the construction of the turns at talk and the responses to them, noting that these are not idiosyncratic to those speakers.

> *What this means*: Although every interaction is unique, there are some systematic properties of talk-in-interaction; therefore, the common/shared forms of language can be identified.

Indeed, it is in looking at the sequence in a more holistic way that you can begin to consider the ways in which the social actions have been achieved by the interlocutors (Pomerantz & Fehr, 1997). Pomerantz and Fehr (1997) suggested that during the analytic process it is important to think about the ways in which social actions implicate certain identities, roles, or relationships for the interlocutors. They proposed that the analyst should question the data in terms of whether the speakers are referring to persons, places, or activities that orient to certain roles or relationships and the obligations that may be expected of them.

Step 6: Collect Several Cases of the Phenomenon

> In CA terms, a **candidate phenomenon** is a tangible, viewable example of something within the data. It is a topic, area, event, or something else specific that you can identify multiple examples of in your data.

Once you have a sense of the ways in which the talk is functioning within your data corpus and you have examined several sequences of talk to gain an overall understanding of your data, it is important that you become more focused in your analysis. Remember that the main aim of CA is to examine and identify *socially organized practices,* as it is through these that people can make themselves understood and manage their social activities (Drew, 2015). There are therefore two stages to making your CA more focused: first, identify a ***candidate phenomenon,*** and second, collect all instances of this phenomenon.

In other words, it is through these two stages that the shared organizations that are present in patterns of talk can be identified, as the patterns become clearer when the analyst collects a range of those instances (Drew, 2015).

Identifying a Candidate Phenomenon

By reengaging in unmotivated looking, you can begin to identify candidate phenomena of interest for analysis (Seedhouse, 2004).

> (!) **It is necessary to collect as many instances of your phenomenon of focus as can be found so that they can be investigated for the properties that they have in common (Drew, 2015).**

For example: A complaint is a candidate phenomenon.

For example: An interruption is a candidate phenomenon.

Through an inductive search across the entirety of your data, you will likely begin to see if you have a collection of the identified phenomenon (Seedhouse, 2004). This is an important stage for a CA study, as it is this identification of a candidate phenomenon that sets the direction of your analysis and defines the focus of that CA. Notably, you may identify multiple phenomena of interest, which may lead to multiple rounds of analysis and different publications. Generally, it is assumed that you will *not* analyze your entire data corpus in one go, nor publish *all* your research in one paper or even an entire thesis or dissertation. See Box 7.2 for a research example.

BOX 7.2
EXAMPLE OF CANDIDATE PHENOMENA IDENTIFICATION

Research Example: Video Data

In a research study conducted by the second author (O'Reilly), a corpus of naturally occurring family therapy sessions was video recorded for research purposes. The research question guiding this project was broad in its orientation. Through an unmotivated trawl through the data, alongside the representative transcripts, a candidate phenomenon of interruptions was identified. The researcher noted that within the data there were many instances whereby one party interrupted another and that this was managed by the interlocutors. Although upon subsequent

(Continued)

(Continued)

in-depth analysis it became clear that these interruptions were different in their usage, it is important to note that at this stage the researcher had simply identified interruptions as the candidate phenomenon of interest for analysis. This led her to engage in the social psychology literature on interruptions, the feminist literature, the CA literature related to interruptions, and the linguistic literature to help develop a better understanding of interruptions.

Example publications of the identified candidate phenomenon include:

1. O'Reilly, M. (2006). Should children be seen and not heard? An examination of how children's interruptions are treated in family therapy. Discourse Studies, 8(4), 549–566.

2. O'Reilly, M. (2008). "What value is there in children's talk?" Investigating family therapists' interruptions of parents and children during the therapeutic process. Journal of Pragmatics, 40, 507–524.

In his original work, Sacks (1992) subscribed to the idea that areas of interest should emerge from the data. In other words, the analyst should find things naturally in the data corpus. So your analytic focus should be driven by what comes out of the data analysis process. In other words, the focus for CA is your commitment to what you are seeing, hearing, and reading in the data as you focus on what the participants are orienting to; that is, you are interested in what the interlocutors are making visible through their interactions with each other (or within the text).

Collection of Instances of the Candidate Phenomenon

Once you have identified the key phenomenon of interest, you can begin the real business of producing a detailed and in-depth analysis. Identifying a single case of the phenomenon can be interesting, but it is necessary to explore the sequential pattern across the cases/instances of the phenomenon. Thus, it is within this step that you need to begin to collect several cases of the phenomenon; that is, you are attempting to generate a *collection of cases* (Drew, 2015).

What this means: Once you have established a collection of cases of the phenomenon, you will be able to explore the features that they have in common.

The purpose of this is to make sense of the patterns in relation to the occurrences of the phenomenon, with the analyst showing how these patterns are methodically produced (Seedhouse, 2004). Generally, you will now need to identify the sequences of talk in which the candidate phenomenon occurs and repeat Steps 1 through 5 on these instances. Broadly, you should closely attend to how the speakers have designed their turns and examine the detail in those turns as you consider how the participants are responding to one another. It is through recursively engaging with the early stages of analysis now in a more focused way that you will be able to note what features the selected segments of data have in common (Drew, 2015).

Step 7: Provide an Account for the Pattern

In this stage of your analysis, you should begin to account for the pattern you have identified. In other words, you are beginning to generate an explanation for the pattern. To develop your analysis in detail, you should determine whether the collection of instances you have identified have any features in common and how the object/pattern you identified arose (Drew, 2015). It is at this point in the analytic process in which you need to provide a detailed analysis of the sequences that have been pulled out of the overall data corpus. It is also during this stage that you need to identify any ***deviant cases*** (Seedhouse, 2004).

A **deviant case** is one whereby the identified case goes against the interactional pattern that you have identified. It is when the established pattern you identified is departed from in some way, and how the speakers orient to this departure (Heritage, 1988).

Identifying deviant cases does not mean your analysis is flawed or inaccurate in any way; rather, this allows you to make a stronger case for your claims. Identifying deviant cases does not mean that there is a disconfirmation of the pattern you have identified, but rather, their special features can help to confirm the genuineness of the identified common pattern (Heritage, 1988). The identification of deviant cases from the identified shared interactional pattern is a useful exercise in CA, as it allows you to see and examine those instances that do not follow the same sequence or content as the others that you have picked out.

Think back to the example we shared with you in Chapter 1 from Sacks's (1992) original lectures:

```
A: This is Mr Smith may I help you

B: I can't hear you.

A: This is Mr Smith.

B: Smith.
```

This example of a telephone call to the suicide center captured his attention, as it did not follow the usual pattern that he had observed in the other telephone calls and thus was a deviant case. Rather than being problematic, this case served to strengthen the claim of normative address that Sacks was making, as the speaker in the interaction oriented to the nonnormative trouble in this case.

Further, some scholars have suggested that the identification of deviant cases is an important aspect of warranting your claims (Antaki, Billig, Edwards, & Potter, 2003); that is, it is part of assuring you generate a quality study (see Chapter 9 for a further discussion of this quality assurance). Additionally, deviant cases are particularly useful, as they can illuminate the kinds of problems that illustrate why a standard or commonly identified pattern takes the form that it does (Potter, 1996b).

What this means: Any examples of the talk deviating from the established pattern are not understood to be exceptions but instead are helpful evidence for the existence of

(Continued)

(Continued)

the pattern. In cases where the speakers orient to a deviation from the norm, it illustrates that the norm should indeed apply.

Step 8: Write Up the Findings

The final stage of your analysis is writing up your findings, which is multifaceted and complex. It is important during this part of the analytic process that your accounting for the phenomenon is clear and includes relevant literature (Drew, 2015). During this stage, you need to select data examples (i.e., representative data extracts) that illustrate the key aspects of your phenomenon of focus, which requires determining how many examples of the phenomenon are required to make your analytic point(s). It is here that you produce an account of how your identified phenomenon relates to the broad matrix of interaction and illuminates the social actions under your analytic spotlight (Seedhouse, 2004).

TABLE 7.1 ● Steps in identifying principal points/patterns and writing up findings	
Step	**Description**
Outline phenomenon	The first step is to describe and outline the phenomenon that is the focus of your analysis. This should be clearly stated, and while a theoretical account may be helpful, it is important not to lose your focus and get lost in theory. What your audience really needs to know is what you have found.
Consult the literature	It is highly likely that some of the literature will be relevant to the topic, method, and nature of your phenomenon, and this should not be ignored. How you do this and the extent of your literature review will depend on the nature of your identified phenomenon. As we have noted previously, reviewing the literature is an iterative that occurs across your applied CA study, not simply at the start. Indeed, even at the stage of writing up your analysis, you will need to once again go back to the published evidence. Anything you write up, whether it be a thesis, dissertation, paper for publication, and so on, will need to include literature related to your phenomenon of focus.
Select examples	As you write up your findings, you will need to be specific in deciding which data examples you want to include and how they might be organized. At this point, it is important that you articulate your analytic points clearly so that your analysis is transparent, and use enough examples to demonstrate that the phenomenon is recurrent and systematic.
Analyze the examples	When you are writing up your analysis of the examples, it is important that you do not simply describe what is being said by the speaker; rather, you need to offer a line-by-line analysis that illustrates what is being produced or performed in and through the participants' talk. As you write your analysis, you should demonstrate the features that play a role in your analytic claims. In so doing, you consider the previous seven stages of analysis and report the relevant aspects in your write-up. Reading examples of how CA scholars write up their findings is helpful in clarifying what is expected when analyzing your data examples within the findings section of your research report.
Draw conclusions	The way in which you develop any critical discussion and draw conclusions will depend largely on who you are writing for and for what purpose. However, make sure that your conclusion provides a summary of the key analytic points and avoids introducing any new data.

Source: Drew, 2015.

Drew (2015) outlined several important steps for writing up the principal points or patterns when analyzing the phenomenon or pattern that you identified, which we outline in Table 7.1.

From the eight steps provided, you should now have a practical understanding of what is involved in carrying out an analysis. While we have provided you with some examples and ideas on how to do an applied analysis, there are also other resources that will help you to learn the art of doing this kind of analysis. Furthermore, when engaging with CA, it is useful to work with others where possible, particularly if you are new to this type of work. Even if you are not new to CA, it is common to engage in collaborative analysis in the form of ***data sessions***. Data sessions serve to provide much-needed support during the analysis process while also acting to increase the quality and veracity of your analytic claims.

> A **data session** is simply where a group of you and your peers come together to examine a segment of your (or their) data for joint analysis. It is usually helpful to do this after you have engaged with some early analysis. Indeed, it is probably most helpful when you have reached Stage 6 of analysis.

It is relatively simple to set up a data session, and they can take many compositions. You may have as few as three people in the group meeting or a large table of many. You might just include your peers (fellow students or colleagues), or you might invite guests or experts to join you. It is important that you have a chair of the data session to keep the conversations on track and guide the discussion of the data, and it is also important to have a focus for the session. This session should be led by a single person who brings examples of his or her data to be analyzed. The number of extracts that you focus on within a data session should be sensible, and, whenever possible (i.e., within the context of your ethical requirements), you should include disguised audio or video of the selected extracts. Typically, a good data session will last 90 minutes to 2 hours.

In addition to reading useful references, such as Drew (2015), and engaging in collaborative data sessions, we also recommend that you complete the activity in Box 7.3.

BOX 7.3
ACTIVITY ON DOING CA

Activity

Professor Charles Antaki of Loughborough University has produced an online tutorial for those who are new to doing CA. This tutorial includes helpful details related to analyzing your data. We recommend that you work through this tutorial to learn more about the analytic process. His tutorial can be found on his home page at http://ca-tutorials.lboro.ac.uk/intro1.htm.

Coding and Using Numbers in Applied CA

While CA is predominantly considered a qualitative approach, it is possible to utilize it more quantitatively by coding the talk. It is important to recognize that conversation analysts are not opposed to counting or coding but argue that such activity should not be at the expense of detailed analysis (Robinson, 2007). Notably, Heritage and Greatbatch (1986) are generally credited as being the first to blend CA with formal coding in their work exploring how politicians generated audience applause at political conferences and reduced these behaviors to categories. In this work, they counted 1,588 events and examined whether or not a sentence in speech contained a contrastive pair or a three-part list.

Coding CA work is something that is attracting more attention. There is now a growing number of projects that utilize mixed methods, combining CA with formal coding, which allows a wider range of research questions to be addressed and different audiences to be reached (Stivers, 2015). Stivers (2015) noted that coding interactions allows analysts to examine whether interaction practices are associated with sociodemographic variables (including age, ethnicity, or culture) or with outcome variables (such as receiving antibiotics from a general practitioner). By bringing together a collection of different types of cases, this can support the analyst's claims about conversational practices (Robinson, 2007).

To undertake statistical analysis on CA data, a formal coding framework is generally developed. It is acknowledged that formal coding procedures reducing social behaviors to codes, such as coding behavior in interaction, can be achieved in CA (Stivers, 2015). Stivers (2015) argued that it is possible to achieve interaction coding in ways that do not sacrifice the approach of CA but instead are grounded in the methodology by quantifying aspects of interactions.

> For example: One way in which CA data can be coded is in relation to the frequencies of occurrences of certain events. An analyst may count the number of wh-questions asked within a police interrogation interview, or the number of times complaints are raised in a couple counseling session, or the number of times a child offers an answer in the classroom.

Stivers (2015) therefore argued that there are two main issues to think about when coding CA data:

1. It is important to be aware that categorizing interactional phenomena requires a clear characterization of what constitutes an instance of your target phenomenon or event, so that your focus is not on the unique element of each aspect of the data but instead on the properties they share.

2. The distributional evidence is a critical aspect of the CA approach, as CA relies on broad patterning properties of the naturally occurring data.

While there are evident benefits from coding CA data and utilizing CA alongside other methods, there are also some limitations to this blending, and it is important that you think about these if you decide to undertake some coding in your own work. We therefore recommend you think about the following difficulties in this sense:

1. Coding imposes hard boundaries on categories of behavior, and behavior is better understood as continuous (Stivers, 2015).

2. The coding scheme you create will necessarily freeze the analytic frame, and this cannot be adjusted once the coding is completed without starting again (Stivers, 2015).

3. Statistical data assume a random sampling design, and in CA, data tend to be nonrandom samples (Robinson, 2007).

4. Rigorous implementation of statistical tests necessitates specific sample sizes, but this can be challenging when dealing with rare practices, as CA is not concerned with the frequency of practices, as frequency does not necessarily indicate an importance (Robinson, 2007).

5. Quantifying CA practices is not always productive or appropriate (Stivers, 2015).

An Interview With Professor Paul Drew

In this chapter, we have introduced you to key considerations related to analyzing your interactional data set within your applied CA study. Notably, in crafting this chapter we have drawn extensively upon the writing and recommendations of Professor Paul Drew (2015) as related to data analysis in CA. Indeed, Drew is arguably a key scholar in CA and has made significant empirical and methodological contributions. As such, we thought it fitting to interview him regarding his current thinking related to engaging in analysis when doing applied CA work. See Box 7.4.

BOX 7.4
INTERVIEW WITH PROFESSOR PAUL DREW   (?)

Paul Drew is a professor of conversation analysis at Loughborough University in the United Kingdom. Professor Drew has contributed to the growing debates on the analysis of social actions in interaction, especially how best to analyze the interplay between verbal and embodied conduct in certain actions (e.g., the recruitment of assistance).

Specifically, he has contributed to many CA texts, and we provide two examples here:

- Drew, P. (2013). Turn design. In J. Sidnell & T. Stivers (Eds.), *Handbook of conversation analysis* (pp. 131–149). West Sussex, England: Blackwell.

- Drew, P., Heritage, J., Lerner, G., & Pomerantz, A. (2015). Introduction. In G. Jefferson (Ed.), *Talking about troubles in conversation* (pp. 1–26). New York, NY: Oxford University Press.

We asked Professor Drew three questions about the practical strategies for analyzing data using applied CA, and his answers to these questions are provided here.

What advice would you give to students who are completely new to CA and are just starting out?

"You will almost certainly have already chosen the setting or kind of interactions you intend to study. You may have been advised to read as much of the research literature on your chosen setting as you

(Continued)

(Continued)

can. My advice is . . . don't. Almost always, PhD students are advised (even required) to do a litera-ture review at the outset of their research. I was advised to do so when I began my PhD, but it was unhelpful—I had no idea, no firsthand knowledge about the social setting I was studying. It is much more fruitful to collect some data (i.e., recordings, whether video or audio, according to the nature of the setting and what access you are granted); do some informal (ethnographic) observation; find out what practitioners want to know; or consider what would be interesting and useful research topics. Then spend some time transcribing (some of) your data, getting to understand it and what's going on in the interactions you've recorded. Consider what people are up to, and why they are up to it. At this stage, don't be intimidated by the 'rules' of doing CA—spend some time looking as closely as you can at whatever catches your attention. But whatever you do, don't read the literature, at least for the first 6 or 9 months; try to observe and absorb and consider the data with fresh eyes. If you come to the data through the eyes of the literature, it will be difficult to find anything fresh in the data other than phenomena or patterns that you've read about—you'll be working along tram lines. Be creative in your approach to the data; when you have an idea of what's there and what's interesting, then read the literature."

What do you think the biggest challenge is for those new to doing applied CA?

"The biggest challenge undoubtedly is doing work that has some applied or practical application and significance. As academics, we are used to following our own interests, hunches, directions—and that is tremendously valuable. It is so important that we continue to pursue our own intellectual and scholarly interests for some part of our careers. But that is doing *applied* research. Most of us doing applied research (e.g., in health care and medicine) work closely with practitioners (cli-nicians, doctors, nurses, etc.). We want to know about their agenda(s)—and by the way, we talk to patient groups to learn what concerns or interests that patients have; so always bear in mind the nonprofessional 'clients' who participate in your setting; do they have agendas? We try then to do research that addresses the interests, concerns, questions, and agendas of practitioners (and lay clients)."

What are the key things to keep in mind when analyzing institutional data?

"Well, there's one—something that in whatever setting you're conducting your research, with what-ever aims or interests, is paramount, which is to consider what are participants *doing* in that setting? What are the key activities in which they are engaged, what are the actions or activities that pret-ty much constitute that setting? I recall the breakthrough moment when I was working on my PhD, studying a quasijudicial inquiry (the Scarman Inquiry) into the disturbances in Northern Ireland that later erupted into 'the Troubles.' I couldn't seem to make any analytic headway until I realized that the lawyer in a section of the cross-examination I was studying was *accusing* a police witness of not having done enough to protect a particular community from attack. Of course, he didn't make an accusation in a single turn at talk; he built up to it, he managed the talk, the question–answer sequences, to lead in a certain direction—to showing that the police officer had acted improperly; in short, to lead up to accusing him of doing nothing.

Similarly, when I was working with colleagues on a study for the Department of Work & Pensions of interactions between Job Centre advisers and benefits claimants (unemployed people), the break-through came when we had identified the key activities in this setting. None of us had any experience of Job Centres, so we had to spend some time to get to 'know' them, to understand the perspectives of both claimants and advisers. We came to terms with the data when we came to realize that some of the key activities that drove these interactions included arriving at a Jobseeker's Agreement and establishing job goals as part of that agreement; asking lone parents about their plans to go back to work; conducting a 'better-off' calculation (designed to encourage a claimant to consider part-time work), and so on. Once we had identified these and other key activities, we then focused on how advisers 'managed,' approached or constructed, these actions/activities. In medical data, especially research into primary care acute visits, some of the key activities are taking the patient's medical history, conducting an examination, diagnosing the problem, and deciding on appropriate treatment. These core activities may not be conducted in such orderly progressive sequences; indeed, they may be interleaved and overlap with one another. But understanding medical interactions is achieved through focusing on these key activities and considering in detail precisely how they are constructed and managed. So the main thing to keep in mind when studying your data is to ask yourself, what is this participant doing, and how are they doing it?"

Chapter Summary

In this chapter, we provided a general overview of the core practices and practical stages of doing analysis in an applied CA research study. As we have noted, there are many ways in which the analytic process within CA has been written about; however, across these perspectives there are several common understandings that we sought to highlight in this chapter. Notably, we first revisited core considerations related to institutional talk, highlighting the importance of attending to turn taking and structural organization. Then we discussed sensitizing practices that are essential during the analysis process, particularly during the earliest stages. Specifically, we described the importance of unmotivated looking, familiarizing yourself with the data set, and reacquainting yourself with the literature. Drawing upon Drew (2015), we presented eight stages of the analytic process, offering data examples throughout. We concluded by considering the place of coding and the use of numbers in CA research. The core learning points from the chapter are provided in the next box.

Learning Points From Chapter 7

- It is important to become familiar with the distinct features of institutional talk prior to beginning analysis.

- When you first begin engaging with your data, it is critical to remember to engage in unmotivated looking, as this will allow you to foreground the data rather than pet theories.

- While thinking about the stages of analysis in an applied CA research study is helpful, it is important to keep in mind that the process is both iterative and inductive.

Recommended Readings

The literature around conducting analysis in CA is quite vast, as there are myriad introductory textbooks, articles, and book chapters that describe the basics of doing analysis in CA research. Thus, we certainly recommend that you turn to key CA textbooks as well as seminal articles and texts written by Harvey Sacks (e.g., Sacks, 1992), Emanuel Schegloff (e.g., Schegloff, 2007a), and others (e.g., Sacks, Schegloff, & Jefferson, 1974). What we recommend here are relatively recent publications that present differing ideas related to doing analysis in a CA study.

- Giles, D. C., Stommel, W., Paulus, T. M., Lester, J. N., & Reed, D. (2015). Microanalysis of online data: The methodological development of "digital CA." *Discourse, Context, & Media, 7,* 45–51.

This article offers important insights for people working with online interactional data. Giles and colleagues discuss which features of CA can be appropriately applied to making sense of online data while also considering some of the key challenges that may arise. For researchers who intend to work exclusively or even in part with computer-mediated communication data, this article is a must read, as it outlines foundational understandings of the relevancy of CA to online data.

- Robinson, J. (2007). The role of numbers and statistics within conversation analysis. *Communication Methods and Measures, 1*(1), 65–75.

An ongoing issue for CA has been the inclusion of numbers—that is, the possible value of counting or coding phenomena within the data. In this paper, Robinson considers some of these debates and outlines how counting and coding in CA might be performed, and why and how this could be done in practice. Indeed, these debates transcend CA and are an issue for qualitative research more broadly, and so you may find it useful to also read general qualitative textbooks that discuss this.

- Sidnell, J. (2013). Basic conversation analytic methods. In J. Sidnell & T. Stivers (Eds.), *The handbook of conversation analysis* (pp. 77–99). West Sussex, England: Blackwell.

In this book chapter, Sidnell provides a baseline discussion of practices central to analyzing data in conversation analysis. He very practically walks the reader through key analytic considerations, with multiple data examples used throughout. Further, Sidnell offers his perspective on the steps of engaging in an analysis in a CA study, which include observing, identifying, and collecting a phenomenon, and describing a practice. We certainly encourage you to carefully review this chapter, as it offers a contemporary perspective on the core features of analysis in CA.

- Stivers, T. (2015). Coding social interaction: A heretical approach in conversation analysis? *Research on Language and Social Interaction, 48*(1), 1–19.

A controversial topic in discussions around analysis in CA has been around the use of coding. Stivers's article addresses questions related to coding in CA while also pointing to mixed methods research that uses CA and quantitative methods. She provides an overview of the ways in which formal codes can be fruitfully applied to study social interaction. Stivers also discusses some of the limitations of formal coding in CA mixed methods research.

8

Using Digital Tools to Support Applied Conversation Analysis Research

> **Chapter Focus**
>
> In this chapter, you will learn how to:
>
> - Describe an (abbreviated) history of digital tools in qualitative research.
>
> - Appreciate the digital changes that have impacted conversation analysis research.
>
> - Recognize the value that audio recording brought to conversation analysis.
>
> - Differentiate the benefits and limitations of audio- and video-recording devices.
>
> - Evaluate the potential of digital tools for supporting transcription and data analysis.

Over the last few decades, there has been an explosion of digital technologies (Paulus, Lester, & Dempster, 2014), which has shaped how researchers conduct applied conversation analysis (CA) research. Indeed, new technologies have allowed researchers to generate important findings based on recording or capturing naturally occurring data, with new forms of data also being made possible. At the most basic level, recording capabilities have allowed researchers to capture the details of people's lives well beyond field notes.

When discussing the role that digital technologies play in applied CA research, it is helpful to contextualize this within the broader field of qualitative research. This is because many of the methodological debates related to capturing data via recording methods, as well as the use of digital tools for analyzing data, stem from the broader paradigmatic concerns within the qualitative community. We thus open this chapter by contextualizing the central debates that have developed in qualitative research about digital tools more generally and consider the relationship between technology and qualitative research.

In this chapter, we focus our discussion on recording interactions via audio- and video-recording devices. As part of this critical discussion, we consider the benefits and limitations of these tools for qualitative research, and specifically applied CA research. We conclude the chapter by presenting a series of digital tools that we suggest are quite useful for generating transcripts as well as engaging in data collection of text-based data (e.g., asynchronous conversations) and completing your data analysis.

Digital Tools and Qualitative Research

Notably, qualitative researchers have long used tools to support their research processes. Whether using pen and paper or video-recording devices, qualitative researchers have relied upon tools to capture data. In the digital age, the relationship between the researcher and digital tools is constantly evolving and, in recent years, has resulted in the generation of new forms of data and ways of generating/collecting such data (Paulus et al., 2014). Yet historically, there have been tensions around the use of digital tools in qualitative research, particularly in relation to using tools to support data analysis (Davidson & di Gregorio, 2011; Paulus, Lester, & Britt, 2013). Despite these tensions, there is a growing body of scholarship that highlights the usefulness and importance of leveraging the affordances of digital tools in qualitative research.

> (!) If you are capturing naturally occurring interactions and recording them, it can still be helpful to take some field notes and be reflexive. Digital tools, such as Evernote, can also support you in generating field notes (Paulus et al., 2014).

The Emergence of Recording Equipment

To explore the human experience, qualitative researchers have often sought to generate more than field notes. Although field notes are important, the increasing availability of recording equipment has meant that research could be more data driven (Speer & Hutchby, 2003). This is because a recording device captures actions that are independent of the analysis, and those actions, at least in part, are visible for all to see (Suchman, 1987).

In the early days of technology, researchers relied upon analog audio recordings of their data, and over time, such recordings would gradually erode and the quality would reduce when copied (Shrum, Duque, & Brown, 2005). Analog recording devices gave way to a new wave of digital technology that even today continues to expand and diversify.

Digital technologies generally provide ultrasharp images and high-quality digital sound, which certainly facilitates a variety of research processes (Murthy, 2008). The commercialization of technology has resulted in more cost-effective options for researchers (Gibbs, Friese, & Mangabeira, 2002), many of which are small and portable. Furthermore, many modern digital devices have a large storage capacity, which means you can capture hours of data onto the device and transfer to your computer (Paulus et al., 2014).

Audio and Video Recording

When you are planning your data collection, you will need to consider the most appropriate means for recording your data. A key decision will be whether you simply capture the audio of the interaction or whether you capture the visual aspects. Audio recordings have historically been the default method, but as video-recording devices have become cheaper and more accessible, as well as more embedded in everyday life, applied CA researchers increasingly rely on video data. There are some benefits of these digital devices, and we list these in Table 8.1.

Of course, any technological device requires that researchers think carefully about the ethical implications, including ways to safely and securely store recorded data. As such, whether you select to use an audio- or video-recording device, it is important to consider both the benefits and limitations. We explore some of these next.

Benefits and Limitations of Audio Recordings

When making your decision as to whether to use an audio-recording device or a video-recording device, it is helpful to weigh the benefits against the limitations. Audio recordings have been used extensively in CA research, as they allow a researcher to capture the actual words of an interaction and take note of how words are spoken in the interactions of interest. We outline some of the benefits of audio recordings next.

- Audio recording allows you to capture the full interaction.

TABLE 8.1 ● Benefits of digital recording

Benefit	Description
Permanence	A digital recording is semipermanent, as it exists until it is actively destroyed.
Editing	Digital recordings can be edited easily, disguised, and sounds and images can be manipulated, which means you may even be able to use your recorded data in presentations (Gibbs et al., 2002).
Ease of operation	Digital recording devices are typically user friendly, with encryption available to make it safe to store securely.
Portability	Many contemporary devices are now small and light, and therefore easy to carry about to field sites.

Modern digital audio-recording devices often come with a great deal of storage; therefore, you can capture an entire interaction on a device, and in some cases, several interactions. These recordings can then easily be transferred to a more secure storage site.

- Audio equipment is relatively affordable.

The price of recording equipment may well be an important concern for you, as digital equipment can be quite expensive if you purchase top-of-the-line devices. While you do need something that will capture the interaction with a high-quality recording, many high-quality audio-recording devices are available at a reasonable price. You may, however, need to purchase an additional microphone. Of course, the type of equipment you need will depend on the nature of the interaction you are recording. If you are recording an interaction in a structured environment where people naturally take turns in an ordered manner, such as a courtroom, then you may more easily capture the interaction on a standard recording device. If, however, you are recording an interaction in a busy place with a significant amount of background noise, you may need a higher-quality device with a noise-canceling function in addition to microphones.

- Some scholars have argued that recruiting participants is more straightforward for a study that uses audio recording than video recording (Themessl-Huber et al., 2008).

This point is somewhat controversial, as there are differences of opinion in the field. Historically, there have been some concerns that the presence of a video camera may make some participants uncomfortable as it visually identifies them; therefore, audio can mitigate against this. Audio recordings do result in slightly less identifiability of the participants and thus could be argued to help promote recruitment, but many people are now used to being video recorded in a range of ways, and this may not be the barrier it once was.

- Many audio-recording devices can be attached to a telephone with a cable.

It may be the case that you wish to record telephone interactions, and this can mean that audio recordings are your main option. Of course, there are now video telephone calls available, such as Skype, Zoom, or FaceTime, which allow for visual data to be collected as well. Traditional telephone calls are still predominantly an audio experience. Notably, technology is available to capture both speakers. Depending on the type of phone you are using, you may need to download a recording application, such as Smart Voice. Alternatively, you may need to purchase a microphone device that allows you to record with a digital recorder. Regardless of choice, it is important to test your equipment prior to beginning data collection.

Indeed, there are many naturally occurring data sets that comprise telephone conversations, and these can be useful in applied CA research.

For example: Consider studies of helpline interactions such as child abuse helplines or counseling helplines, or consider organizational telephone interactions such as insurance companies or complaints lines.

To help you understand what telephone data in an applied CA study might look like, we quote directly an example from Hepburn and Wiggins (2005, p. 631). Here they examined the issue of body weight raised in telephone calls to a child protection helpline in the United Kingdom, the National Society for the Prevention of Cruelty to Children (NSPCC) helpline.

```
CPO:      .Hh I mean ↑how do they appea:r I m'n a- are they
          ↑thin: or:: win      [((inaudible))]

Caller:                        [ Oh NO ]: no [no' at] all.

CPO:                                      [No::?]

Caller:   [no Tim-] (0.2) Bob is [thin but Tim] is

CPO:      [No:? ]                [.H h h ]

Caller:   a little po(h)rk(er. Huh ↑huh=

CPO:      = So they're ↑not failing [to thri:ve then.]

Caller:                             [↑OH NO:. No:. ]
```

There are indeed many applied CA research publications that have relied on audio recordings, and this work has made a valuable contribution. However, this benefit should be offset against the limitations audio-recording devices bring. We therefore consider some of these limitations.

- A common limitation cited of audio-recorded data is that you cannot see the participants and therefore are unable to capture other elements of their interaction, such as nonverbal gestures.

When examining applied settings, there is a great deal of interaction that is not in the form of spoken language. There are many paralinguistic features, such as nonverbal gestures, which may contribute to the meaning of an exchange.

For example: Consider the case where a child nods in response to a question. For the analyst with an audio recording only, there is the risk that this may be reported as a nonresponse as there was nothing captured on the audio recorder. While the uptake from the recipient may demonstrate this, it may not.

- When an interaction has multiple parties, it can be difficult to differentiate who is speaking without additional visual information.

When using an audio recorder, the device will only capture sound; therefore, if lots of people speak at once or if people sound alike, it may be difficult for you to be sure who is speaking.

Benefits and Limitations of Video Recordings

The use of video recordings in applied CA research studies has certainly grown recently, and more researchers are tuning in to the power of video to capture data. Video recordings capture the actual words spoken in the interaction and provide a visual representation of an interaction. Next, we outline some of the benefits.

- Video recordings can be useful for capturing naturally occurring data, as it means you can capture more of the environment and context (Heath, 2004).

As you are now aware, applied CA research generally relies on naturally occurring data; therefore, the analyst relies heavily on the recording to analyze all available aspects of the interaction. Being able to see where people are looking when they speak and any reference to institutional notes, forms, or documents is often helpful. Broadly, such a recording can help the analyst to better understand the institutional context in which the participants are interacting.

- Video equipment is becoming smaller.

Historically, there have been concerns that video-recording devices can be intrusive for participants, particularly when such devices were quite large. However, in the digital age, video-recording devices are becoming increasingly smaller and are far more discreet. This smaller size means that they are less of a focal point for participants.

- Using video recordings allows you to capture both verbal and nonverbal interactions.

(!) **Just because the device is small does not mean it is hidden. Remember that ethically you must have consent to record.**

CA researchers focus on talk-in-interaction, and while talk may be the primary focus, the whole interaction (not just what is said) is equally important. In interaction, much of what is happening is nonverbal, and gestures, gaze, and other paralinguistic aspects can be important for analysis. If you have a video recording of your interactions of interest, then you will be able to add in multimodal features to your analysis.

In Chapter 6 we provided a visual example from Dickerson and Robins (2015, p. 65). Central to their study was the visual aspect as they examined interactions between a robot and a child diagnosed with autism spectrum disorder. Given the centrality of the visual, the authors included images from the video as well as the spoken words, with matching descriptions of the visual. We reproduce that same example from Chapter 6 here so you can see how video images can be embedded to facilitate analysis.

```
"+ ↓((C gazes at K))
1  B  You-you You'll decide what you want you want him happy
      or sad
2  B  Look at (it)
↓((All gaze at control pad, CP))
3  - - - - - - - - (0.8)
```

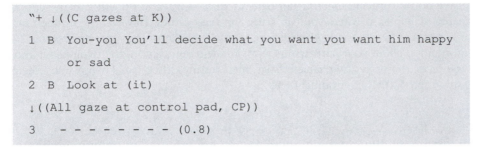

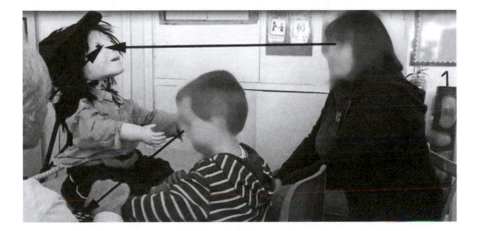

```
(1.1)
((Ben pushes button with C's finger))↓ (1.1)↓((A & B look
at K))
4.  B  Ahh the blinking (0.5) this is the blinking (0.3) look
at his eyes"
```

(Dickerson and Robins, 2015. Reproduced with permission.)

Although valuable for applied CA research, the benefits of video recording should be offset against the possible limitations of using video-recording devices. We thus consider some of these limitations next.

- Video-recording devices tend to be more expensive than audio-recording devices.

Generally, a quality video-recording device is more expensive than a good quality audio-recording device. However, it should be noted that over time the cost of these devices has reduced significantly, and, in many cases, it is now possible to purchase such a device for a reasonable price, or you may be able to borrow one.

- Using video recordings raises additional ethical issues.

We do not provide much detail here, as there is a section on this in the ethics chapter (Chapter 4) where you can reflect on these issues. However, it is important to note that by using video-based data, you will be capturing a greater volume of information about your participants. Not only will you capture their voices but also their faces, their physical characteristics, their gestures, their facial expressions, their fashion sense, their environment, etc.

> *What this means:* Ethically, this means that your participants are much more iden-tifiable. If the interaction is delicate, embarrassing, or sensitive in any way, this can create further ethical concerns. This also has implications for data protection, data security, and risks of disclosure.

If you have vulnerable populations in your data, this is especially important to think about in terms of their capacity to understand the implications of your work (as discussed in Chapter 4).

- The scope of the camera needs to be considered, as it may not capture all parties.

A single static video camera will be limited in terms of what it can capture. Further, the larger the room/environment and the more parties present, the less likely a static video camera will be able to capture everything you need. To overcome this limitation (at least in part), you may be able to use a camera with a wide-angle lens, use multiple cameras, or even gain access to a camera that includes a 360° spherical curved lens. Gomoll, Hmelo-Silver, Šabanović, and Francisco (2016), for instance, used a PixPro 360 camera to capture interactions in an after-school robotics club (A. Gomoll, per-sonal communication, August 2017), with this device allowing them to view the recorded interactions in a 360° globular view or in a flattened view. Regardless, it is very important to consider what a given camera affords you, as well as how and where you position your camera.

While we have not been exhaustive in our list of benefits and limitations of audio- and video-recording devices for an applied CA project, we have given you some important things to think about. We now encourage you to turn your attention to the activity in Box 8.1, which invites you to locate what you have read so far in relation to your own research project.

Regardless of whether you choose to use an audio- or video-recording device, there are some things to be cautious of when you are setting up to record your data. It is important that you take steps to counter any difficulties or problems in the recording of data. We present some of these cautions in Table 8.2.

Selecting a Recording Device: Things to Consider

Once you have decided whether to use an audio- or video-recording device, you should turn your attention to the equipment itself. We have already alluded to some

BOX 8.1

ACTIVITY ON CHOOSING AUDIO OR VIDEO

Activity

It is helpful to contextualize considerations related to audio- and video-recording devices in relation to your own research study. In your research diary, write down a list of pros and cons of both audio- and video-based devices, specifically in relation to what you plan to do and what you need to achieve from your research. Also, take note of any ethical considerations; you might want to read Chapter 4 again at this point.

TABLE 8.2 ● Cautions of digital recording

Caution	Description
Testing	Do not forget to familiarize yourself with the equipment you plan to use. Practice with it and know what buttons serve what function. Make sure it works, and make sure you know what you are doing with it.
Quality	It is very important that you think about the quality of your recording. You will need to think about where you place your device and your microphone (if you have an external one), and think about where the participants will be in the room (Heath, Hindmarsh, & Luff, 2010).
Background noise	Remember that background noise can be quite intrusive and may interfere with the quality of the transcript, and subsequently the quality of the analysis. Thus, you should plan for how you will manage background noise. For instance, will you use a recording device with a noise-canceling mechanism and/or will you use multiple recording devices, etc.
Data security	Make sure you keep your recording device safe and, as soon as possible, transfer your recorded data to an encrypted device such as a password-protected hard drive or USB stick. When you are certain it has copied over fully, you need to delete your recording from the recording device, as this is likely something you will be carrying around with you, and you need to keep your data safe.
Battery life	If your device relies on batteries rather than a main cable, make sure you have a spare battery or a battery charger with you.

of the issues of quality that you need to think about, and in this section, we expand on this preparation. As noted, transcription will be a more straightforward task if your recorded data are of high quality; thus, an essential feature of any device is simply ascertaining whether it produces a quality recording. Notably, the quality of the microphone in your device will be a central contributor to the quality of your recording. While many devices tend to have a built-in microphone, you may want to invest in an external microphone to improve the quality.

In addition to the quality of the recording, you also need to think about how much data you can fit onto the device. Applied CA research studies often include large volumes of data, particularly as you record things as they happen. Thus, you should anticipate your recorded data requiring significant digital space. Many devices have large storage capabilities and a means to transfer the data easily to encrypted devices and computers (Paulus et al., 2014). Perhaps most important, when thinking about data storage it is critical that you protect the data. The data should not be left on the recording device for too long and need to be transferred to a portal where they can be protected by a password. One possibility is to store your files virtually through an Internet storage center such as iCloud or Dropbox. However, depending upon your ethics board requirements and the nature of your data, this might not be allowable.

One possibility is the use of a mobile/cell phone, such as a smartphone. Mobile technologies have resulted in researchers no longer being required to gather their data in fixed environments (Hagen, Robertson, Kan, & Sadler, 2005). Smartphones, for example, have been instrumental in allowing for a fluidity in the data collection process. These kinds of devices usually have a recording capacity of both video and audio, and for some projects this may be sufficient for your research purposes (Paulus et al., 2014). Using a phone, however, generally has implications related to storage capacity, as some phones have SD cards and others have internal storage. Also, remember that phones are at greater risk of theft and thus your data will be at risk too, so it is advisable to transfer the recording to a more secure device as quickly as possible and delete from the phone.

Digital Tools for Supporting Transcription

With the rise of new recording technologies has come new possibilities for generating transcripts. From the advent of foot pedals to the emergence of voice recognition software, there is now a plethora of digital tools that you can use when creating a Jefferson transcript. Of value to applied CA scholars is the possibility of working with a *synchronized transcript*.

A **synchronized transcript** is a transcript that is directly linked or synchronized to the audio or video recording.

By working with a synchronized transcript, you are able to move from one section of your recorded data to another by simply clicking on the desired segment of your transcript. In this way, you are staying close to your data.

Paulus et al. (2014) highlighted four transcription software packages that can be used to support you in generating your transcript, including Express Scribe, Audio Notetaker, InqScribe, and F4/F5. In Table 8.3 we provide an overview of some of the primary features of these transcription software packages.

There are other packages that may be particularly useful and more accessible to you, such as ELAN or even computer-assisted qualitative data analysis software packages that support transcription (e.g., NVivo). Regardless of the package you adopt, we

TABLE 8.3 ● Transcription software packages and their features

Package	Description
Express Scribe (http://www.nch.com.au/scribe/index.html)	• Free trial version • Mac/PC platform • Supports audio and video data • Fee-based version supports foot pedal use • Hot keys available to control playback • Integrates with word processing programs • Works with voice recognition software
Audio Notetaker (https://www.sonocent.com/en-us/audio-notetaker)	• Free trial version • Mac/PC platform • Supports audio data only • Supports foot pedal use • Audio recording can be represented visually with colored bar segments for navigation, editing, and organizing • Works with voice recognition software
F4/F5 (https://www.audiotranskription.de/english/f4.htm)	• Free trial version • Mac/PC platform • Supports audio and video data • Supports foot pedal use • Minimally functional with voice recognition software • Can create a synchronized transcript • Hot keys available to control playback and insert timestamps • Integrates with word processing programs and with some computer-assisted qualitative data analysis software
InqScribe (https://www.inqscribe.com)	• Free trial version • Mac/PC platform • Supports audio and video data • Supports foot pedal use • Works with voice recognition software • Can create a synchronized transcript • Supports creating shortcuts and snippets, which is particularly useful when generating Jefferson transcripts • Can insert subtitles on video data

Source: adapted from Paulus et al., 2014, p. 108.

strongly encourage you to work with synchronized transcripts as you engage more deeply in the analysis process.

Notably, while voice recognition technologies (e.g., Dragon Naturally Speaking, Google Voice, etc.) are becoming increasingly more accurate, they still do pose challenges for applied CA researchers. Many of these technologies still only recognize one voice, and thus it is difficult, if not impossible, to generate verbatim transcripts of multiparty interactions. Indeed, such technologies do not generate detailed Jefferson transcripts, while also raising questions related to the methodological implications of such technologies for the transcription process (particularly when and if they become more fully developed).

Given the importance of transcription within applied CA research, adopting a transcription software package is an important part of your research process. Thus, we encourage you to complete the activity in Box 8.2, as it provides you with an opportunity to begin exploring which transcription software package(s) might be best for your research needs.

BOX 8.2
ACTIVITY ON TRANSCRIPTION SOFTWARE PACKAGES

Activity

As you plan to use transcription software, it is helpful to begin exploring the various packages that are available. Go to one or more of the transcription software packages' websites and download the free trial version. Explore the package and practice transcribing with the main features. As you do so, consider how these features might shape your transcription process.

Digital Tools for Supporting Analysis

Since the 1980s, more and more scholars have been using computer-assisted qualitative data analysis software (CAQDAS) to support their qualitative analyses. Yet the relationship between CAQDAS and qualitative analysis has not been a straightforward one (Davidson & di Gregorio, 2011; Paulus et al., 2014). Widely varying views on CAQDAS have been offered, with some scholars suggesting that CAQDAS packages result in nothing more than quantification of qualitative data or that such packages are primarily useful when using grounded theory (Davidson & di Gregorio, 2011).

Within the CA literature base, there has been little discussion about the use of CAQDAS. A few exceptions include concerns being voiced about the functionality of code and retrieve features within such packages (Gibbs et al., 2002). In the last decade, other scholars have noted the limitations of transcribing data within many of the CAQDAS packages (e.g., ten Have, 2007). However, it is important to mention that Konopasek (2008) and others have noted that CAQDAS packages go well beyond code and retrieve functions. Notably, there are packages that some have even argued are particularly useful for researchers working with interactional data, such as Transana (Mavrikis & Geraniou, 2011; Woods & Dempster, 2012), Leximancer, and Discursis (Angus, Rintel, & Wiles, 2013).

More recently, Paulus and Lester (2016) offered a detailed illustration of how ATLAS .ti, a CAQDAS package, can be used in a CA study for "transcribing and synchronizing transcripts with media files, engaging in unmotivated looking through creating quotations, and conducting a close, line by line analysis through writing memos" (p. 405). While acknowledging that technology is not neutral, Paulus and Lester also noted that their experience with using CAQDAS has been like what Kimmel (2012) argued:

> While the tool itself decides nothing for you, it systematizes the procedure via checks and good workflow management, provides utilities for making decisions, facilitates multi-level categorization, and provides leverage on large corpora. Software makes hermeneutic skills reflexive and encourages the systematic presentation of what sometimes appears as research "alchemy." (p. 30)

Paulus et al. (2014) have also argued that CAQDAS packages can be used to support the entire qualitative research process, from the early stages of organizing data to conducting a literature review to transcribing data to engaging in a close analysis to generating findings sections/reports. In addition, some of these packages support you in extracting social media data, such as Facebook data or YouTube data. We align with this position and have found in our own work that CAQDAS packages are particularly useful for providing us with a means by which to carry out all or even part of our research processes.

Paulus et al. (2014) suggested that ATLAS.ti, MAXQDA, and NVivo are three particularly popular CAQDAS packages. Indeed, there are other packages available with a range of features provided, some of which we highlight in Table 8.4.

The degree to which you might have access to a CAQDAS package will vary and likely be dependent upon the institution in which you work/study and the funds available. However, we strongly encourage you to begin exploring what might be possible, engaging in CAQDAS training when possible, and taking note of which packages might work best for your needs. As such, we suggest you complete the activity in Box 8.3.

BOX 8.3
ACTIVITY ON EVALUATING CAQDAS PACKAGES

Activity

A growing number of CAQDAS packages are available to choose from. It is thus helpful to spend time examining various packages and identifying which package may be best for you. Go to one or more of the CAQDAS packages' websites and download the free trial version. Explore the package and practice organizing, transcribing, and analyzing your data. As you do so, consider how the package's various features might shape your research process. Further, explore which package(s) may be accessible at your institution.

TABLE 8.4 ● Considerations for selecting a CAQDAS package

	ATLAS.ti	QSR NVivo	MAXQDA	Dedoose	Quirkos	Transana
Platform	Windows; Mac since 2014	Windows; Mac since 2014	Universal Windows/Mac since 2014	Cloud-based	Windows, Mac, & Linux all have the same interface	Cross-platform since 2007 and open source since 2005
Mobile app	Mobile for Android / Mobile for iPad	No	MAXApp for Android and iOS	Yes	No	No
Support text data	Yes	Yes	Yes	Yes	Yes	Yes, in version 3.0 / Yes, in version 2.6 with Coding Shapes
Supports video/image data	Yes	Yes	Yes	Yes	No	Yes, designed for video analysis
Supports transcribing	Yes	Yes	Yes	Yes	No	Yes, designed to support transcription, though transcription is not required
Supports incorporating survey data	Yes	Yes	Yes	Yes	Yes	No
Supports extracting social media data	Yes	Yes [Facebook, Twitter, YouTube, LinkedIn]	Yes [Tweets]	No	No	No
Citation management system integration	Yes	Yes	Yes	Yes	Yes	No
Collaboration	Asynchronous	NVivo for teams or asynchronously	Asynchronously	Real-time web-based via the cloud	Asynchronously	Multiuser version since 2002 or synchronously

Source: adapted from Paulus, 2016, n.p.

An Interview With Professor Trena Paulus

In this chapter, we have introduced you to the ways in which digital tools can support your applied CA research. We have situated our discussion in relation to the broader debates about using digital tools in qualitative research. Relatively little of this research is written specifically in relation to applied CA research, yet much of it is relevant and applicable. One of the leading scholars in this area is Professor Trena Paulus, who has written extensively around digital tools in qualitative research and for CA research. Thus, we interviewed Professor Paulus, inviting her to offer her perspective on using digital tools to support applied CA research. Her responses are presented in Box 8.4.

BOX 8.4
INTERVIEW WITH PROFESSOR TRENA PAULUS

Trena Paulus is a professor of qualitative research in the Department of Lifelong Education, Administration, and Policy in the College of Education at the University of Georgia, United States. Professor Paulus is a leading scholar in technologies and qualitative research methodologies. She has also written about the ways in which digital tools can support CA research as well as research using a discourse analytic approach. In particular to the use of CAQDAS for CA research, Professor Paulus coauthored the following publication:

- Paulus, T., & Lester, J. (2016). ATLAS.ti for conversation and discourse analysis. *International Journal of Social Research Methodology, 19*(4), 405–428.

Given her expertise related to digital tools and qualitative research generally, and CA more particularly, we invited Professor Paulus to respond to three questions about digital tools and CA research.

What digital tool(s) do you typically use when carrying out a CA study?

"Both digital tools and digital contexts have impacted the CA work that I do. When working with face-to-face contexts and participants, I use a variety of digital *tools* to record, transcribe, store, and analyze the conversations that I will treat as data. However, I also need to consider digital *contexts*—online spaces in which important conversations are taking place—because disciplines are often overlooking this kind of talk. I use a voice recorder on my smartphone to record face-to-face conversations, and I have used ATLAS.ti and NVivo's social media import tools to collect online talk. I have used both InqScribe and Transana to transcribe recorded conversations. Both allow you to synchronize the recording with the transcript so that you can quickly listen to how something was said by clicking on that portion of the transcript. Transana has the bonus of having Jefferson transcription symbols available within the software.

(Continued)

(Continued)

ATLAS.ti is the qualitative data analysis software I use to both manage and analyze the data—using the memo, coding, and visualization tools to perform a close analysis. My collaborators and I can easily share the data as well as our analysis with each other by exchanging ATLAS.ti files. We store the files using password-protected cloud storage—usually Dropbox—so that it is instantly backed-up and accessible via my computing devices."

What are some key ethical considerations for using digital tools when carrying out an applied CA study?

"Digital contexts are often publicly visible (e.g., Twitter or online communities). Even though many institutional review boards therefore do not consider analysis of online talk to be human subjects research, members of these communities do not necessarily consider what they are writing in these spaces to be public. So deciding to treat this online talk as data needs to come after careful consideration. Protecting the identity of both the face-to-face and online speakers is critical—online conversations are easily Googleable, for example. Ensuring that your data storage devices are secure should also be a priority when handling sensitive data."

For those new to digital tools, what are some suggestions for where and how to start?

"I would recommend starting with our book, *Digital Tools for Qualitative Research* (Paulus, Lester, & Dempster, 2014), and to pick just one or two tools at first. Learning new technology can be overwhelming, so starting small and experiencing early success will keep you motivated. Software companies usually have helpful video tutorials, blog posts, and social media accounts that are valuable learning resources. Also, find out what your institution supports and what your colleagues are using. If you find that your colleagues all use NVivo to analyze social media data, there's no real point in learning ATLAS.ti all by yourself—and vice versa."

Chapter Summary

In this chapter, we introduced you to considerations related to the digital tools that might support you in collecting, transcribing, and analyzing data. We began by briefly contextualizing our discussion in relation to the larger discussion related to digital tools and qualitative research. Recognizing that many of you are likely to use audio- or video-recording devices, we overviewed some of the key benefits and limitations of such devices. We then provided an overview of some of the digital tools that can support you in transcribing and analyzing your data. We summarize the key points in the next box.

Learning Points From Chapter 8

- The semipermanent nature of recorded data requires that you think carefully about how to securely store your data.

- Digital tools that support creating a synchronized transcript allow you to stay close to your data, particularly as you engage in deeper levels of analysis.

- You can use CAQDAS packages across the entirety of the research process.

Recommended Readings

As noted, there is a growing body of literature focused on the use of digital tools in qualitative research. Much of this writing can be directly applied to considerations related to applied CA research. Thus, what we suggest next is simply a useful starting point, as we encourage you to move well beyond what we have summarized in this chapter.

- Heath, C., Hindmarsh, J., & Luff, P. (2010). *Video in qualitative research: Analysing social interaction in everyday life*. London, England: Sage.

This book contains a great wealth of information about recording equipment, with a specific focus on the use of video. The authors do refer to CA in the book and draw upon their own experiences of recording interactions. The book is filled with practical advice for researchers and provides examples of the kinds of issues that might arise when using video-recording devices. Heath and colleagues draw attention to both ethical and practical issues that may arise when recording data and offer case examples to illustrate their points.

- Paulus, T., Lester, J. N., & Dempster, P. (2014). *Digital tools for qualitative research*. London, England: Sage.

This book offers a fairly comprehensive overview of how digital tools might be used across the entirety of the qualitative research process. From conducting literature reviews to representing findings, the authors discuss a variety of digital tools and illustrate their points in relation to real-world examples written by qualitative researchers from a variety of disciplines. While this book is not specifically written for applied CA researchers, the discussions are relevant to the everyday work of researchers engaged in qualitative research of all kinds.

- Paulus, T., & Lester, J. (2016). ATLAS.ti for conversation and discourse analysis. *International Journal of Social Research Methodology, 19*(4), 405–428.

(Continued)

(Continued)

In this paper, Paulus and Lester offer a series of concrete examples of how to use ATLAS.ti for carrying out a CA study or a study using a discourse analytic approach. Specifically, they illustrate how ATLAS.ti can be used to document analytic decisions and make visible a reflexive and transparent research process. Paulus and Lester include screenshots throughout that provide examples of features within ATLAS.ti, including transcribing and synchronizing transcripts, using quotations, and conducting line-by-line analysis, among others. While the authors focus exclusively on ATLAS.ti, much of what they offer can be applied when thinking about the ways in which other CAQDAS packages might be levered within an applied CA research study.

9

Establishing Quality in Applied Conversation Analysis Research

Chapter Focus

In this chapter, you will learn how to:

- Critically assess the debates about quality in qualitative research.

- Evaluate different perspectives about quality in the literature.

- Describe issues of quality in conversation analysis research.

- Recognize the indicators of quality in an applied conversation analysis study.

- Discuss the criticisms of conversation analysis research.

Within the qualitative community, discussions surrounding assuring quality in qualitative research indicate that it has been a rather contentious issue. In quantitative research, ensuring that a piece of research is robust is perhaps more straightforward, at least in the sense that there are several agreed-upon markers to which researchers generally conform. In qualitative research, however, there is more tension regarding how to judge a research study. While there has been some consensus in terms of key quality indicators in recent times with several overlapping ways of ensuring rigor (see Ravitch & Carl, 2016), there remains some tension in places. Yet in applied conversation analysis (CA) research, various audiences often demand to understand how well conducted a study was, and these understandings shape the degree to which they judge the findings. In other words, regardless of the debates about quality in qualitative research, you are likely to be asked to justify that you generated a quality study. Thus, this chapter begins with some of the broader ideas related to quality in qualitative research, and more specifically on key ideas related to establishing quality in applied CA research.

Notably, CA is a qualitative approach, and thus we argue that it is particularly helpful to contextualize quality concerns specific to CA within the broader arguments about quality in qualitative research. As such, the first part of this chapter provides you with contextual information as we introduce you to four main positions on quality that have been voiced within the qualitative community. When discussing these different positions, we note the implications for applied CA researchers where relevant. Furthermore, we discuss some of the criticisms that are often made about the approach and provide the reasons these are insufficient. We conclude the chapter by more specifically discussing considerations common in establishing quality in CA research.

Qualitative Research and the Problem of Quality

In theory, any audience should be able to ascertain from reading your research whether it is quality work, as well as whether your work conforms to the underlying assumptions of your given methodological approach. For various audiences to fairly judge your work, there needs to be some sense of what markers or indicators of quality they are judging a given piece of work against. In other words, the criteria to make a fair judgment must be clear. In qualitative research, there is not universal acceptance of a set of quality criteria, although some consensus has been achieved on some of the key indicators. There remain some tensions, however, regarding the most appropriate ways to judge the quality of a qualitative research project.

This reality is further problematized by the broader academic community's oft minimal understanding of the heterogeneity of qualitative methodologies. Indeed, many scholars who judge applied research assume that there should be a straightforward (and single) way for judging the robustness of a qualitative study. The foundation of this tension relates to whether qualitative research can be judged by quantitative criteria, which is complicated further by the lack of consensus about exactly what qualitative research is (Mays & Pope, 2000). We would point out here that what distinguishes qualitative from quantitative research is the nature of the data and the methods used, and not an underpinning dichotomy between the two. Furthermore, there is now a greater acceptance of the value of mixing methods in various ways to address related problems, and therefore, applied CA can be combined with other approaches for a larger-scale project (although there are some challenges to consider; see O'Reilly & Kiyimba, 2015, for a full discussion).

Quality Matters in Qualitative Research

We argue that it is important for a range of audiences to be able to make judgments about the quality of an applied CA study. Funding reviewers, journal article reviewers, article readers, conference delegates, etc., will expect to see that the work being presented to them has followed the procedures of the methodology and conforms to the relevant criteria.

Some of the criteria relevant to an applied CA study are those that are general to qualitative research. Although there are tensions as to how quality can be judged in qualitative research, there is general agreement that it is necessary to evaluate qualitative research in terms of assessing the robustness of the approach used, the quality of the analysis, and the theoretical interpretations (Freeman, deMarrais, Preissle, Roulston, & St. Pierre, 2007). While there is agreement that quality is important in qualitative research, it is argued that qualitative research should be judged on its own terms rather than in comparison to criteria common to quantitative research (Lincoln & Guba, 1985). This is especially important in applied fields, such as health, law, and education, where evidence-based practice is prominent and the quality of qualitative evidence is especially important (Lester & O'Reilly, 2015; Morse, Barrett, Mayan, Olson, & Spiers, 2002).

Indeed, qualitative research has a different focus from quantitative research, with unique theoretical bases, methods, and analytic techniques. As just one example, qualitative researchers generally position the role of the researcher as integral to a study (Stenbacka, 2001), and this therefore needs to be reflected in any judgment about quality. Qualitative researchers have recognized the need to distinguish the meaning(s) of *quality* from quantitative research, which has resulted in the development of various quality frameworks. Such developments have occurred for many reasons:

- It is necessary to prevent qualitative research from being inappropriately judged by quantitative quality criteria (Anastas, 2004). This is essential, as it is not possible to judge qualitative work in the same way as quantitative methods, particularly given that qualitative research is generally flexible, unstructured, and iterative (Davies & Dodd, 2002).

- Qualitative researchers submit their work to be published, aiming for the value of their work to be recognized. In applied research, particularly, researchers often seek to demonstrate how their findings might be implemented in practice. If researchers are to convince various audiences of the importance and value of their work, they need to demonstrate that their work is robust and has quality parameters guiding it, and this is important for applied CA researchers who seek to inform practice in some way.

- Qualitative researchers often seek funding to be able to undertake their research and thus need to convince a funding body that their work is worthy of the financial support. Quality criteria generally help a funding body to ascertain the worthiness of proposed work. Applied CA researchers work within a funding envelope and also need to convince funders to provide economic support for the work.

- The qualitative community has worked hard to demonstrate its credibility in academic and practice-based fields, which for many scholars has been facilitated by the promotion of quality frameworks.

- Researchers have an ethical obligation to demonstrate the integrity and rigor in their research (Angen, 2000), and this is also true for applied CA.

Arguments About Quality

The key issue we wish to draw your attention to is that while there is agreement that quality criteria are needed for judging qualitative research and recently more consensus as to how this can be achieved, there is still some tension in the field. In their recent book on qualitative research, O'Reilly and Kiyimba (2015) summarized the vast literature on quality in qualitative research. These arguments reflect the four key positions in the literature about quality in qualitative research and are broad overviews of the ways in which quality is considered in that paradigm. Based on their conceptualizations of this issue, we summarize the key arguments in Table 9.1, which is followed by a more detailed discussion of each argument.

TABLE 9.1 ● Four arguments about quality in qualitative research	
Argument	**Description**
Adaptation argument	Some scholars have argued for the use of quantitative vocabulary with an adaptation to the meaning of those key markers for qualitative research.
Universal markers argument	Some scholars have argued that distinctive criteria are needed for qualitative research and that these should be universal.
Heterogeneity argument	Some scholars have argued that due to the great methodological diversity in qualitative research, each qualitative approach needs its own criteria.
No criteria argument	Some scholars have argued that it is inappropriate to have criteria for quality in qualitative research.

Source: O'Reilly & Kiyimba, 2015.

Position 1: Adapting Quantitative Criteria

The first position O'Reilly and Kiyimba (2015) outlined was based on the qualitative literature, which has used quantitative terminology to establish quality while transforming or modifying the meaning of such terms in some way. The main argument has been that the core concepts of quality from the quantitative research practices can be used to assess qualitative work.

The first of these core concepts that has been adapted and utilized is that of **validity**, which has been central to judging the credibility of quantitative research for many decades.

In terms of qualitative research, the translation of the quantitative concept of validity relates to whether the claims to knowledge being made

Validity often refers to the credibility of the claims being made. In quantitative terms, validity demonstrates that the study has measured what it set out to measure.

by an author are an accurate representation of reality (Spencer, Ritchie, Lewis, & Dillon, 2003), although the very notion of what constitutes reality is of course more flexibly conceptualized in qualitative research. Notably, it is important to recognize that the iterative nature of the qualitative research process should be accounted for in the conceptualization of validity (Onwuegbuzie & Leech, 2007).

For qualitative researchers who use validity as a key indicator for quality, two main areas where it is relevant are in data collection and data interpretation (O'Reilly & Kiyimba, 2015).

> *What this means:* From this perspective, qualitative researchers should be concerned with validity at the stage of data collection, assuring that their selected method is appropriate to address the research question. They also need to be concerned when engaged in data interpretation and consider how to present their data to ensure that their interpretations can be verified by a given audience.

For those scholars who advocate for the use of the concept of validity in qualitative research in the data collection stage, it is the relationship between the researcher and the researched that is essential in ensuring the quality of the data itself (Stenbacka, 2001). In qualitative terms, validity in data analysis relates to the trustworthiness of the interpretations made by the analyst (Stiles, 1993). For validity to be demonstrated, the audience requires the necessary information to be able to evaluate the analytic claims made by an author. For some qualitative researchers, this can be achieved through the technique of *member checking,* while others have argued for the use of *intercoder reliability,* both of which rest on assumptions that are not entirely congruent with CA.

The second of the core concepts adapted and used has been that of *reliability,* which has also been central to judging the credibility of a quantitative study for many decades.

In qualitative research, reliability is generally understood in more complex ways than the quantitative definition, which generally refers to the extent to which replication of the study might be

● **Member checking** is a technique used by some qualitative researchers and refers to the process whereby researchers corroborate their findings with the participants (Corden & Sainsbury, 2006).

● **Intercoder reliability** is the process of establishing consistency of findings through more than one coder (Armstrong, Gosling, Weinman, & Marteau, 1997). This encourages interrogation of the data and provides an account of how the analysis was developed (Barbour, 2001).

● **Reliability** in quantitative approaches refers to the need for research to be replicated or repeated (Golafshani, 2003).

possible (Spencer et al., 2003). For qualitative research, the notion of reliability has been modified and considers the degree of consistency between different researchers on the same occasion or of the assignation of the same category by the same researcher on different occasions (Silverman, 2013).

What this means: From this perspective, there is an assumption that the feelings, thoughts, and opinions of the participants can be accessed and interpreted, and that all researchers would draw similar conclusions from the data.

For qualitative researchers, then, reliability may be realized through the demonstration of a clear audit trail and a transparent account of how the research was conducted, allowing audiences to see for themselves how the findings were derived (Sandelowski, 1993). Reliability is therefore achieved through a process of demonstrating transparency.

Generalizability refers to the extent to which the results from the study might be generalized to the broader population.

Assertional logic is analytical generalization whereby the researcher identifies the differences and the similarities between situations and utilizes a relevant theoretical framework for the interpretative understandings that support the generalizable claims (Collingridge & Gantt, 2008).

Moderatum generalization refers to the confines of any claims that can be made in terms of the applicability to the other participant groups as opposed to making any sweeping statements to a range of cultures or periods of time (Payne & Williams, 2005).

The third and final core concept adapted and used is that of *generalizability*, which has also been central to judging the credibility of a quantitative study for many decades.

In qualitative research, the study is not considered to be generalizable in the same way as a quantitative research study; rather, the concept has been adapted to mean that it is possible to make connections across studies to establish the applicability of a given piece of work (Freeman et al., 2007). For qualitative research, it has been argued that generalizability is based on *assertional logic* and not probabilistic logic (Kvale, 1996).

Qualitative research studies are often limited to a time frame and a specific context (Payne & Williams, 2005). In this sense, generalizability is confined in terms of its applicability. This has been called *moderatum generalization* in qualitative terms (Williams, 2000).

Many qualitative scholars have suggested that to achieve generalizability in qualitative work, it is necessary to treat it as representational in the sense that the study is not able to make wider inferences to other settings but instead can consider the findings from the study as representative of the phenomena under investigation (Lewis & Ritchie, 2003).

The adaptation of a quantitative criteria argument has received a great deal of attention in qualitative circles. In the qualitative research articles that you read, you might find reference to the key quantitative indicators of validity, reliability, or generalizability, but the exact meaning of the concept is likely to have been modified in some way to have relevance to the qualitative approach. It should be noted, however, that not all qualitative scholars agree with this line of reasoning, and some criticisms have been presented against this view of quality:

- A criticism of using validity as a quality indicator is that this notion has an assumption that reality can be revealed and that social life can be represented in an accurate way, and this is not a position that is typically congruent with qualitative approaches (Hammersley, 2007).

- It has been argued that the concept of reliability for the qualitative researcher is misleading, and it is instead more appropriate to consider quality through enabling intersubjectivity in a description of the research process (Stenbacka, 2001).

- It has also been argued by some that generalization is not actually possible in qualitative research, as evaluation is context specific and the meanings are not free from context (Schwandt, 1997), but others have argued that theoretical generalization is possible, that is, generalization to a theoretical explanation (see Demuth, 2018 for detail).

Our own position here is that the argument of adapting quantitative criteria is not entirely appropriate for CA work, especially applied CA. We would argue that the underpinning theoretical assumptions that are tied to markers of validity, reliability, and generalizability are not congruent with the practical or theoretical foundation of the approach.

Position 2: Universal Markers

One of the main reasons that the argument to adapt quantitative criteria for use within qualitative research has been so influential is because of its presumed ability to be applied across the range of qualitative approaches—that is, its universality. However, some scholars have claimed that it is possible to have a universal approach to quality without being held to the quantitative paradigm and its vocabulary. Rather, it has been argued that there can be a set of quality criteria that may be used for all qualitative methodologies.

This universal marker perspective has gained popularity in the qualitative community, and over time, several different frameworks have been developed. In some ways, this argument orients to qualitative methodologies and methods as homogeneous, as it promotes the idea of holistic criteria spanning across a range of different methodologies, or at least recognizes that despite the differences there are some core features of these approaches that are similar (O'Reilly & Kiyimba, 2015). Despite the tensions and questions that surround this perspective, there has been some acceptance of qualitative quality frameworks that have the goal of identifying "good" practice for qualitative researchers (Spencer et al., 2003). In their work, Spencer et al. (2003) reviewed the literature on quality and developed a general taxonomy of principles, arguing that often qualitative scholars prefer to have guiding quality principles instead of fixed standards. Their four overarching principles are outlined in Table 9.2.

TABLE 9.2 ● Guiding principles of quality	
Argument	**Description**
Contributory	Researchers should have the goal of advancing wider knowledge and understanding.
Defensible	Researchers should generate a research design that includes strategies to address the research question.
Rigorous	Researchers should conduct studies that entail a transparent and systematic collection of data, analysis, and interpretation.
Credible	Researchers' claims should be credible and include plausible and well-grounded arguments related to the significance of the evidence generated.

Source: Spencer et al., 2003.

Spencer et al. (2003) further added that the relationship between the researcher and participants needs to be accounted for and that the work should be carried out in an ethical way.

These kinds of frameworks have promoted the idea that all qualitative research can be judged by a universally applicable set of standards; thus, there have been some efforts to establish a gold standard of quality indicators. In this pursuit of a universal set of markers, many different suggestions have been made.

For example: Tracy (2010) suggested eight markers of quality, which were designed to unite the quality principles from the debates surrounding quality in qualitative research.

For example: The Consolidated Criteria for Reporting Qualitative Research (COREQ) was a framework designed for interview studies. This checklist is one that was designed to help reviewers judge the standard of qualitative interview work (Tong, Sainsbury, & Craig, 2007).

Indeed, there are numerous published frameworks focused on establishing quality in qualitative research. A useful way to make sense of how arguments have been conceptualized is to gain familiarity with a variety of frameworks, whether you align with the argument of universal markers or not. Thus, we encourage you to complete the activity in Box 9.1, as this will support you in acquiring broader familiarity with universal markers.

Collectively, there is a wide range of markers that could be argued to be universal indicators of quality in qualitative research. While there are far too many to deal

BOX 9.1

ACTIVITY ON GAINING FAMILIARITY WITH QUALITY FRAMEWORKS IN QUALITATIVE RESEARCH

Activity

Appreciating the broader argument of universal criteria in qualitative research requires further reading around the subject. A good starting point is Tracy's (2010) eight markers. After reviewing her suggestions, reflect on whether you think any of the markers are applicable to CA.

- Tracy, S. J. (2010). Qualitative quality: Eight "big-tent" criteria for excellent qualitative research. *Qualitative Inquiry*, *16*(10), 837–851.

with in this chapter, we introduce you to some of the more commonly accepted markers, particularly those that are most relevant to applied CA research.

Transparency is considered an important marker for qualitative research and can be realized in different ways depending on the methodological approach being used.

To be transparent in your research, you need to clearly demonstrate all of the stages of your research process and provide relevant information to outside readers so that your primary audience can examine and assess your assertions and interpretations (Freeman et al., 2007). A common way in which transparency is achieved is by using verbatim quotations from your data, and in qualitative research, this is a common way of representing your participants' perspectives (Corden & Sainsbury, 2006). In applied CA research, this is also true. CA researchers include verbatim excerpts of their data (in the form of Jefferson transcripts) in their research reports so that their primary audience can see what was said and link this to the analyst's observations. Furthermore, the very nature of the transcript in CA research allows analysts to show not only what was said but how it was said. In this way, transparency is also realized in an applied CA research study through making evident the *what* and *how* of the social interaction of focus. Given that CA researchers base their analytic claims on the interaction itself, including data extracts in the form of detailed transcripts allows for readers/evaluators to judge whether the analyst's claims are indeed grounded in the data.

Reflexivity is also considered to be an important general marker for quality in qualitative research.

> To achieve **transparency** in your qualitative research means that you provide a full and honest account of your work, providing your audience with a complete description of what you did, as well as giving an explanation and justification for the decisions you made (Spencer et al., 2003).

> **Reflexivity** in qualitative research is argued to be the process by which researchers reflect on their own role and influence on the research process.

In qualitative research, it is generally understood that researchers should account for their role in the process of data collection and data analysis (Mays & Pope, 2000). Researchers need to be mindful of how their theoretical positions and social locations might influence and shape the way the research is conducted. For instance, applied CA research studies are heavily influenced by the guiding theoretical framework that underpins the research process, and this requires some reflection. However, the collection of naturally occurring data usually requires less involvement of the researcher in its collection, but that does not mean the researcher is completely removed from the process; thus, some reflection on the motivations and impact remains essential. Indeed, in a literature review of discourse analysis and CA research in therapy, Tseliou (2013) argued that CA researchers often do not report the reflexive aspects of their study and yet noted this is a critical aspect to this kind of work.

Trustworthiness relates to the relevance and value of the research findings in terms of the degree to which they can be accepted.

Trustworthiness has also been a priority in the quality literature, which is a broad concept in qualitative research and encompasses a range of more specific criteria.

Broadly speaking, trustworthiness is a demonstration that your findings are important and relevant. Lincoln and Guba (1985) argued that trustworthiness is demonstrated through four key indicators:

- Transferability—the degree to which your findings might be relevant and applied in other settings and contexts.

- Credibility—the confidence that an audience might place in your findings.

- Confirmability—the extent to which your findings can be corroborated by others.

- Dependability—the idea that your study is accurate and consistent, with your data being viewed as stable across time and contexts.

For a CA study, trustworthiness is bound to the methodological process, with variation of the four features of trustworthiness depending on the nature of the study. However, for applied CA research, there is typically some effort to demonstrate that the findings are relevant across institutional settings, or at least within one setting across practices. Further, the confidence in the findings is generally demonstrated through the microattention to detail, with analytic claims being illustrated by making visible your interpretation to readers/audiences. It has been generally argued that by displaying your line-by-line interpretation, readers/audiences are likely to come to the same conclusions you came to, perhaps pointing to how confirmability might be conceptualized within an applied CA study.

We recognize that there is certainly some value to developing and using universal criteria for quality, and some of these are relevant to CA work, but we also argue that the heterogeneity should be accounted for in addition. This is because some scholars have argued that the use of general checklists simply does not account for the diversity within the landscape of qualitative research.

> For example: Barbour (2001) argued that "if we succumb to the lure of 'one size fits all' solutions we risk being in a situation where the tail (the checklist) is wagging the dog (the qualitative research)" (p. 1115).

CA is a good example of this, as its theoretical framework and analytic procedures are very specific to the approach; thus, there are ways of judging the quality of a CA study that are most relevant to CA research yet far less relevant to other approaches to qualitative research. This can be problematic when reviewers are judging a CA study against criteria that fail to map onto the approach. For instance, the COREQ was designed for interview studies (see Tong et al., 2007), but CA relies on naturally occurring data; however, some journals use this checklist to judge quality regardless of the type of data collected. Likewise, the notion of data saturation to assure sampling adequacy works well for interview studies that draw upon thematic analysis (Braun & Clarke, 2006) but is not an entirely appropriate concept for CA research (O'Reilly & Parker, 2013; see Chapter 3 for our discussion of sampling in CA). Thus, while a broad list of general indicators is both relevant and helpful for quality, it is also necessary to acknowledge the heterogeneity in the application of some quality principles.

Position 3: Heterogeneity Argument

A popular argument within the qualitative research community has been the necessity to account for the heterogeneity of the qualitative paradigm, even when accepting some of the broader general markers. It has been argued that the general markers of quality proposed can be applied where they are relevant (and only where relevant) to the approach being judged. However, it is widely recognized that each individual methodology should be judged against the specific quality criteria developed for a given approach. Fundamentally, the argument for universal markers has resulted in a collapsing of methodologies, data collection, and analysis practices, which is problematic (Dixon-Woods, Shaw, Agarwal, & Smith, 2004). In that it is not possible to identify a single qualitative methodology, universal criteria are difficult and perhaps inherently counterproductive to generate; therefore, an argument for the heterogeneity of qualitative research has emerged (Rolfe, 2006). Advocates of the heterogeneity argument have emphasized that the diversity within the field of qualitative research necessitates considering quality in diverse ways as well as in ways specific to a certain methodology. Unlike quantitative research, which has some consistency in theoretical frameworks, methods of data collection, and analysis, qualitative research has huge within-group heterogeneity on all levels (Meyrick, 2006), and the epistemological spread within the landscape of qualitative research is far too broad for a single, all-encompassing criteria checklist (Sandelowski & Barroso, 2002).

Indeed, qualitative approaches cannot be understood as unified in that there is great diversity in the ideological, philosophical, political, and ethical assumptions espoused within varying methodological approaches (Moccia, 1988). From this perspective, quality criteria can be only idiosyncratically applied (Caelli, Ray, & Mill, 2003), and thus it is arguably more appropriate for each methodological approach to have its own clarity about what constitutes a quality study. CA research does have its own quality indicators, although they are not always explicitly written about in CA textbooks. There are, however, ways of recognizing a quality CA study, and there is guidance regarding how to report this work, which we discuss in the section in this chapter titled "Critical Considerations for Establishing Quality in Applied CA Research."

Position 4: No Criteria Argument

An argument that has predominantly emerged within the social sciences is that there is no need for a quality checklist in qualitative research, nor is it necessary to conform to quantitative ideological ways of doing research. Thus, the claim within the no criteria argument is that it is inappropriate to develop quality criteria (Hammersley, 2007).

> (!) The no criteria argument advocates have called for an end to "criteriology," as it is argued that such an imposition on researchers squashes creativity (Schwandt, 1996) and minimizes the need for judgment (Hammersley, 2007).

Smith (1990) was one of the first scholars who questioned the growing conformity of creating checklists for qualitative research. Indeed, Smith argued that qualitative research is philosophically distinct from quantitative research, and it is this philosophical foundation that means that quality criteria are generally inappropriate. This argument is grounded on the understanding that developing checklists is founded on the assumption that there exists a correct set of procedures, which certainly is not possible for qualitative approaches. It should be recognized that the no criteria argument operates broadly at a theoretical level and focuses on the issue of the existence of reality.

The no criteria argument makes an important contribution to the debates about quality and is one that should not be ignored. It has merit at a metaphysical level and recognizes the importance of the theoretical aspects of qualitative research. However, for applied researchers, it can be difficult to sustain this position even if you agree with it. In applied research, you face the real challenges of publishing your work and seeking funding to conduct it in the first place, as well as convincing practitioners, commissioners, and managers that the recommendations your work produces have some merit and value.

> For example: Policy makers, commissioners, practitioners, and other audiences must have some confidence in the quality of your work to judge its value for practice (Dixon-Woods et al., 2004).

> *What this means*: Reviewers of submitted work to journals have a responsibility to assess that the methodological practices of the author are consistent with the methodological tradition within which the work was produced (Easterby-Smith, Golden-Biddle, & Locke, 2008).

Critical Considerations for Establishing Quality in Applied CA Research

We began this chapter by introducing the four positions that have surrounded establishing quality in qualitative research. In doing so, we sought to situate a discussion of quality in applied CA in relation to these arguments. Specifically, we suggest that the heterogeneity argument is most productive for thinking about how you establish quality in applied CA research, as it foregrounds the notion that individual methodologies bring with them assumptions while accepting that some indicators are applicable/universal to most qualitative approaches, including CA. These underlying assumptions should and do shape how concepts such as quality are conceptualized and actualized in practice. As such, while what we share here may have applicability to other qualitative methodologies, at least in part, we suggest that some of the ways in which CA researchers commonly establish quality are quite idiosyncratic to CA as a methodology. For instance, one of the practices we discuss next is the idea of validation through "new turn" proof. In Chapter 2, we have defined and described the next turn proof, noting its foundational role in analyzing and interpreting what is happening in social interaction. While other methodologies may do something similar, this practice is specific to CA. In other words, what counts as a quality CA study is built into the very assumptions of the methodology.

Drawing upon Peräkylä (2011), we discuss six issues related to quality in CA research:

1. "the transparency of analytic claims";

2. "validation through 'new turn' proof";

3. "deviant case analysis";

4. "questions about the institutional character of interaction";

5. "the generalizability of conversation analytic findings"; and

6. "the use of statistical techniques" (p. 367).

Peräkylä used the term *validity* rather than *quality*, and thus you will see this term woven throughout the next discussion as we take each of these issues in turn.

The Transparency of Analytic Claims

CA researchers should aim to display "apparent validity" (Kirk & Miller, 1986, p. 22); that is, people who engage with your interpretations of your data set should be convinced of their veracity. In this way, you should never move too far away from your data. One concrete way in which this is done is in the reporting of CA findings. CA researchers do not simply present a series of data excerpts and then broadly describe them; rather, they provide a thorough line-by-line analysis and sequential examination of each data excerpt, making visible how they oriented to and made sense of the data. By thoroughly and transparently presenting how each claim is supported by the data, you provide space for the reader to evaluate your claims.

Validation Through "New Turn" Proof

An underlying assumption in CA is the idea that the next turn in a conversation will make clear whether the interactants orient to the utterance in ways similar to the analyst (Sacks, Schegloff, & Jefferson, 1974). In other words, your claims can be subjected to the "proof procedure." While this is an important practice, it is helpful to keep in mind that some interactions are incredibly messy and next turn proof may be a bit ambiguous. Nonetheless, as Peräkylä (2011) noted, "the 'proof procedure' provided by the next turn remains the primordial criterion of validity that must be used as much as possible in all conversation analytic work" (p. 369).

Deviant Case Analysis

We first introduced you to the relevance and usefulness of deviant cases in applied CA in Chapter 7. Deviant case analysis is central to CA research. In seeking out negative instances/deviant cases or variability, you aim to attend to inconsistencies and diversity within the natural talk of the participants. Peräkylä (2011) noted that deviant case analysis is like analytic induction, which is often used in ethnographic studies. While through your analysis you will note regular patterns of interaction, deviant case analysis pushes you to consider where "things go differently" (Peräkylä, 2011, p. 369). This will lead you to engage in a deeper analysis of your data and not assume that the pattern you noted is stable; rather, you will return to your data again and again as you aim to show how a deviant case may offer support or countersupport to the regular interactional pattern you may have identified.

Questions About the Institutional Character of Interaction

In applied CA research, it is critical to avoid assuming the institutional context is present in the data simply because the data were produced in a context. As such, of concern for applied CA research studies is the following question: "What grounds does the researcher have for claiming that the talk he or she is focusing on is in any way 'connected to' some institutional framework?" (Peräkylä, 2011, p. 371). Notably, simply because data are collected within an institutional setting, an analyst cannot assume that this determines whether they will have a certain institutional character (Drew & Heritage, 1992). Thus, a critical consideration related to quality in an applied CA study is found in the very way in which the analyst explains the data. Indeed, we must not assume that institutional roles or practices are a given simply because the data were produced within an institutional context. Rather, the goal is to show "exactly how the things said brought forward the context" (Peräkylä, 2011, p. 373).

The Generalizability of Conversation Analytic Findings

A common question that people unfamiliar with qualitative research often pose is: How generalizable are your findings? While we do not attempt to unpack the various meanings of generalizability, we do note that CA researchers have historically dealt with questions around generalizability in very particular ways. Peräkylä (2011) noted, however, that for CA researchers the question of generalizability is posed in a very particular way, which is: "Do the findings of a particular study hold true in settings other than the one that was studied in this particular case?" (p. 374). CA researchers address this question in varying ways depending upon the nature of their research design as well as their own conceptualizations of the very meaning of generalizability. For instance, some CA researchers might engage in comparative studies across institutions, while others may turn to cumulative research produced about particular types of institutions. Furthermore, it may be possible to generalize from a single case (Demuth, 2018). Peräkylä also suggested that a researcher might simply point to the *possibility* that a practice may be used in specific institutional settings. Regardless of the approach you might take to addressing questions of generalizability, it is critical to spend time reflecting on

1. how you conceptualize the concept of generalizability in your applied CA study (or any qualitative study for that matter) and

2. how you might respond to questions raised from outsiders about the applicability of your work to other contexts.

Indeed, in applied CA research, questions about the applicability of your findings to other contexts are likely to arise, regardless of the position you take on the concept of generalizability.

The Use of Statistical Techniques

Some applied CA researchers may generate large data sets in which statistical analyses may be useful. For some scholars, such techniques speak directly to questions related to the generalizability of their findings. Notably, there are several examples of applied CA research studies in which statistical techniques have been applied (e.g., Robinson, Tate, & Heritage, 2016; Stivers & Majid, 2007). Using statistical techniques within a CA study, however, is not without challenges. As we have noted in Chapter 7, Stivers (2015) wrote about both the potentiality of coding and counting interactional data sets as well as some of the challenges. Indeed, coding social interaction is not a straightforward endeavor! Further, as Schegloff (1993) suggested, some social interactions may be orderly only "at the level of single occurrence" (p. 177) rather than at an aggregate level (Peräkylä, 2011). Consequently, the degree to which statistical techniques may be wielded will be dependent upon the nature of your research design.

Reading published CA literature is a particularly useful way to acquire a sense of how conversation analysts not only establish quality in their research but also (implicitly and explicitly) discuss the measures they took to assure it. Thus, we encourage you to complete the activity in Box 9.2, as it will allow you to generate a broader understanding of the varying ways in which CA researchers pursue and describe quality.

BOX 9.2

ACTIVITY ON EVALUATING QUALITY IN PUBLISHED APPLIED CA RESEARCH

Activity

Identify four to five published applied CA studies. After reading each study, consider the following questions:

- What evidence does the author provide that allows you to determine whether this is a quality CA study?

- Who was the primary audience for the publication?

- How might the audience have shaped the ways that the author(s) made visible and/or wrote about the quality of their research?

Common Criticisms of CA and Counterarguments

In any discussion promoting a specific methodology, it is important to consider the limitations and/or criticisms that surround a given approach. Applied CA is no exception and, like any other methodological approach, has been subject to critical questions from the broader academic community. We would point out here that all methodologies have their critics, and what matters is how these are circumnavigated by authors and responded to. Prior to reading about some of these critiques, take a moment to complete the activity listed in Box 9.3.

BOX 9.3

ACTIVITY ON THE CRITICISMS OF APPLIED CA RESEARCH

Activity

Methodology in itself is a construction—one crafted by people with particular interests and perspectives. We would be remiss to suggest that methodology of any kind is without limitations or constraints. As you have read through the previous chapters in this book and perhaps even carried out your own applied CA project, what are some of the limitations, constraints, or questions that have arisen for you regarding applied CA? If possible, we encourage you to discuss these with colleagues who are familiar with applied CA and consider carefully how you might address these limitations, constraints, and/or concerns.

In his recognition of some of the core challenges of CA, ten Have (1990) outlined three central and common critiques of CA:

1. Concerns related to the restricted nature of CA databases

2. Concerns about the interpretive practice common to CA

3. Concerns related to quantification

Drawing on the contributions of ten Have (1990), we consider each of these concerns in turn.

The Use of Restricted Databases

The criticism: Ten Have (1990) noted some scholars have claimed that recordings of naturally occurring interactions result in a restricted data corpus and thereby create a limitation related to the validity of CA findings. Typically, such critiques are underpinned by commitments to macrosociological concerns and result in claims that a naturally occurring data corpus lacks contextual information (e.g., participant age, gender), which some scholars argue is important information for substantiating analytic claims (see Cicourel, 1981).

> For example: Some critics have argued that CA's focus is too narrow and therefore fails to account for the sociopolitical consequences of participants' orientations (Wetherell, 1998).

The response: Ten Have (1990) argued that this criticism is not reasonable, as a basic assumption of CA is that the analyst works to substantiate his or her analytic claims in the data themselves. Schegloff (1998) also argued that CA focuses on participants' concerns, and thus any macroconcerns are only of relevance if/when oriented to by the interlocutors. Thus, within CA, there is a commitment for the analyst *not* to impose macroconcerns or to interpret the data with preconceived ideas about context.

> *What this means:* This means that the microfocus and data-driven foundation of CA's analytic procedure is what makes the approach unique and, some would argue, valid.

The Interpretive Practice of CA

The criticism, Part 1: Ten Have (1990) noted that one of the criticisms levied toward CA is that it is nothing more than a "meaning producing context," as CA relies on an interpretive framing of the data grounded on the assumption that the analyst possesses specialized knowledge of a given conversation. Thus, ultimately, analysts must account for their own contributions to the findings.

The response: In his response to this critique, ten Have (1990) was cognizant that this difficulty cannot be solved in principle but rather must be solved in practice. He argued that an analyst is only able to attempt to design procedures that produce a valuable reading of what happened in a conversation, and the interpretive frame of a CA researcher is indeed different from the participants in the data or a lay observer. In other words, the analyst transforms the knowledge displayed within the interaction into a discursive type of knowledge, which presumably requires specialist knowledge, which is not necessarily (immediately) available to participants.

> *What this means:* The analyst has a privileged position of observing both the lay members of the interaction and the professional practitioner members of an interaction, and closely attending to the details of the interaction as he or she identifies the conversation practices that occur.

The criticism, Part 2: Related to this is further critique often presented by those who work in ways similar to CA. Cicourel (1981) and Lynch (1985), for instance, questioned whether conversation analysts are truly able to understand the conversational data set when they do not have intimate knowledge of the participants and their circumstances. The critique rests on an assumption that CA assumes the analyst possesses a rather general conversational competence, with critics noting that specialized contexts often result in social activities that may not be accurately understood or interpreted by an outsider. More particularly, Lynch (1985) argued that the application of CA concepts is somewhat separated from the more comprehensive investigation of the original settings in which the data were produced and thus reveals only conversational aspects of the talk and not the nature of the tasks produced within a certain setting.

The response: Ten Have (1990) responded to the critiques of Cicourel (1981) and Lynch (1985) by highlighting the record of CA research focused on talk produced in institutional settings. Notably, he pointed to how institutional talk is studied by making sense of how it is different from mundane conversations. In this way, a conversation analyst may begin by comparing institutional talk with mundane conversations.

> *What this means:* CA research on mundane conversations allows for an understanding of the general practices of lay participants within institutional settings and thus serves as a useful analytic starting point when considering institutional talk, particularly when this talk is produced in a context that the analyst may or may not be familiar with.

The criticism, Part 3: Ten Have (1990) noted that another concern is whether a conversation analyst can conduct cross-cultural research. Can, for instance, an analyst with no insider knowledge of a given cultural context fairly interpret conversational practices? Given that CA is grounded in the general competence of the analyst, some scholars have questioned whether it is possible to research conversations produced in different settings.

The response: Although doing cross-cultural CA work is challenging, particularly due to issues related to translation and transcription, the growth of CA across the globe has meant that there is now a range of studies whereby the participants' first language, and in many cases the analyst's native language, is not English. Even back in the early 1990s, ten Have recognized that CA was possible and useful for studies of interaction in different cultures, as he argued that CA can produce findings that are potentially applicable across contexts. Yet such findings must be grounded in an intimate knowledge of the culture from which the interactions are produced, often resulting in the analyst engaging in broadly ethnographic research.

> *What this means:* Challenges are inevitable when engaging in CA work across cultures and often result in analysts familiarizing themselves with the conversational norms and relevant contextual features of a given context through ethnographic work.

The Problem of Quantification

The criticism: Ten Have (1990) noted that CA risks being identified as another form of constructive analysis, a type of analysis that constitutes its own object of study but fails to account for this object. He noted that if we think of the possibility of CA being used as a quantitative enterprise, we risk simply spotting conversational structures (i.e., our object of study) and coding/counting them. In reporting CA findings, authors may also write in a way that suggests quantification, using phrases such as *frequently, often,* and *commonly* (ten Have, 1990). This approach to writing may result in readers assuming that data were simply quantified, with the context of the interaction presumably lost.

The response: Recently, these arguments have been addressed by conversation analysts who recognize some audiences find quantification useful. For example, Robinson (2007) argued that conversation analysts are not opposed to counting/coding, but this should not be at the expense of detailed line-by-line analysis. In other words, exploring frequent patterns can allow the identification of social practices across the data set. Yet it is the detailed analysis that matters, and therefore, if the analyst decides to code/count, he or she is simply acquiring additional information. Notably, however, ten Have (1990) cautioned against coding/counting outside of context, remarking that an analyst who relies solely on this may ultimately ignore the sequential environment of a given interaction and/or overlook how the interactional environment might be implicated in the coding process.

What this means: The conversation analyst must attend to the sequential nature of the talk, which requires attending to that which precedes and follows an utterance (Sacks et al., 1974).

Other General Critiques of CA

Several additional criticisms of CA have been offered that are far more pragmatically oriented. We discuss five such criticisms in turn.

CA Is Time Consuming and Costly

The criticism: A criticism sometimes levied at CA is that it is time consuming and can require expensive resources (such as recording equipment, specialist transcription support, and so on), and is therefore impractical.

The response: There is no doubt that CA is time consuming if it is conducted properly, but we argue that this is a strength, not a limitation. Further, recording equipment of decent quality is relatively accessible and even at times free or available to borrow from one's home institution. Anything worthwhile takes time and resources.

CA Requires Specialist Skills and Training

The criticism: It is common for critics to suggest that CA is inaccessible and complicated to learn, and requires specialized training. Furthermore, researchers are expected to engage in data sessions with others, which means networking is required and may not be easy for some scholars to access.

The response: We argue that to carry out any qualitative methodological approach in a grounded and thoughtful way, training and careful study are required. Although some approaches perhaps require less specialized training, many are very specialized in different ways. In other words, learning how to engage in a quality analysis of any kind requires time, training, and commitment.

Jefferson Symbols Make a CA Transcript Difficult to Read

The criticism: The high level of detail common to Jefferson transcripts can be complicated for audiences to understand, particularly when unfamiliar with it. Given that applied CA research is often disseminated to those who work in areas of practice, such a complicated transcript can make this especially difficult for others to access.

The response: While we did consider this point in Chapter 6, we return to it here as it is often positioned as a limitation of CA. While CA does rely on a technical transcript that demonstrates how things were said as well as what was said, it is possible to make sure that the transcripts are explained and readable by novice audiences, which may require slightly adapting the level of detail you present.

A Quality CA Study Relies on the Quality of the Recordings

The criticism: A quality CA study relies on a quality recording. It can be challenging to achieve quality recordings, especially as CA often relies on collecting naturally occurring data that may include significant background noise or multiparty interactions.

The response: While this may have been a valid criticism when researchers relied on analog recordings of data, in contemporary practice researchers often have access to high-quality digital devices and microphones, which make higher-quality recordings possible. Although generating quality recordings can still be a challenge in environments that are noisy, the use of software can also help to isolate sounds and cancel out background noise.

The Use of Naturally Occurring Data Can Make a CA Project Ethically Complicated

The criticism: The ethics of qualitative research are often positioned as more complex and certainly different from quantitative research. However, CA raises additional ethical complexities due to its preference for recording naturally occurring events and/or harvesting naturally occurring texts.

The response: We have addressed this difficulty in Chapter 4 but remind you that while it may be more challenging to implement ethical strategies to manage the different types of risks that naturally occurring data raise, it is still possible. There are steps you can take to ensure the safeguarding of your participants.

An Interview With Professor Anita Pomerantz

In this chapter, we have introduced you to key considerations related to establishing quality in applied CA research. We have situated our discussion in relation to the broader debates regarding establishing quality in qualitative research. While there is a robust literature base surrounding general discussions of quality in qualitative research, there is far less literature specifically addressing quality in applied CA research. Notably, some CA scholars, such as Professor Anita Pomerantz, provided some of the earliest discussions of how conversation analysts might think about quality when engaged in CA research. Thus, we interviewed Professor Pomerantz, inviting her to share her perspective on establishing quality in applied CA research. You can read her interview in Box 9.4.

BOX 9.4

INTERVIEW WITH PROFESSOR ANITA POMERANTZ

Anita Pomerantz is professor emerita of communication at the University of Albany, United States. She is recognized for her significant contributions to CA, with one of many of them focused on generating important considerations related to quality.

While her publication record is vast, a particularly useful reading related to quality in CA is the following:

- Pomerantz, A. (1990). On the validity and generalizability of conversation analytic methods: Conversation analytic claims. *Communication Monographs*, *57*(3), 231–235.

We asked Professor Pomerantz two questions about establishing quality in CA research, and her answers to these key questions follow.

What are some of the key considerations for establishing quality/validity in CA research?

"Conversation analysts have no simple formula or recipe for guaranteeing quality or validity. However, certain practices contribute to our producing high-quality research: making our method-ological choices in relation to the goals and intended claims of the project, attending to the details of the interactions in their sequential context, and reflecting on the assumptions associated with our analytic language. Given space limitations, I will not address those issues but rather limit myself to discussing a crucial stance: our willingness to change our conceptions and claims while developing analyses.

One kind of shift comes about when we discover that instances we put into a collection because they initially look similar in fact function differently. When that happens, we change our conception of the project, our collection, and/or our findings. Another kind of shift may involve initially looking for a regularity or pattern and then accounting for it. This may take us to exploring the rights and obliga-tions associated with that conduct or the principles participants use in producing and interpreting it. A third kind of shift may involve broadening our focus from the conduct in question to the interactional task which the conduct addresses and then contrasting the alternative ways of dealing with that inter-actional task."

How can an applied CA researcher promote quality?

"For high-quality research, it is crucial to maintain a stance of openness and flexibility. As Jefferson (2004b) wrote:

> And in my experience this is a fact, and a pleasure, of collecting instances: Inevitably one comes across materials that don't fit under the heading one has set oneself to collect on some particular data-run, but which seems to be related; "ballpark phenomena" that might cast some light on the focal phenomenon and/or point to independently interesting issues. (p. 134)

The stance of flexibility has been important in a current project on which I am collaborating. Our initial goal was to examine the inferential work of dispatchers during 911 emergency calls. As we analyzed the calls, we found cases in which the dispatcher inferred that a piece of the reported event was missing or misrepresented. However, we also found cases in which the dispatcher had trouble figuring out which emergency service was needed. Given the different sequential contexts, constraints, and inferential methods occurring in the two groups of instances, we recast our project as two projects. Regarding dispatchers' figuring out which service was needed, we broadened the focus of the study to examine how dispatchers generally and unproblematically infer which service is needed and, in that context, how and when it becomes problematic. My point is that as our investigation proceeded, we found we needed to refine our sense of the project, alter our collections, and push ourselves in unanticipated directions."

Chapter Summary

In this chapter, we introduced you to important considerations related to establishing quality in applied CA research. To contextualize our discussion, we began the chapter by offering a general perspective on the various arguments that have been made regarding quality in qualitative research. Specifically, we introduced you to four arguments commonly noted in the literature: (1) adaptation argument, (2) universal markers argument, (3) heterogeneity argument, and (4) no criteria argument. Throughout this discussion, we sought to make links to the potential applications of a given argument to applied CA research. Notably, we argued that the heterogeneity argument is perhaps the most useful when considering quality in CA. From this perspective, we offered several key considerations related to establishing quality in an applied CA study. Drawing upon Peräkylä (2011), we discussed six issues related to quality in CA research: (1) "the transparency of analytic claims"; (2) "validation through 'new turn' proof"; (3) "deviant case analysis"; (4) "questions about the institutional character of interaction"; (5) "the generalizability of conversation analytic findings"; and (6) "the use of statistical techniques" (p. 367). We concluded the chapter by noting some of the common criticisms of CA. We summarize the key learning points in the next box.

Learning Points From Chapter 9

- There is a lack of consensus about how to judge the quality of qualitative research.

- There are four common arguments about quality in the qualitative research literature.

- Quality in CA research is often established through one or more of the six practices outlined by Peräkylä (2011).

Recommended Readings

As we have noted, there is a relatively small body of literature around establishing quality in applied CA research. We include here four suggested readings, noting that each will provide you with important foundational understandings of how to engage in the practices common to establishing quality in an applied CA research study.

- Antaki, C., Billig, M. G., Edwards, D., & Potter, J. A. (2003). Discourse analysis means doing analysis: A critique of six analytic shortcomings. *Discourse Analysis Online, 1*. Retrieved from https://extra.shu.ac.uk/daol/articles/open/2002/002/antaki2002002-paper.html

Antaki et al.'s article is indeed a classic that focuses broadly on critical considerations for generating a quality discourse analysis study. While the article explicitly focuses on the broad area of discourse analysis, we argue that there are many relevant points for applied CA researchers as well. For instance, one of the six shortcomings the authors warn against is "analysis that consists in simply spotting features" (n.p.). We strongly recommend that you spend time with this article and think about ways in which you can incorporate the authors' suggestions into your own applied CA work.

- Peräkylä, A. (2011). Validity in research on naturally occurring social interaction. In D. Silverman (Ed.), *Qualitative research* (3rd ed., pp. 365–382). London, England: Sage.

As we have noted previously, Peräkylä's chapter provides an incisive and instructive overview of critical considerations for establishing quality in a CA study. We suggest that you view this chapter as one of the key guides on how to conceptualize and carry out a quality CA study. Further, you can certainly use the key considerations presented by Peräkylä to support you when evaluating published applied CA research.

- Pomerantz, A. (1990). On the validity and generalizability of conversation analytic methods: Conversation analytic claims. *Communication Monographs, 57*(3), 231–235.

Pomerantz's article provides readers with a clear understanding of the kinds of claims that conversation analysts make. She illustrates how these claims should and can be justified in relation to one's interactional data set, as well as how these claims function to make visible the validity of a given CA research study. We view this article as essential reading and encourage you to spend time thinking about the implications of Pomerantz's discussion for your research.

- ten Have, P. (1990). Methodological issues in conversation analysis. *Bulletin of Sociological Methodology/Bulletin de Méthodologie Sociologique, 27*(1), 23–51.

In this seminal article, ten Have guides the reader through some of the core critiques of CA, particularly the fundamental challenges that are endemic to the process of doing analysis. In so doing, ten Have outlines the counterarguments presented by CA to demonstrate how valuable (despite the critiques) CA is as an approach. This article is one we encourage you to gain familiarity with, as you are likely to encounter one or more of said critiques as you carry out your applied CA research.

Disseminating Your Work

PART III

10

Doing Applied Conversation Analysis Research in an Evidence-Based World

Chapter Focus

In this chapter, you will learn how to:

- Describe what is meant by *evidence* in research terms.

- Appreciate the history of evidence-based practice.

- Evaluate the value of qualitative evidence.

- Critically assess the notion of evidence hierarchies.

- Evaluate the relevance of evidence arguments for applied conversation analysis research.

The term *evidence-based practice* is relevant to applied researchers. Yet it is a relatively new concept in relation to the field of research, and one that has only recently begun to impact researchers who practice applied conversation analysis (CA). In a modern society, there has been a consistent drive to ensure that research in most fields has some applicability to the practice/field in which that research is conducted. More recently, there has been a growing emphasis on the idea that research should be relevant for practice and/or policy so that those who work in a specific field can be informed by research findings in some way. This reality has created some tension, as there is still arguably a legitimate claim that there is value in the generation of theoretical knowledge that does not immediately require real-world application, and thus researchers may undertake research to inform practice and/or to inform theory (O'Reilly & Lester, 2017).

If you are planning to do an applied CA research study, it is reasonable to assume that your findings should be applicable to the field or practice you are studying. By its very nature, applied CA often involves the study of real-world institutional settings, often, if not typically, with a goal of demonstrating the interactional practices within a given setting in order that some lesson may be understood or learned from it. Generally, applied CA researchers do have a goal of informing practice and usually disseminate their findings both in applied fields for practitioners and for the CA research community, reporting on the sequential or organizational aspects of the talk.

The underlying focus on *applied* CA often means that you will disseminate some of your research findings to practitioner audiences. To do that effectively, we believe it is important to be familiar with the evidence-based movement, which has been growing over the last few decades. Thus, in this chapter, we introduce you to the key concepts of this rhetoric, debating the very meaning of evidence, the notion of implementing evidence into practice, and the implications of superiority that this tension has created in certain fields. For context, we consider how the evidence-based practice rhetoric has been embraced by qualitative researchers and what this means for those practicing applied CA. To contextualize this, we provide one example from the field of health, specifically therapy.

Examining the Notion of Evidence

To consider what is meant by evidence-based practice, we must first start to unpack the notion of **evidence**.

Evidence can be defined as that which either proves or disproves a premise of an argument being put forward.

(Source: Dictionary.com)

In the field of law, notions of proof and evidence have tended to be treated synonymously, while in research, the idea of proving a hypothesis or point of view has always been more contentious. In research terms, therefore, evidence is argued to refer to the knowledge that has been generated from different sources. Further, this knowledge is presumed to have been subjected to a degree of testing and therefore thought of as credible (Higgs & Jones, 2000).

What this means: You should bear in mind that the aim of research is often to generate knowledge or social theory (Rolfe, 1998), and the knowledge that is generated can be used as evidence.

Although in this chapter we focus on evidence generated by research, it is important to bear in mind that not all knowledge and evidence come via research. There are different types of evidence sourced from different arenas, and, for context, we briefly draw your attention to these. Arguing from the context of health-based evidence but applicable to many fields, Rycroft-Malone et al. (2004) argued that there are four broad categories of knowledge, which we summarize in Table 10.1.

As we have noted, Rycroft-Malone et al. (2004) presented their argument from a health care perspective, and yet this is arguably translatable and applicable to most areas of practice. Certainly, in other areas such as education, social care, youth work, and so on, there is a range of different evidence that informs practice and guides policy development and implementation. These four types of evidence and knowledge demonstrate a broad view of what counts as evidence.

> *What this means:* In your research practice, you can take a broad view of the meaning of evidence. Indeed, it is argued that evidence should be thought of as a spectrum that includes research, practitioner experience, expertise, and audit information (Fox, 2003).

Notably, we argue that there are certainly other forms of evidence and knowledge that are not captured in Rycroft-Malone et al.'s (2004) typology and, perhaps most important, point to evidence that is generated in ways outside of Western-dominated conceptions of research, being, and knowing. Thus, we encourage you to consider additional forms of evidence by completing the activity in Box 10.1.

TABLE 10.1 ● Four types of evidence and knowledge

Type	Description
Research knowledge and evidence	In Western culture, the evidence generated by research is often considered most credible and subsequently tends to be given priority over other types. This includes evidence from quantitative and qualitative research studies.
Professional practice and life experience	An important type of evidence is referred to as *practice-based evidence*. This is evidence that is expressed through and embedded in practice. This tends to be tacit and intuitive, and in order to be taken up by others, it must often be subjected to some type of analysis and critique.
Lay, service user, and individual knowledge	This type of evidence refers to the knowledge and experiences of those individuals relevant to practice, and it has been argued that their opinions and preferences should be central. Generally, we know far less about this knowledge.
Local context	This type of evidence relates to the context of practice from which evidence and knowledge are drawn. It is argued that practitioners can draw upon local audit and performance data, consumer narratives, and knowledge about the organization and culture, as well as social and professional networks, local policies, and feedback from key stakeholders.

Source: Rycroft-Malone et al., 2004.

BOX 10.1
ACTIVITY ON OTHER FORMS OF EVIDENCE

Activity

Notions of evidence and knowledge have often been conceptualized in Westernized frameworks in which only certain ways of being-knowing have been privileged. As a result, it is common for conversations around evidence to exclude expansive understandings of knowledge. Take a few moments to consider types of evidence and knowledge that are perhaps omitted from Rycroft-Malone et al.'s (2004) typology listed in Table 10.1. Develop an expanded list and reflect upon the implications for research practice.

What Is Evidence-Based Practice?

As we have questioned the meaning of the notion of evidence, it is perhaps obvious that defining ***evidence-based practice*** is contentious. The call for evidence in practice came originally from the field of health/medicine, and over time many other disciplines have followed suit. The concept of evidence-based practice was introduced by David Eddy during his early work in the 1990s (Eddy, 2011).

Evidence-based practice in simple terms means a practice that is informed by the best evidence available.

What this means: For evidence-based practice to be implemented, practitioners need to apply their knowledge gained from engaging with research to improve their work in the field.

In the field of health (broadly defined), over time an important change has occurred wherein there has been a noticeable investment in the infrastructure needed to increase the promotion of interventions being delivered to patients based on "best" evidence (Rycroft-Malone et al., 2004). Consequently, practitioners are presumed to have some level of certainty regarding the potential outcomes of interventions while integrating clinical expertise and patient values when making critical health-related decisions (Sackett, Rosenberg, Gray, Haynes, & Richardson, 1996). More recently, the evidence-based practice movement has gained influence, becoming a particularly powerful force across a range of different applied fields. There is now a pervasive belief that research evidence should inform practice and guide decision making in a range of areas, including

- Medicine

- Health care

- Psychiatry and psychology

- Social care

- Education (children and adults)

- Law and criminal justice

- Forensic science

- Children and youth services

- Mediation

- Media

> (!) **Although earlier ideas about evidence-based practice included practitioner expertise, consumer values, and qualitative research, the evolution of the meaning of evidence has resulted in a greater leaning toward scientific evidence and standardization.**

Consequently, the evidence-based movement has impacted the way research is conducted, interpreted, and applied, as well as how research is viewed by society at large. In practice, this has meant that there has been a drive to create greater levels of quality control and more uniformity, and this has promoted a range of standards being created, particularly for both health-related research and clinical practice (Timmermans & Berg, 2003).

A consequence of the reliance on conceptions of evidence has been the emphasis on the ***randomized controlled trial (RCT)***, which is frequently argued to be the most credible and reliable way of setting standards. An RCT is usually used for medical research but can and has been used in other fields.

This gradual shift to favor the RCT is argued to be misrepresentative, as it may mislead audiences to believe that if an intervention is not supported by an RCT then it should not be used in practice (Swisher, 2010). Swisher (2010) and others have argued that this is problematic, as it has created an overreliance on the scientific method and an emphasis on cause and effect. However, other forms of evidence are still valued in most fields, including health, and a lot of work has been generated to demonstrate this.

> ● A **randomized controlled trial** is a form of scientific experiment that has the goal of testing a new treatment. Participants in the trial are randomly allocated to the standard treatment group or the intervention group. RCTs are used to test the effectiveness of an intervention.

> *What this means:* The emphasis on the RCT has led to a rhetoric of hierarchies and superiority of evidence that has raised arguments in the field about the value and place of other forms of evidence, such as qualitative research, practitioner expertise, consumer values, and so on.

Arguments of Superiority

The drive for standards of evidence has implications for methodology and arguments about quality indicators (Nutley, Powell, & Davies, 2013). The different perspectives about evidence have led to a creation of hierarchies of evidence leading to some research designs being favored by some scholars, and in some cases funding bodies too. It was as early as 1979 that it was agreed that evidence ought to be ranked, and this notion was popularized by the Canadian Task Force (Sackett, 1986). Problematically, ranking evidence has created a superiority rhetoric, which has meant that there has been a reduced appreciation of the ways in which research evidence interacts with practitioner experience, contextual factors, and consumer experience (Rycroft-Malone et al., 2004). Most hierarchies of evidence that have been developed have ranked evidence in terms of effectiveness of interventions being focused on the outcome of a service or treatment (Evans, 2003). In practice, therefore, RCTs have often been positioned as the gold standard, an idea subjected to much criticism (Grossman & Mackenzie, 2005).

> *What this means:* Research that focuses on outcomes has historically been favored more than other types of research.

These hierarchies of evidence have been visually represented in various forms, such as tables or pyramids; commonly, RCTs are at the top, with expert opinion and qualitative evidence often positioned toward the bottom (Turner, 2013). Such ranking of evidence in terms of superiority takes a homogeneous view of evidence and is problematic in terms of the relevance of evidence to practice and the superiority of certain research designs. We would argue that ranking evidence in terms of superiority has created problems, particularly for qualitative research (and this includes applied CA work). Indeed, there are several issues that have resulted. These were outlined by Nutley et al. (2013), which we describe in Table 10.2.

We argue that the notion of hierarchies is unhelpful, and different types of evidence serve different purposes. What may be a useful form of evidence in one context may be the worst type of evidence in another (Marks, 2002). We also suggest that qualitative evidence is important, equal to the RCT, as it addresses different types of problems and answers different types of questions. Indeed, qualitative evidence can complement, inform, or facilitate evidence gained from an RCT. Furthermore, we argue (like others; see Ravitch & Carl, 2016) that treating quantitative and qualitative evidence as an opposing dichotomy is not helpful.

> For example: If an RCT demonstrates that drug A is more effective than drug B for diabetes, qualitative research can show what patients feel about the drug, the regime of taking it, the side effects they suffer, and their experience of the condition, among other things.

TABLE 10.2 ● Problems with viewing evidence as a hierarchy	
Argument	**Description**
It neglects important and relevant issues around evidence.	Traditional hierarchies that place scientific evidence generated from RCTs at the top are focused on the methodological design of the research. This means they tend to fail to critically consider how the design was implemented and if or how that fits with other studies focused on the same issue.
It underrates the value of useful observational studies.	Some observational studies deliver estimates regarding the effects of an intervention. These types of studies score high on external validity as they tend to involve large representative samples.
It tends to exclude all studies except high-ranking ones.	By excluding all other studies, it risks losing useful and important evidence. Thus, the hierarchy serves as a filtering device, and this means that the value or relevance from other types of studies tends to remain unexamined.
Insufficient attention is paid to the need to understand what works and why.	It is problematic that these hierarchies tend not to examine what works, who it works for, and under what circumstances. Often, social programs are multifaceted, and local context can be important.
It provides an insufficient basis for recommendations.	It is notable that the hierarchies do not provide a sufficient basis for practitioner recommendations regarding whether the intervention should be used in practice. So the translation of evidence into practice is not necessarily a direct link.

Source: Nutley et al., 2013.

For example: If an RCT demonstrates that a computerized test is more effective for promoting children's learning than standard curriculum design, then qualitative research may help researchers and practitioners understand teachers' and children's views on the changes, the policy implications and potential challenges of implementation, and the resource implications for schools, among other things.

What Is Practice-Based Evidence?

When working in areas of practice, it is important to also think about the benefit of *practice-based evidence.*

Practice-based evidence is an important form of evidence and promotes a focus on translation and dissemination of research into practice (Green, 2008). Questions have been raised about ways of making evidence more useful to practice, and practice-based evidence is one of the ways in which this can be achieved. This is because practice-based evidence

Practice-based evidence is that produced by examining the real world of practices, observing the real-world practices, often by practitioners themselves.

pays more attention to external validity, often employs action and participatory approaches that can be tailored to specific settings, and promotes the involvement of practitioners in the generation of evidence (Green, 2008). Because of this, the evidence has more real-world authority for practitioners, as practitioners have been directly involved in the development of questions with applicability to their setting in mind (Fox, 2003).

Qualitative Evidence

Quantitative evidence has an important place in informing practice, as it provides useful indicators of outcomes relevant to a certain field that can be compared against one another to demonstrate efficacy and effectiveness. Equally important, qualitative research provides the framework by which the processes of how those outcomes are achieved can be investigated and can be achieved in both evidence-based and practice-based ways. While qualitative research is now recognized as making an important contribution to the evidence, the ways in which research is funded and the journals that articles are published in have been influenced by the rhetoric of evidence-based practice with some orientation toward favoring outcomes.

Consequently, efforts to legislate scientific practices have the potential to reshape the boundaries of what constitutes science and risk devaluing qualitative findings (Freeman, deMarrais, Preissle, Roulston, & St. Pierre, 2007), relegating qualitative research to a secondary position (Freshwater, Cahill, Walsh, & Muncey, 2010). Arguably, any misinterpretations about evidence and its value could hinder the ways in which qualitative research is viewed by those outside of academia (Lester & O'Reilly, 2015), particularly in applied fields. More broadly, it has been argued that this has potential consequences for how and when qualitative methods are taught in universities, when qualitative research is published in high-ranking journals, and if qualitative studies are funded (Morse, 2006a). Consequently, the lack of focus on qualitative evidence may then impede advances in practice (Morse, 2006b); thus, it is important that we maintain the status that qualitative research has achieved and continue to recognize that this type of evidence addresses different kinds of questions to the RCT.

(!) "If the goal is generalizability, quantitative methods are accepted to be superior, but if the goal is a rich understanding of a particular phenomenon, then qualitative methods are indispensable" (McNeill, 2006, p. 151).

To maintain the status achieved in the field, we encourage qualitative researchers, including applied CA scholars, to continue to engage in critical conversations and activities that serve to promote the use of qualitative evidence. Particularly in applied fields, it remains paramount that qualitative researchers maintain a strong presence, serving to promote and advocate for the meaningful nature of qualitative evidence (Lester & O'Reilly, 2015).

Further, when writing up research, scholars have argued that qualitative researchers need to ensure that their writing is palatable and understandable for the practice-based audiences they are aiming to reach (Green, 2008). This, we suggest, is particularly pertinent to applied CA researchers who engage in rather specialized analytic practices that could easily become inaccessible to those audiences who might benefit the most from the research findings. It is thus important to keep in mind that CA brings its own specialized vocabulary, and this vocabulary might need to be unpacked for practice-based audiences who have little familiarity with the details of CA. It will be up to you to make sure that your audience(s) can understand the key messages of your work. Before you continue reading further, we invite you to reflect on what the arguments about qualitative evidence might mean for applied CA researchers by completing the activity in Box 10.2.

BOX 10.2
ACTIVITY ON CA AS EVIDENCE

Activity

We would argue that CA evidence is essential for informing practice and makes a very important contribution to any field. In the next section of this chapter, we consider the ways in which it might do this. Prior to reading further, write down at least three reasons that applied CA research has a place in an evidence-based world and why it is important.

Engaging With Arguments About Evidence in Applied CA Research

We believe that applied CA research has the potential to make significant contributions to the evidence base of any discipline. As we highlighted in Chapter 1, there are different types of applied CA, ranging from foundational applied CA to interventionist applied CA, among others. Fundamental to applied CA is the application of findings of "pure CA" studies to the study of institutional interactions and a common (but not required) focus on applying CA findings to offer practical advice to organizations. In fact, there are a growing number of examples of applied CA scholars working directly with practitioners to address practice-based problems. In such cases, there is an inherent assumption that the applied CA study will generate evidence that directly informs and potentially even changes practice.

More specifically, there are several considerations for applied CA researchers engaged in arguments around evidence. First, it is often useful to keep in mind that the nature of the data common to CA generates useful evidence directly linked to practice. Historically, CA scholars have assumed that the privileging of naturally occurring data allows for a deeper understanding of how people engage in their actual everyday social activities. In other words, CA is based directly on the observable properties of conversational data and within such a focus examines how interaction is organized, patterned, and systematic (Drew, Chatwin, & Collins, 2001). Evidence, therefore, is commonly generated by observing/collecting actual social events of interest rather than inviting people to retrospectively talk about their practice, for instance. As such, the evidence common to an applied CA study is such that it is well grounded in actual practice and therefore has the potential to generate insights closely aligned with in situ understandings.

Second, and perhaps most closely connected to interventionist applied CA research, applied CA research studies can be designed to generate evidence directly linked to a problem of practice. While CA researchers do not always directly provide recommendations for what might work better, they do often provide details regarding what is going on in the data, thus encouraging practitioners to make assessments about what might work better. Thus, they make recommendations about things that need to be changed or done differently but cannot be certain that if the changes are implemented it will result in better practice, as this is something that will need more attention. Stokoe's (2011) conversation analytic role-play method, for instance, is an excellent example of how data generated in a CA study can be used as evidence for generating a training model and potentially informing and even changing practice. Thus, as you work to design your CA studies that engage with applied fields, your work may meaningfully impact practice and thereby further legitimate the valuable nature of the qualitative evidence your CA study produces.

An Example: CA Evidence and Health

In this chapter, we have provided you with information about the arguments around evidence-based practice and linked this to practice-based evidence. To help you better understand this area in relation to applied CA, we now provide you with one key example and show how applied CA research has contributed to a particular field. Specifically, we discuss health research broadly and demonstrate some of the ways in which applied CA has supported health practitioners, and then focus more particularly on applied CA research in therapy.

In terms of the field of health, evidence refers to data and knowledge generation from research, from experts or service users, and from evaluation or anecdotal information (Bartgis & Bigfoot, 2010). Health practitioners are now being encouraged to engage with evidence, and they are becoming better skilled in questioning the value of research (Thorne, 2009). Health is a practical discipline and a specialized activity that focuses on both physical and mental health conditions. Qualitative evidence is important in this field, as it provides insights into the patients' experiences and enables practitioners to treat and communicate with them in more sensitive ways (Kearney, 2001).

In our example of the value of applied CA, we focus on therapeutic interaction. There is increased pressure on mental health professionals to work in an evidence-based way, and they face increased challenges in working in the field. The language of evidence in relation to mental distress suggests quality, validity, science, and robustness, and this is a discourse applied to prevention and treatment of mental health conditions (O'Reilly & Lester, 2017). Such evidence is used to determine the cost-effectiveness of certain treatments, and this influences commissioning decisions (Hoagwood, Burns, Kiser, Ringeisem, & Schoenwald, 2001). We argue that applied CA as a form of evidence has a lot to offer the world of therapy and counseling, and we turn now to demonstrate how and why.

An Example: Applied CA and Therapy

Mental health is an important aspect of the field of health, and although it is an area that is considerably underfunded for both practice and research (McCrone, Dhanasiri, Patel, Knapp, & Lawton-Smith, 2008; Ngui, Khasakhala, Ndetei, & Weiss Roberts, 2010), it is an area that has received attention from applied CA researchers. CA researchers often view mental health from a different perspective than more traditional quantitative approaches. As we noted earlier in the book, CA takes a social constructionist view and treats mental states as constituted through interpersonal interactions (Georgaca, 2014). In terms of therapy, therefore, this position allows for greater flexibility in understanding the ways in which therapists and their clients make sense of the process and in terms of how the language of mental illness is used. In the context of counseling and therapy, then, CA offers a rigorous approach for examining the nuances of how therapeutic interaction unfolds in a turn-by-turn way between the therapist and the client (Kiyimba & O'Reilly, 2016a). CA provides a useful way for examining the clinical processes that are constructed throughout the course of therapy (Georgaca & Avdi, 2009).

CA does not aim to evaluate therapeutic practices, and neither does it dictate to therapists how they should conduct their therapy; instead, it seeks to reveal how therapeutic interactions operate in practice (Streeck, 2010). CA researchers therefore avoid focusing on therapists' insights or assumptions within the therapeutic protocol and focus instead on how the therapeutic conversations work (Madill, Widdicomb, & Barkham, 2001).

> *What this means:* CA examines the practices through which the therapist and the client produce a therapeutic reality (Streeck, 2010), and it is through dialogue that both parties find new understandings and ways of progressing (Strong, Busch, & Couture, 2008).

From this discussion, we hope you can now see why CA can offer an important insight into the field of therapy. It should be clear that applied CA work can operate as a basis for making recommendations to therapists and counselors based on their research findings. This is important, as therapy and counseling as funded disciplines have to demonstrate their efficiency and effectiveness by drawing upon empirical evidence (Streeck, 2010). Thus, it is important to demonstrate evidence of therapeutic change for these disciplines to indicate their worthiness. Clearly, it is reasonable to argue that examining the interactional processes between therapists and clients is the most direct route for assessing that process (i.e., the conversation) and the outcome (i.e., the evidence of change), as these are inseparable (Strong et al., 2008).

In therapy, the therapeutic relationship is a central feature, and this is just as important as the therapeutic modality itself (Kiyimba, 2016). For example, in research we conducted using discursive psychology (which aligns with CA), we demonstrated how the process of therapeutic alignment is instigated and maintained to promote therapeutic progressivity (Parker & O'Reilly, 2012). Paying attention to what happens in therapy can be useful in training initiatives and to help those working in the field. By bringing CA findings to therapists, it can encourage them to be mindful of their use of language (Strong et al., 2008). Additionally, this close attention to the actual talk occurring within the therapeutic environment provides opportunities for practitioners to reflect on any in situ decisions they made (Kiyimba & O'Reilly, 2016a). Indeed, as these examples illustrate, CA findings provide important evidence for therapists and counselors, as well as other practitioners.

An Interview With Dr. Nikki Kiyimba

In this chapter, we have introduced you to some of the key arguments around evidence-based practice as well as the idea that applied CA research generates evidence useful for practice. Clinicians familiar with CA are well positioned to share insights on the ways in which evidence produced via a CA study might inform practice. Thus, we invited Dr. Nikki Kiyimba, a clinical psychologist who also studies and writes around CA, to share the ways in which she engages with findings from applied CA research. See Box 10.3.

BOX 10.3
INTERVIEW WITH DR. NIKKI KIYIMBA

Nikki Kiyimba is a senior lecturer at the University of Chester and a chartered clinical psychologist. Dr. Kiyimba is a program leader for the master's course in Therapuetic Practice for Psychological Trauma, and she has experience working with adults with a wide range of mental health difficulties. Her research has tended to focus on mental health and has used a range of qualitative approaches, including CA. Dr. Kiyimba has written CA research articles specifically aimed at practicing clinical professionals. For example, she has written for mental health nurses working with children and families:

- O'Reilly, M., Kiyimba, N., & Karim, K. (2016). "This is a question we have to ask everyone": Asking young people about self-harm and suicide. *Journal of Psychiatric and Mental Health Nursing, 23,* 479–488.

We asked Dr. Kiyimba three questions about why CA is an important form of evidence.

As a clinician, in what way does qualitative evidence inform your practice?

"I find that most of my reading of research evidence is qualitative, purely because it informs me about the depth and breadth of people's experiences in a way that quantitative research doesn't quite get to. As a clinician, I know that there are interventions and approaches that are helpful for lots of people, but every person that I work with is a unique individual with a unique history, unique interests and circumstances, and unique challenges. So while I am intrigued by human nature on a broad level, in my day-to-day practice I am primarily concerned with the idiosyncratic ways that each person makes sense of their life from their own perspective. Qualitative research is exciting because it enables an understanding of individual people, their personal life, experiences, ways of making sense, and ways of talking about and interacting with others."

How have you used findings from CA research to inform your clinical practice?

"Using conversation analysis as a researcher has first of all made me very attentive to the specific words that clients use, as it makes me consider 'why is that word there?' It also leads me to be really attentive to the sequential organization of the turn-by-turn interaction I have with clients. CA gives me a perspective of my work that means I know it is not without meaning that certain ways of expressing things can lead to certain kinds of responses. I find CA endlessly fascinating in relation to ordinary conversation, and the added bonus in terms of my clinical work is that CA helps me to really 'tune in' to clients' talk in a much more informed way."

What suggestions do you have for applied CA researchers who aim to position their research findings as informing practice-based evidence?

"That's a really good question. It is exciting to attend conferences where there are more and more academics seriously engaged in CA research that has a direct application to clinical practice. I wholeheartedly support this trend and am grateful to those researchers who are collecting data from practice-based settings. In my experience, it sometimes feels challenging to find journals that practitioners access that also welcome research using CA. My suggestions for journal editors would be to include some members on the board who have CA experience so that they feel more confident about accepting CA research. For researchers themselves, please keep up the good work, and keep adding to the growing evidence base for using CA to empirically inform practice."

Chapter Summary

In this chapter, we introduced you to the concept of evidence as it relates to research practice. We noted that historically, evidence has been defined in varying and at times conflicting ways. Related to this, we discussed the history of the evidence-based movement and the impact this movement has had on understandings of qualitative evidence. We noted how this movement resulted in the development of evidence hierarchies in which research designs were positioned as superior to others. Notably, qualitative research has been described as producing evidence at the bottom of the evidence hierarchy. Unsurprisingly, we argued against this positioning and pointed to the useful and practically important nature of qualitative evidence. More particular to this book's focus, we highlighted how applied CA researchers may engage with these debates around evidence, noting that applied CA research is fundamentally focused on practice. To conclude, we offered an example of a body of CA research that has served to inform practice. In doing so, we sought to highlight the very real ways in which applied CA work might inform and, at times, change practice. We provide a summary of the key points from the chapter in the next box.

Learning Points From Chapter 10

- Evidence-based practice has resulted in an ongoing debate around what counts as evidence and how said evidence should and can be legitimately produced by researchers.

- Hierarchies of evidence have generally favored evidence produced via RCTs, with qualitative evidence sometimes inappropriately positioned at the bottom of the hierarchy.

- The best form of evidence for a problem is that which addresses the questions asked and the problem at hand. Sometimes this will be quantitative, and sometimes this will be qualitative.

- Applied CA research typically produces a certain kind of qualitative evidence that can be used to inform practice.

Recommended Readings

The literature around evidence-based practice and qualitative research has primarily been published in more general qualitative research literature rather than in relation to CA. Nonetheless, given that applied CA research studies are generally situated in relation to problems of practice, it is important to gain familiarity with scholarship, offering general considerations related to evidence and qualitative research. The following two publications are useful starting points.

- Lester, J. N., & O'Reilly, M. (2015). Is evidence-based practice a threat to the progress of the qualitative community? Arguments from the bottom of the pyramid. *Qualitative Inquiry, 21*(7), 628–632.

This article offers a contemporary read of the impact(s) of the evidence-based movement on the qualitative community. In it, we highlight the current and (potential) future challenges to the qualitative community. The article offers a brief and useful overview of the history of the movement and its impact while also pointing to potential responses by the qualitative community. It serves as a useful starting point for those new to the debates and arguments around evidence.

- Morse, J. M. (2006). Reconceptualizing qualitative evidence. *Qualitative Health Research, 16*(3), 415–422.

Morse's article provides an incisive call to qualitative researchers to examine how their work might be positioned against and within evidence-based perspectives. She highlights how evidence-based medicine and qualitative inquiry may have conflicting agendas. Morse argues that by attending to these differences, we can move closer to legitimating the value of varying perspectives. Indeed, this article is a useful starting point for engaging with the debates around evidence and qualitative research, particularly for those engaged in health-related research.

Disseminating Applied Conversation Analysis Research

Chapter Focus

In this chapter, you will learn how to:

- Recognize the reasons for disseminating an applied conversation analysis research study.

- Evaluate the ethical implications of dissemination.

- Describe the process of publishing in journals.

- Describe the process of preparing and defending a thesis or dissertation.

- Recognize what is involved in presenting at a conference.

- Evaluate the benefits of using the Internet for dissemination.

A central aspect of any academic endeavor is writing up and sharing your research. The process of sharing your work requires several important considerations, from who your primary audience is to your overall purpose in writing or presenting, among many other considerations. Your primary audience, for instance, may be (in the near term) the members of your thesis or dissertation committee, and/or may include scholars and/or practitioners in the wider community. Further, you may be at the earliest stages of your research study and thus presenting the first iteration of your work.

For example: You may be writing up a thesis or dissertation proposal, or, in contrast to this, you may be preparing a final iteration of a journal article you hope to submit for publication.

The focus of this chapter is on disseminating applied conversation analysis (CA) research as well as providing you with concrete suggestions for how to think about completing a thesis or dissertation. Thus, for some of you, there may be sections of this chapter that are less relevant to your current situation (e.g., you are well beyond the master's or dissertation defense/viva process). Thus, we encourage you to read selectively while noting that the broader discussion around dissemination is relevant to all readers regardless of their current position (e.g., master's student, PhD student, faculty member, practitioner, etc.).

As an applied CA researcher, you have many options available to you for presenting your findings, and while it is beyond the scope of this chapter to deal with all of them, we do consider the most common and most likely methods you will use. The chapter opens with some general information about dissemination. Additionally, before moving on to the more specific types or ways of disseminating, we examine some of the ethical implications of disseminating scholarship. More particularly, we recognize that many readers may be amid a master's or PhD program and therefore required to write a thesis/dissertation. Although all educational institutions have their own specific rules, we outline some general advice related to developing work for the purposes of a thesis/dissertation. Aligning with this, we also offer some practical advice for planning for a defense/viva. Beyond this, it may be the case that you elect to publish your work through more public channels, such as journal articles, conference presentations, or via the Internet or social media. Thus, we very briefly offer critical considerations related to publishing in journals, presenting at conferences, and disseminating research via the Internet and/or social media.

An Overview of Dissemination

Dissemination is an important part of any research project, and if you are undertaking an applied CA research study, there is a high probability that you will disseminate your work in some form or another.

Dissemination of your work refers to a process of identifying the core messages and communicating them to a targeted group(s). In so doing, it is important to demonstrate the main implications of those messages for that selected audience.

The targeted audiences for CA research can range from practice-based professionals to policy makers and commissioners to patients/service users/clients to key stakeholders to academic audiences (including other CA scholars), to name just a few. It can be easy to forget about dissemination during the process of collecting and analyzing your data, as it is quite common to become engrossed in the data. Nonetheless, disseminating your work is an important aspect of the research process. This is particularly true of applied CA work because of its inherent applied nature. Dissemination, however, is not as straightforward as one might assume; therefore, we suggest that it requires a detailed process of decision making and planning. Furthermore, dissemination is likely to require different types of output for varying audiences, and the way in which these variations are approached generally requires you to adapt and modify the way you communicate. Further, the norms and expectations around the dissemination of research is often specific to a given discipline, and thus we

BOX 11.1

ACTIVITY ON THE REASONS FOR DISSEMINATING APPLIED CA EVIDENCE

Activity

We would argue that applied CA research has a practical purpose because of its general focus on applied settings. It is useful to write a more specific list about your own research project and why it is important that audiences read about your work. Thus, using your research diary, take some time to write down some of the key reasons sharing your work with a broader audience matters. As you do so, consider the following questions:

- Who is my primary audience?

- What are the implications of my research findings?

- Considering the implications of my work, who are the people who might be most interested in learning about my research?

encourage you to become familiar with the norms of the discipline(s) you participate within and/or hope to contribute to.

Reasons to Disseminate

As you undertake an applied CA project, it is highly probable that your focus includes an area that has implications for practice. Furthermore, it is likely that practitioners and/or service users from practice-based settings (or participants like this) are part of your study. In that sense, therefore, your findings have potential for impact and might have important messages for those audiences, among others. In applied research, there is now an increased expectation that the work carried out is presented and published in a way that generates a wider reach (Cleary & Walter, 2004). We invite you to think about why this is the case with the activity in Box 11.1.

From writing your own list of reasons specific to your project, you should have some sense about why it matters that applied CA findings are consumed by a range of audiences. Some of these reasons relate to academic obligations, some relate to personal motivations, and some might relate more to the institutional environments that are linked to a given study. There are several general reasons for dissemination, and we present these in Table 11.1.

The Ethics of Disseminating Your Applied CA Research

When you begin making plans for disseminating your research, you should also consider carefully ethics surrounding any dissemination activity. Beyond the ethical

TABLE 11.1 ● Reasons for disseminating applied CA research

Reason	Description
To improve and increase knowledge and understanding of a subject area or issue	It is often the case that researchers disseminate their work to various audiences so that the knowledge base can be increased. In so doing, there is often the goal of promoting better judgments or better informed decisions in future practice. Applied CA research can contribute to the evidence base in a certain area of practice—and in so doing informs best practice.
Researchers have a responsibility to disseminate	Arguably, when carrying out research, researchers use resources, take participants' time, place a burden on the workload of ethics committees, and put in a great deal of personal effort to complete a project. Consequently, some would argue that researchers have a responsibility to disseminate what they find for the greater public good. This is often conceived of as including an ethical responsibility to share findings so that others can learn from a given study. This is the case whether the findings project a positive or negative message, as both types of findings tell wider audiences something important.
To raise awareness of the issue or topic, as well as the methodology	It is not unusual for researchers using CA as an approach to want to show how helpful it is to explain a social phenomenon by attending to the sequential detail of social interaction. By disseminating your work, it is possible for you to educate and explain the methodology as much as you do the substantive issues related to the topic you explored.
To influence policy and practice	Applied CA, as we have already noted, is especially interested in institutional applied settings (e.g., medical clinic). Thus, it is common for researchers using this approach to be motivated to produce findings that may help to improve practice or the delivery of services, as well as improve the knowledge of institutional practitioners. Most practice-based areas also have policies that influence thinking and decision making in those areas of practice, and with effort, it is possible that the key messages from your applied CA project could be included in current and future policy discussions.
To invite feedback and academic/practice responses	Your applied CA project focusing on a specific problem, area, or question will be just one of many that have examined an institutional setting or applied issue. In other words, there will be a community of academics and possibly practitioners who also do applied CA work in the general topic area related to your own; thus, by disseminating your work you invite interest and feedback from the broader scholarly community. In this way, dissemination can be used to generate dialogue. Similarly, dissemination can be used to promote collaboration and serve as a route for sharing knowledge and generating future research partnerships.
To promote transparency and quality assurance	By disseminating your findings, you are promoting transparency of your research processes. By disseminating your findings, other scholars can judge if the research is of an acceptable standard and if it has adhered to the quality parameters of CA research. Additionally, and perhaps most important, this allows you to reflect upon the status of your research study while also making explicit any potential conflicts of interest that may have arisen during your research process.
For personal motivation reasons	One of the reasons that you might disseminate your work is for self-promotion. In general, academics engage in research practices that often serve to further their careers. Disseminating your research may result in recognition and attention being given to you as a scholar. Further, disseminating your work either publicly (e.g., a conference presentation) or for the purposes of completing your PhD requirements (e.g., dissertation defense) can be quite rewarding and lead to a sense of self-satisfaction.

principles discussed earlier, there are some ethical issues specific to the process of disseminating your research findings that you should return to.

> *What this means:* It is your responsibility as a researcher to continue thinking about ethics, even when you write up your research findings and share them with various audiences. In other words, ethics is an ongoing process.

For the dissemination phase of your study, there are several things you should think about:

Do Not Waste Your Participants' Time

Collecting naturally occurring data often relies on the goodwill of participants and institutions to help you and/or give you access to institutional contexts. Of course, there are contexts that are publicly available and incur less effort on the part of participants, but quite often, multiple people must contribute their time for your data collection process to be successful. There is little point in using resources and participants' time if you are not going to share the findings beyond your own needs.

Protect the Participants' Identities

When you begin to publish your research, whether in the form of a thesis or dissertation, or in another format, there is always a risk that others may be able to identify participants if you do not take sufficient steps to safeguard their identities. There is a further risk that those who know the participants personally may recognize the anecdotes, stories, examples, or experiences that are familiar to them; thus, you must consider the risk of ***deductive disclosure***.

> **Deductive disclosure** refers to the possible identification of participants by people known to them as they recognize the features of the narratives spoken. In other words, those who know your participants may be able to deduce from the richness of your data who the person speaking was (Stein, 2010).

Declare Any Conflicts of Interest That You May Have

Most often, you will not have any conflict of interest. However, if it is the case that you do have a conflict of interest, it is important that you acknowledge this. The most obvious conflict of interest is a potential funding source, as some funders may have political or commercial interests, and some may actively try to prevent negative findings or negative messages about services from being published.

Be Transparent About Your Research Process

To be ethical, it is necessary that you are transparent in the dissemination process. In other words, when you are explaining your applied CA study to an audience, you should demonstrate what you did, what you found, and what you concluded. The analytic process of CA is grounded in the data, and it should be clear from your writing and/or speaking what analytic claims you are making and how they align with CA.

Your Findings Should Be Accessible to the Relevant Audience(s)

You have an ethical responsibility to assure that your applied work has a message for those who work in the related area of practice. There are many ways by which you increase the accessibility of your findings—for instance, perhaps writing a short report or conducting a workshop for relevant stakeholders. Importantly, you need to keep in mind that writing for audiences who have no specialized training in CA means that you need to think about how you demonstrate your findings. For instance, should you include all the detailed transcription symbols? How should you write and/ or speak about different aspects of the social interaction? In other words, should you use CA-related terminology (e.g., turn construction units)? Further, if you do decide to collect feedback from your participants (see Lester & Paulus, 2015, for an example), you need to think about how to share the key messages and invite meaningful critique and varying perspectives from your participants.

Completing Your Applied CA Thesis or Dissertation

Often, a researcher's earliest experience with dissemination is in the form of a thesis or dissertation, typically at undergraduate, master's, or PhD level. Quite often, the expectations of your program determine the structure and length of such a report. Yet generally, you can expect this kind of writing to be a large undertaking. You are likely to have to put considerable time into the project beyond the traditional working day. Nonetheless, this can be exciting and enjoyable as you learn new things from the data and make good progress with the project. We offer next several considerations for how you might approach the task of completing and ultimately writing your applied CA thesis or dissertation.

When considering how to approach your CA thesis/dissertation, it is important that you make a careful plan. You may only have 6 or 7 months for a small-scale undergraduate project but may have up to 6 years for a part-time PhD at some institutions. Regardless of the time frame you have, it can feel challenging, particularly if you have a large corpus of data, pages of transcription, mounds of analytic memos, etc. Indeed, you may feel overwhelmed and be unsure about how to begin your writing process. It is therefore important that you make a plan and break down the overall task into manageable chunks. Whether you have a self-set or externally determined deadline, it is important to establish clear writing goals and develop a defined time frame. We recommend consulting with your adviser/supervisor each step of the way, as he or she can give you invaluable guidance.

The way you develop your plan will need to reflect the way you work best. If you respond well to checklists, then write down several of these. Break up larger tasks into their respective parts and cross them off the list as you achieve them. If you are more of a visual person, perhaps you can create a brainstorm cloud and craft categorical tasks that originate from the central image/task. Of course, there are other ways to represent your goals, and we suggest that you simply find a way that works for you.

Writing a Thesis or Dissertation

Academic writing is very much about building an argument. Further, it generally brings with it a certain style—one which is directly related to your audience(s). Writing for academic audiences, which is typically the case when crafting a thesis/dissertation, certainly requires practice, time, and dedication. As such, writing up is not something that you should leave to the end of your studies. Rather, engaging in an applied CA study means that once you have your data, you should spend extensive time engrossed in analysis *and* simultaneously begin writing up sections of your thesis or dissertation. Further, drafting and redrafting, particularly after receiving feedback from your adviser/supervisor, is also a central part of the writing process. Thus, as you develop your plan, building in time for drafting and redrafting is essential.

> ① Remember that the educational institution and/or program where you are studying will have guidelines for how to format your thesis or dissertation.

More particularly, your thesis or dissertation will generally include specific sections, which we outline next in turn.

Title Page: It is important that your thesis has a title that makes explicit to a reader that your work is an applied CA project. Your title should be original, reflect your topic and approach, and be clearly stated. Generally, your title page displays the title of your thesis, lists your name, and the degree you are studying for. Your educational institution is likely to have a title page template.

Acknowledgments: It is probable that during your studies many people will provide support, ranging from your adviser/supervisor to your fellow graduate students to your family and friends to your study's participants to funders, among others. It is thus appropriate to have an acknowledgments page where you thank those people, even if some of this must be done anonymously (e.g., your study's participants).

Table of Contents: In a thesis or dissertation, you will likely have several chapters, and each chapter will have subsections. Therefore, as a rule, it is appropriate to include a contents page as well as a contents page for any tables and figures you include.

Abstract: Your abstract plays an important role, as it provides a summary of the project for the reader. This section tells your audience what you did, what you found, what you concluded, and the implications of the findings. In your abstract, you can demonstrate the value of using applied CA for the study of your chosen topic area and provide methodological details in this section.

Introduction: The introduction section generally introduces your thesis or dissertation, provides some context for the topic, provides general reasons for undertaking the study, and outlines the structure. It is here that you often include a problem statement and indicate the significance of your study (Kilbourn, 2006), generally in a relatively small number of words. Also, it is here that you should aim to include a narrative hook. In other words,

> ① Some software, such as Microsoft Word, can create a contents page for you.

!

For an applied CA project, you may also find it necessary to provide some historical accounts of CA and how CA studies have contributed to the understanding of your topic area.

write in a way that captures your readers' attention and highlights for them the importance of your work.

Literature Review: The literature review demonstrates where and how you position your study in relation to the larger literature base(s) (see Boote & Beile, 2005, for discussion). Thus, the literature review provides an important foundation for your overall argument and serves to point to the gap in knowledge. Within your literature review, it is important that you provide a critical appraisal of the relevant evidence, not simply a general summary.

Method: The method section is likely to attract attention from your committee members/outside examiners, as all your methodological choices should be described in detail. This section describes the approach and why it is valuable for addressing the kind of research question(s) you have posed. Further, you should describe your naturally occurring data sources, outline your recruitment process, offer a description of the research site and participants, and describe your analysis process. You should also discuss any ethical issues that were relevant to the study and the ways in which you assured that you produced a quality study.

Analysis/Findings: A particularly crucial part is the discussion of your findings. Quite often, this is written in the form of multiple chapters, particularly for PhD-level dissertations. The structure across and within the findings chapter is important, as you need to demonstrate an analytic argument. For CA, you need to provide detail and depth, offering essentially a line-by-line analysis of representative extracts. Indeed, for an applied CA study, presenting your findings in this way illustrates your commitment to transparently reporting your interpretative process and grounding your claims in the data themselves.

Discussion and Implications: The discussion section provides a contextualization of your findings and places them in relation to the literature you cited in your literature review. Your discussion is likely to start with a clear summary of the findings and will broadly conceptualize the salient issues at stake for the topic area. Further, you should consider the wider implications and applications of your work. Given that applied CA studies often have direct implications for practice, it is a good idea to highlight the implications for practice when relevant. Indeed, you may also discuss the general value of applied CA in addressing certain types of research problems, while acknowledging the possible limitations as well. As applied CA is a qualitative approach, it will also be necessary to include a section on researcher reflexivity to reflect on the role you played in the process. A strong conclusion that summarizes the core arguments should finalize this section.

References: A great deal of literature will be cited, and thus it is essential that you provide a clear listing of your references. These should conform to the guidelines set by your educational institution and often entail using a certain style (e.g., Harvard, American Psychological Association, etc.).

Appendices: It is likely that you will have several documents that need to be referred to in your thesis or dissertation. All the additional documents that you cite within the main text can be given an identifier (either a number or letter) so that they can be easily located as an appendix. Organize these carefully in the back of the thesis and check the guidelines to see if they are included in your word count. There are a range of appendices you may choose to include.

> For example: You may include a blank copy of your consent form, a copy of the information sheet you gave to your participants, a copy of the letter confirming approval from your ethics committee, a copy of the letter of invitation, and any other useful information.

Producing the Final Version

Once you have written each chapter, produced several drafts, and attended to constructive feedback, it will be important to generate the final version. It will be important to reread your institution's guidelines to make sure you have complied with their regulations but also to get some information about the submission process. It is probable that you will be required to submit a copy electronically, but you may also have to get a copy bound to submit in print. Further, many institutions ask you to submit your final version only after your defense/viva. Regardless of the specific process, it is generally important to

- proofread your thesis and check for errors,
- include line numbers on the extracts of data,
- assure that you have appropriate headings throughout,
- be consistent in your formatting, and
- abide by the formatting regulations set by your institution.

The structure of your work is important, and we recommend you undertake the activity in Box 11.2 and reflect on how you will do this. Finally, as you prepare your final version, it is critical to assure that you have no instances of plagiarism. Your examiners will certainly be mindful of this, as they will be experts in the field and thus likely to notice if you have copied the work of others. Furthermore, the electronic copy of your thesis or dissertation may be run through antiplagiarism software upon submission. And perhaps most important, the aim of writing and disseminating your work is to foreground what you learned—in your words! It is therefore crucial that you credit the sources that you cite and reference them appropriately. Be under no illusion: Plagiarism is not accepted in educational institutions, and the consequences of copying the work of others and trying to take credit for it is considered a serious academic offense.

Preparing for Your Defense/Viva

Defending your work can be challenging, and undertaking an applied CA PhD will mean that you need to consider the decisions you have made and be well prepared. Quite often, the final step is the defense/viva. This process does not look the same across academic institutions, disciplines, or geographies. For instance, in some U.S.-based institutions, individuals (1) defend a proposal, (2) carry out their study, (3) submit

BOX 11.2

ACTIVITY ON THESIS AND DISSERTATION FORMATS

Activity

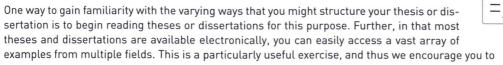

One way to gain familiarity with the varying ways that you might structure your thesis or dissertation is to begin reading theses or dissertations for this purpose. Further, in that most theses and dissertations are available electronically, you can easily access a vast array of examples from multiple fields. This is a particularly useful exercise, and thus we encourage you to

- search for recently published CA theses or dissertations;

- read the identified CA theses or dissertations;

- focus as you read on how the argument was structured and note what information was included; and

- develop a document that lists key structural features you noted that you would like to incorporate in your approach for structuring your thesis or dissertation.

their final version to their committee members, and (4) orally defend their work. This oral defense typically takes place with three to five committee members and may or may not be closed to the public. In some institutions, there are also external examiners who review the final piece. For defenses, it is common for PhD candidates to give a brief presentation about their work and then begin fielding questions from the committee members. At some institutions, the norm is that after presenting and fielding questions, PhD candidates are asked to leave the room so that committee members privately converse related to the status of the dissertation. After conversing, PhD candidates are invited back into the room where they are told whether they passed or failed the oral defense as well as what revisions must be made to their dissertation.

Notably, this process varies significantly from one institution to another and one country to another. For example, in the United Kingdom there is some variation in the processes by which students are tracked throughout their studies but commonly undertake a viva at the end of the process. For some students doing a professional practice-based doctorate, the viva will be slightly different as the focus will be on the area of practice to which the doctoral thesis relates. For a PhD, it is usual for the student to be tracked through the process by the supervisory team (usually two supervisors) and by the university where he or she is registered, and that may require annual reports or panels of experts to comment as the student proceeds. The viva itself typically involves an examiner internal to the institution and an external examiner from an outside university. Typically, this verbal defense and the decisions made throughout the project will continue for approximately 2 hours but may be as short as 90 minutes or as long as $3^1/_2$ hours. This is not intended to be an interrogation but an intellectual and critical discussion of the research project whereby the student defends his or her work. The decision regarding whether the student has passed outright or requires minor or major revisions (or has failed to convince the examiners of the quality of the work) will be deliberated while the student is sent out of the examining room and delivered when called back in. United Kingdom universities usually have clear regulations that examiners must follow in conducting the viva and in the paperwork that has to be completed.

Regardless of the nature of your defense/viva, it is important to be well prepared. More specifically, we suggest you keep the following ideas in mind as you prepare:

- Reread your full thesis or dissertation a few days prior to your defense/viva date. It is a good idea to have a break from it after you have submitted your work and come back to look at it fresh near your viva date.

- Do a practice defense/viva with colleagues and/or peers in which you field questions and (if relevant to your process) give a short presentation.

- In some cases, your adviser/supervisor will be willing to offer feedback on your presentation, and you should take advantage of this opportunity.

- If you have been asked to prepare a short presentation, keep in mind that CA studies emphasize doing analysis rather than just talking about it. Thus, it will be important to think about how you might selectively show excerpts from your data and then show your interpretation of them.

- If you were required to complete a thesis or dissertation proposal defense, be sure to review the feedback you received. If you have been involved in a process whereby your studies were tracked by your supervisors or expert panels, use the feedback from those to make sure you can answer key questions about your project. Your committee members will expect that you have addressed their earlier concerns and considered their suggestions when carrying out your thesis or dissertation study.

- In some institutions and/or disciplines, thesis and dissertation defenses are open to the public, and this is common in some European countries as well as in the United States. If this is the case in your situation, it is helpful to observe as many of these events as possible, as it gives you a sense of the process and common expectations. In those cases where public viewing is not an option, we encourage you to speak with colleagues who have recently completed the process. They will likely have valuable advice to offer.

- Talk to your supervisors, as they will be able to offer you some reassurances.

Working With Your Adviser/Supervisor

Throughout the process of carrying out a study, you will likely work rather closely with an adviser/supervisor. In some cases, this individual may be referred to as the *chair* and/or *director* of your dissertation. Your relationship with your adviser/supervisor will be central to the progress you make, and thus it is important to establish and build this relationship early on. It may be the case that you select your adviser/supervisor by approaching someone directly. In such cases, it is critical that this person has expertise in applied CA and (preferably) your chosen topic if he or she is to provide you with the skills you need. There are several things you should bear in mind about the supervisory relationship, and these include:

- Advisers/supervisors should encourage students to be innovative, and should be patient and flexible in their approach (Magnuson, Wilcoxon, & Norem, 2000). Equally, it will be important for you to be patient with your adviser/supervisor and express your creativity so that he or she is aware of your thoughts.

- Advisers/supervisors should give you frequent feedback on your performance and progress (Abiddin, Hassan, & Ahmad, 2009).

- Remember that you are an independent learner, and it is not the job of your advisers/supervisors to give you all the solutions or to do the work for you (Thompson, Kirkman, Watson, & Stewart, 2005).

- You and your adviser/supervisor should establish boundaries early on in your relationship so that you both know what your expectations are and how they can be met (Magnuson et al., 2000).

- Advisers/supervisors need to recognize the needs of their students (Magnuson et al., 2000), but students may have to help them to see what their needs are. Thus, being open and honest about current needs and expectations is critical.

(!) **Your supervisor will do his or her best to support you and facilitate your skills, comment on your work, guide your analysis, and generally be there for you. However, the overall responsibility for your research rests with you (Abiddin et al., 2009).**

As a student, there are several things you need to think about to facilitate your relationship and help you develop your research skills. Although written in the context of research with children, O'Reilly, Ronzoni, and Dogra (2013) outlined some practical tips for good supervision, and we outline these in Table 11.2.

Writing for Journal Publication

One of the especially desirable ways of disseminating your work is through publications in recognized academic and practice-based journals in the form of a **journal article** (sometimes referred to as *academic papers*). In Chapter 3 we listed a range of journals that actively publish applied CA studies.

Journal articles are typically a short report focused on a certain area published in a specialist journal. Journals are publications that specialize in a subject area and/or methodological approach(es) and often contain editorials, journal articles, and book reviews. Such publication outlets tend to be published regularly and thus are designed to give up-to-date information.

Writing for publication in journals is a good way of making your research accessible to academic and practitioner audiences. For the most part, journal publications are generally considered by academics to be a credible and an important way of sharing empirical research.

An **impact factor** is the marker assigned to journals based on the number of citations that are generated from it.

It is important to note that journals tend to be ranked, with this ranking (or even perceived ranking) based on their ***impact factor.***

TABLE 11.2 ● Practical hints for good advising/supervision	
Practical Hint	**Description**
Before advising/supervising, think of your questions.	Before you attend your meeting with your adviser/supervisor, write down all the questions you want to ask. You may write these down over the course of time as you work through a specific problem.
Develop an agenda and e-mail this ahead of your meeting.	It can be helpful to prepare an agenda prior to meeting with your adviser/supervisor. Talk to your adviser/supervisor early on about this, and if both of you agree, then it can be helpful to e-mail an agenda to him or her a few days prior to a scheduled meeting so that you are both clear about what needs to be discussed.
Be mindful of your supervisor's/mentor's time.	Remember that your supervisor/mentor will be busy like you and is likely to have several students needing his or her attention. It is important when you do have time together that you prioritize what needs to be attended to and what can wait for a later time. Also, bear in mind that your adviser/supervisor will have a large workload, so if you submit something for feedback on a Friday evening, it is not likely that you will get feedback on Monday morning. It is important to set up expectations, even around how much time is needed to provide feedback.
Keep notes from all meetings with your adviser/supervisor.	Throughout the course of your thesis or dissertation study, you will have multiple meetings with your adviser/supervisor. It is important that you keep notes on these meetings and perhaps even maintain them in an electronic folder that both you and your adviser/supervisor can access. Some institutions have a specific template for generating supervision notes while others do not. Regardless, be sure to gain familiarity with the norms and expectations of your institution and discipline.
Keep to the boundaries of the supervision.	It is helpful to be clear regarding the boundaries of supervision from the beginning. Your institution may have a code of practice that you should follow. However, your institution may not have such a code. Regardless, you should be thoughtful about maintaining the boundaries that surround an adviser/supervisor relationship. For instance, if you have personal problems that are affecting your research, it may be helpful to seek outside advice and support, recognizing that many academic institutions have counseling centers.

Source: O'Reilly et al., 2013.

However, be mindful that this does not necessarily reflect how widely read a given journal is by practitioners, and some lower-ranking journals may be more commonly accessed by practitioners in comparison to those with higher ratings.

The impact factor of journals is used by institutions to measure the level of impact that work has in the wider sphere. This is the measure of frequency with which the average article has been cited in a certain year and determines the contribution of that journal in a specific field. As a measure of impact, however, there have been some concerns about using impact factors as a judgment on research. This is because impact factors are based only on quantitative information based on the number of citations of a journal, which fails to account for the other ways in which research is shared. Furthermore, scholars do not have to publish their work in journals for it to be influential, as sometimes people can be influenced in other ways.

If you are new to publishing in journals, it can feel quite challenging to even contemplate writing a journal article let alone submitting it for external review. It is therefore often useful to acquire help from more experienced scholars. There are also several decisions you will need to make when planning to publish your work, including:

- *Choosing the most appropriate journal:* It is important that you assure that the aims and objectives of a journal are relevant to your work. You can often acquire a sense of this by reviewing the details of a journal posted on the journal website. Quite frequently, editors do a "desk reject" without sending a submission out to review if they feel that the work does not match their aims. In the case of an applied CA study, you first want to assure that a journal publishes qualitative research. However, sometimes taking a risk and submitting a manuscript to a journal that does not typically publish CA research may result in an acceptance and the emergence of a new conversation within a certain discipline. Indeed, this has been our experience in autism research (see O'Reilly, Lester, & Muskett, 2016, for an example).

- *Read the author guidelines very carefully:* Journals will have a clear set of author guidelines that outline very specifically how to prepare your work in line with their expectations. These will be clear guidelines about what should be included in your manuscript, from the title page to the number of words within your abstract to the nature of the headings to the total word count, etc.

- *Formatting:* It is important that you format your work in the way that is expected by the journal. Journals vary considerably in their requirements and have their own formatting styles. They tend to be very specific about how they want the article to look.

- *Audience:* You need to think about who you are writing for. If you are submitting your work to a journal that is designed for conversation analysts, you will not need to do as much explaining about the associated terms you are using. However, if you are writing for practitioners or more general qualitative research audiences, some of the concepts of CA will need to be well explained and possibly simplified.

- *Read papers from the journal:* One of the best ways to help you write your journal article is to read papers that have already been published in that journal.

(!) Be mindful that some open access journals (and a small number of other journals) charge a fee to publish your work.

Once you have made the decision about which journal you are aiming for and you are familiar with the journal guidelines and aims, you must write your article (if you have not already begun to do so). As we noted earlier, we suggest that you work with a more experienced scholar, perhaps even collaborating to generate a journal article. Throughout the writing process, there are some practical tips to consider, some of which we consider next.

Start Writing

While it may seem like an obvious thing for us to state, it is important to get started. It can be easy to allow anxiety, doubts, and procrastination to prevent you from beginning your writing process. Nonetheless, you will be very familiar with your data by the time you plan to publish them; you should have spent many hours listening to the recordings or reading the text and have a quality Jefferson transcript to work with. It is therefore necessary to develop a specific idea for your first article and, once you have your idea, start writing your paper (Bourne, 2005).

Take Your Time

When you start planning, it is important that you take your time and plan it out carefully in terms of the key messages and structure. When making your writing plans, try to take small incremental steps to reduce the chance of becoming overwhelmed (Cleary & Walter, 2004). Further, it is helpful to keep in mind that with interactional data sets, such as you will have within your applied CA study, it is common to generate multiple articles. Thus, as you develop your first article, be thoughtful about not trying to accomplish too much within the confines of one article.

Decide On the Authorship Order

If you are working collaboratively, establish the order of authorship at the start of your project. Keep in mind that just because the project or data set is your project does not automatically mean that you will be the first author on a paper. This decision relates to who does the *most* work; who leads the paper; who develops the ideas; and who does the formatting, editing, and tidying of the final version. It is essential to decide the order of authors before much work is undertaken, as you want to avoid misunderstandings.

Think About Your Language

It is important that you write your article in a clear and accessible way (Cunningham, 2004). There are different ways in which you need to be mindful of your language. First, you need to be careful that you do not have spelling or grammatical errors. Second, be mindful not to use language that may be conceived of as sexist, racist, ableist, or ageist (or any other discriminatory style). Third, avoid using technical jargon, particularly when writing for audiences less familiar with CA. It can be challenging to maintain the robustness of the approach while simplifying the language for unfamiliar audiences (of course this is not necessary for CA-specific audiences).

There Is Often a Word Limit

All journals specify the maximum number of words that an article can be. Sometimes these word counts include the abstract, references, and tables, and sometimes these are excluded from the final count. Journals that are designed specifically for qualitative research, including those that specialize in CA-related methods, tend to have higher word counts than those that are more general.

The Review Process

After submitting your article to a journal, the editor will determine whether it is an appropriate topic and method for the journal. If your article passes this initial editorial review, the editor will then send it out for peer review, typically inviting two or three reviewers to engage in a blind review of your article.

> *What this means:* This means that there will be a delay from when you submit your work to when you receive a final decision. It takes time for editors of journals to collect feedback from multiple reviewers and to convey this feedback to you, as well as offer their final decision (e.g., revise and resubmit, reject, etc.).

Craswell (2005) prepared a list of questions that reviewers generally ask when reviewing an article, and although these are not specific to applied CA research, they are quite useful to think about. Craswell argued that reviewers will

- assess the abstract to ensure it is informative and concise,
- check that the article is congruent with the aims of the journal,
- check to see if your article contributes innovative insights,
- assess the clarity of the aims and objectives of your article,
- identify whether quality indicators of the methodological approach have been pursued and are evident within your article,
- determine whether your findings have been transparently and coherently presented,
- check whether references are accurately used,
- complete an overall assessment of whether the article is well written and coherently presented, and
- assess the main strengths and weaknesses of your article.

It is not uncommon for articles to get rejected, and even senior scholars experience this. It is important not to take a rejection personally. If you pursue a career that requires you to publish, it is likely that you will face many rejections, particularly if you are aiming to introduce CA to a discipline that is less familiar with it. There are many reasons for rejection, and Greenhalgh (1997) outlined some of these as being:

- Lack of originality of the article
- Failure to address an important issue
- Inappropriate methodology for the question

- Inappropriate procedure or transparency in the methodology

- Poorly written or constructed article

Other reasons may relate to editors feeling that the article does not fit well with the aims of the journal (even if it is well written). If your article is rejected, we suggest that you use the rejection as information and continue moving forward with your project. For instance, if your article has been rejected from one journal, you can use the feedback generated from the reviewers to improve the article and subsequently submit it elsewhere.

Presenting at Conferences

A common way of disseminating research findings is presenting at conferences, and often, students are encouraged to participate in conferences. While there are some CA-specific conferences (e.g., the International Conference of Conversation Analysis) as well as language-oriented conferences (e.g., National Communications Association), many scholars present their work at substantively focused, topic-specific, or discipline-specific conferences (e.g., annual meeting of the American Education Research Association, British Psychological Society conference). Regardless of where you present your work, conference presentations often serve to further develop your ideas, raise critical issues related to your study, and expand who engages with the findings of your research.

Depending upon the nature of your applied CA study, you may decide to present at conferences to introduce your findings to certain audiences. Alternatively, you may seek to present at a conference to garner critical feedback on your study's design and findings. Thus, an important early consideration related to presenting at conferences is (1) the purpose and scope of a certain conference and (2) primary audience(s). Once you decide to present at a conference, you typically must prepare a conference abstract, with your submitted proposal often being reviewed by peer reviewers. If accepted, you are often assigned to present a paper and/or poster, with some conferences also designed to facilitate panels or symposiums, workshops, and even data sessions. Furthermore, some conferences have sessions especially for those new to a method, and it can be useful to attend these rather than aiming to present at them. Like developing a journal article for a publication outlet, prior to developing your proposal and final conference presentation, you should become familiar with the norms and expectations of the selected conference.

For those readers who are new to applied CA research, we strongly recommend participating in CA-specific conferences as well as those that may have a high number of CA-related presentations, as this is one way to generate familiarity with the norms of presenting a CA study and develop a network of colleagues engaged in work methodologically like your own.

For example: The authors presented together at the last large international CA conference with over 450 delegates attending. O'Reilly and Lester (2014) presented at a symposium looking specifically at epistemic rights of children in mental health settings. This conference attracted mostly academic scholars who undertook CA work in a wide range of different disciplines and topic areas. This was a useful event for hearing about CA work and engaging with other interested people.

- O'Reilly, M., & Lester, J. (2014, June). Epistemic claims to psychiatric matters in child mental health settings: Children's claims to knowledge regarding their mental health experiences and professionals' renegotiation of the problem. In T. Stivers (Chair), *Symposium: Knowledge management in institutional interaction.* Symposium conducted at the International Society for Conversation Analysis Fourth Annual Conference, Los Angeles, California.

Remember that there are some conferences that are designed for postgraduate students or have a strand of the conference specifically for students, and this can be a useful starting point for you if you have not presented before. Further, given that applied CA research may be aimed at directly impacting practice, it is helpful to pursue presenting research at conferences that draw a broad audience of practitioners—those working in the field you are interested in. Presenting at such venues serves to disseminate your research findings to those you likely hoped to target at the start of your project as well as provide you with important insights related to how to make your work more accessible to broader audiences.

> For example: Recently O'Reilly (second author) and Karim (2016) presented a paper about child mental health assessments at a local United Kingdom conference designed for child mental health practitioners. This was a small-scale conference especially designed to target practical recommendations from research evidence for those working in child mental health professions. The paper focused on questions asked in assessments, and using CA (with an accessible vocabulary), O'Reilly demonstrated some of the lessons learned about asking children questions.

- O'Reilly, M., & Karim, K. (2016, July). *An investigation of the reality of clinical assessments with children and families: Question design and child-centered practices.* Paper presented at Children and Young People's Mental Health Conference, Northampton, England.

Using the Internet and Social Media for Dissemination

Alongside the emergence of new technologies has come the possibility for disseminating your research to broader audiences via the Internet (e.g., websites) and social media platforms (e.g., Twitter). Indeed, there is a growing body of literature around the importance of crafting your online academic identity (e.g., Paulus, Lester, & Dempster, 2014), becoming networked scholars (e.g., Paulus & Lester, 2017), and moving beyond the confines of academic publication outlets and conferences (Vannini, 2012). Indeed, it can be very useful for you to publicize your research through blogs, Twitter, or other digital channels. Some scholars have argued that the move toward digital scholarship serves to "enhance the impact and reach of scholarship," as well as results in "more equitable, effective, efficient, and transparent scholarly and educational processes" (Veletsianos & Kimmons, 2012, p. 166). Certainly, academics use social media for varying reasons, with such use often resulting in increased visibility for scholars and their work, and the generation of new scholarly networks across shared personal and professional interests (Stewart, 2015). Scholars have noted, however, that leveraging technologies requires academics to reenvision the very nature of engaging in scholarly practice (Esposito, 2013). Indeed, the norms of academia include a merit system built around the expectation of disseminating research in traditional ways (e.g., journal publications). Yet as Vannini (2012) and others have noted, the privileging of such traditional dissemination outlets has resulted in most research being inaccessible to the broader populace.

For an applied CA study, we see great value in leveraging the affordances of technologies to increase the reach of your research. From developing a website that highlights core messages drawn from your research findings to sharing newly published articles or upcoming presentations via Twitter, there are myriad ways in which you might expand who engages with your research and how. There are many contemporary examples of CA scholars using such technologies to share their work with broader audiences. For instance, Kimmo Svinhufvud, Chloé Mondémé, and Charlotte Lundgren are leading an applied CA study focused on social interaction used in equine-assisted therapy, or horse-assisted therapy. As part of their project, they maintain a website, Moving With Horses: Resources for Social Interaction in Equine-Assisted Therapy (see http://moving withhorses.org), which provides key findings and resources relevant to practitioners. As another example, a relatively robust number of applied CA scholars maintain active Twitter accounts in which upcoming training, talks, recent publications, and even critical dialogue about research are shared (e.g., @rolsi_journal and @LizStokoe).

An Interview With Dr. Amber Warren

In this chapter, we have noted the varying ways in which you may go about disseminating your work. Indeed, for those who are graduate students, a significant aspect of this process involves writing a thesis or dissertation, which brings with it all the norms and expectations common to an institution, program, and even adviser/supervisor. As time passes, the feelings of walking into a defense/viva and/or crafting a thesis or dissertation become distant. Thus, we invited Dr. Amber Warren to share her experiences, as she recently completed and defended her PhD dissertation. Her responses are shown in Box 11.3.

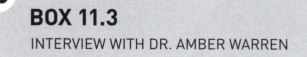

BOX 11.3
INTERVIEW WITH DR. AMBER WARREN

Amber Warren is an assistant professor of teacher education for teaching English language learners at the University of Nevada, Reno, United States. Dr. Warren has an emerging line of research focused on the study of online education talk. In the summer of 2016, she completed and successfully defended her dissertation:

(Continued)

(Continued)

- Warren, A. (2016). *Respecifying teacher beliefs in second language teacher education: A discursive psychology approach to analysis* (Unpublished dissertation). Indiana University, Bloomington, IN.

We asked Dr. Warren three questions about her experiences carrying out a CA study for her dissertation research.

What are some practical suggestions for how to craft a dissertation proposal that draws upon CA?

"While CA's methodology is common in some fields (e.g., second language acquisition), scholars from adjacent fields may be less familiar with it. For my proposal, I found it important to carefully articulate the theoretical and methodological grounding of CA in relation to other language-oriented approaches, like discourse analysis, to demonstrate what CA was bringing to the table. Depending on how the dissertation proposal process is set up at your institution, it may be necessary to plan for changes to the focus of the dissertation as you become more enmeshed in the data: The process of unmotivated looking may send you in unexpected directions. Therefore, it is important to find out about this process at your institution and to discuss plans for this with your chair and in the dissertation proposal defense."

What aspects of your dissertation did you find to be most challenging?

"Writing a dissertation is a profoundly individualized experience. I can't be sure that the parts I found challenging would be challenging for others. However, I will say that I found it extremely important to have colleagues both familiar and unfamiliar with CA methodology read parts of my findings at various stages. Readers familiar with CA helped me think through the line-by-line analysis, while colleagues from other research backgrounds helped me to ensure that my findings were readable to an audience not already familiar with CA. Applied CA also assisted me in thinking about how my findings could be translated into useful recommendations for my audience."

What are some key considerations for preparing for a CA dissertation defense?

"Of course, all the standard advice for preparing a dissertation defense applies here too. Read the dissertation and refamiliarize yourself with parts you may not have visited in a while. The presentation is generally not the time to think about presenting your data in a new way, so be careful that the language used in the defense matches that of the dissertation. Thinking about how to best present findings is an important consideration. For example, do I include extracts? How do I introduce them? How much of CA's methodology do I need to explain or justify in the defense? In answering these questions for yourself, think carefully about perspectives in CA as well as the perspectives of your committee members."

Chapter Summary

In this chapter, we introduced you to the importance of disseminating your research and the varying ways by which you might do so. We highlighted how there are various purposes of dissemination yet noted that regardless of your purpose, it is a critical part of engaging in applied CA research. We also noted that writing and presenting a thesis or dissertation is a common aspect of dissemination. Recognizing that this process brings with it norms and expectations, we discussed some of the key considerations related to carrying out and defending a thesis and/or dissertation. Further, we described the process of publishing in a peer-reviewed journal and presenting at conferences. Finally, given the rise of emergent technologies and the increasing attention being given to their role in public scholarship, we briefly noted how applied CA research may be disseminated via the Internet and various social media platforms. We summarize the key learning points from the chapter in the next box.

Learning Points From Chapter 11

- Dissemination of research findings is a central aspect of completing applied CA research.

- There are varying purposes for disseminating research findings.

- Dissemination may involve completing and defending a thesis or dissertation, writing for and publishing within a journal publication outlet, presenting at a conference, and sharing research on the Internet or a social media platform, among other possibilities.

Recommended Readings

There are several articles that are useful for thinking further about the writing process. While the readings we note next are not specific to applied CA research, they do offer insights that are useful across methodological perspectives. Thus, we encourage you to explore the three publications described, particularly as you further develop skills related to disseminating applied CA research.

- Bourne, P. (2005). Ten simple rules for getting published. *PLoS Computational Biology, 1*(5). Retrieved from https://doi .org/10.1371/journal.pcbi.0010057

This is a relatively short and simple journal article that outlines a list of 10 simple tips for getting your work published. It is a useful starting point to consider when you are first planning your journal article.

- Craswell, J. (2005). *Writing for academic success: A postgraduate guide.* London, England: Sage.

This is a useful book that will help guide you through the dissemination of your thesis and/or dissertation. It is a practical book with hints and tips on how to approach the writing process, and it offers tips on academic writing skills. Within this book, Craswell covers a range of topics, including time-management strategies and preparing for an exam. The book includes case studies and activities, and is suitable for those who are writing a thesis or dissertation across a range of disciplines.

(Continued)

(Continued)

- Murray, R. (2006). *How to write a thesis* (2nd ed.). Berkshire, England: Open University Press.

This book focuses specifically on the production of a thesis (PhD level), and the author offers practical advice and tips for how to approach this task. Murray includes summaries and checklists as a way of helping students to stay on track and make sufficient progress. Different types of writing are presented in the book, as well as strategies for dealing with writer's block and procrastination.

12

Considering Empirical Examples of Applied Conversation Analysis Research and Future Directions

Throughout the book, we have provided you with practical ideas and tools for carrying out an applied conversation analysis (CA) study in a theoretically and methodologically grounded way. Notably, we have emphasized the importance of being reflexive and ethical while attending carefully to how you might go about generating a quality applied CA research study. To illustrate these points, we have provided you with examples and definitions to explicate core concepts and processes in this type of research. Although we have separated out the main steps and procedures of carrying out an applied CA research study, we encourage you to view an applied CA research study in a holistic way. Indeed, engaging in applied CA research is iterative, cyclical, and generally nonlinear.

Thus, to illustrate this further, the first portion of this chapter is devoted to providing four empirical examples. By drawing upon a range of research examples, we aim to demonstrate the versatility and flexibility of applied CA research, particularly when applied in a range of institutional settings. Unlike the previous chapters in this book, we do not end the chapter with a single interview; rather, we weave throughout four interviews with the primary scholars whose work we offer as useful examples of applied CA research. Second, we point to some of the future directions that we envision for those interested in pursuing applied CA research. We conclude the chapter by offering an abbreviated summary of the book and drawing some final conclusions.

Examples From Applied Fields

To broaden your understanding of the varied ways in which researchers conceptualize and carry out applied CA research, we provide four examples from the literature. These four examples demonstrate how findings from applied CA research contribute in different ways to the qualitative evidence base and more generally inform disciplinary practice.

An Example From Media Research

Talk and text in traditional media, such as television, newspapers, and radio, provide an interesting source of naturally occurring data. There has been a range of applied CA studies examining different media, and Professor Ian Hutchby has published several articles examining talk on the radio. In doing so, he examined a range of social interactions, including political interviews and phone-in chats invited by radio hosts. In an analysis exploring the argumentative interaction in *hybrid political interviews*, Hutchby (2011) reported on how nonneutrality is sequentially achieved when the speech exchange system shifts into the aggravated opposition characteristic of a political interview.

A **hybrid political interview** is a genre of interview talk whereby the radio talk positions the radio speaker not neutrally but as a sociopolitical advocate.

Data from the project were taken from news interviews broadcast on a U.S. show where major political candidates (including Barack Obama) gave extended interviews with the host. The focus of analysis was to explore whether the hybrid political interview had distinctive discursive features and revealed the ways in which nonneutrality was achieved in different ways. Hutchby examined what was said as well as the way it was said to do this. He noted there were shifts in the talk from interview to argument frames involving the use of third-position rejoinders, contrast structures, and personalization through stance taking (please refer to the paper for details).

In other radio-based CA work, Hutchby (2001) investigated radio talk shows whereby members of the public could phone in to the show. In so doing, Hutchby explored the discursive devices employed to legitimate or authenticate opinion about the news. Specifically, the analysis focused on examples identified where there was an orientation to the importance of *witnessing*, defined as claims to firsthand knowledge, as a way of legitimizing the claims made about the news. Hutchby noted that witnessing refers to a range of actions related to claims to personal experience or knowledge, direct perceptual access, or categorical membership. By examining the sequential nature of the interaction, Hutchby demonstrated how firsthand knowledge could function to legitimate the status of a caller's contribution but also undermine it at times.

> *What this means:* Speakers use discursive devices to formulate a version of events that they present as credible or at least as hearable to an audience as credible.

Hutchby argued that such witnessing can involve claims to firsthand knowledge or can involve the mobilization of collective experience.

> For example: Hutchby (2001) examined when firsthand knowledge was invoked as a form of witnessing and how this authenticated the claim, and also when categories were drawn upon to demonstrate a collective experience. Consider the following two data examples quoted directly from page 486 of the article.

> Example 1:
>
> Caller: One day **I actually saw** a lady owner allow her dog to do
>
>   its business right in the middle of my gateway.
>
> Example 2:
>
> Caller: **I'm a pensioner** myself of seventy two

Hutchby noted that such devices are a form of legitimation for a contribution to the show debate. He argued that the witnessing claim is produced within a sequential context, and this interaction is important. This is a way of introducing the firsthand knowledge of the event and demonstrates relevance to the topic in hand. He noted that in this type of interaction, the callers participate as lay speakers on the radio show who are calling into the show to contribute to an existing institutional setup.

To gain a sense of how Hutchby analyzed his data and grounded his claims, we recommend that you read:

1. Hutchby, I. (2011). Non-neutrality and argument in the hybrid political interview. *Discourse Studies*, *13*(3), 349–366.

2. Hutchby, I. (2001). "Witnessing": The use of first-hand knowledge in legitimating lay opinions on talk radio. *Discourse Studies*, *3*(4), 481–497.

To facilitate your study of Hutchby's scholarship in this area, we interviewed him to learn more about the process that informed the development of his research around media talk. His responses can be seen in Box 12.1.

BOX 12.1
INTERVIEW WITH PROFESSOR IAN HUTCHBY

Ian Hutchby is professor of applied linguistics at the University of Leicester. Professor Hutchby has published widely using CA and is interested in topics including media, technology, and health communication.

What motivated you to examine radio talk?

"When I first encountered conversation analysis in the late 1980s, I had really been developing my ideas as a political sociologist. Political sociology is concerned, among other things, with studying debate, persuasion, and the construction of competing versions of reality, and I initially wanted to use CA to analyze these things in detail. But then I became more interested in the wider question of how people go about having arguments, not just about politics but about anything. I was faced with the problem of how to reliably gather naturally occurring data containing arguments. I wanted quite a lot of arguments, not just the odd one that might crop up around a dinner table. This was in the early days of the "shock jock" talk radio phenomenon, and there were numerous British talk radio hosts who were noted for the aggressive and argumentative style of their programs. It just struck me that this would be a place where I could be pretty sure of recording a collection of arguments to work on. As in a lot of research projects, therefore, serendipity played a significant part."

What kind of planning did you undertake before you started?

"It was very basic. The show I chose to record was broadcast daily, so I went out and bought a little bit of technology you could get in those days, which combined a radio and a cassette tape recorder, some tapes, and marked on my calendar a random set of days over about 3 months when I would record the show. My reasoning was that this method would pass the so-called dead social scientist test; that is, what appeared on the tape would have taken place in the way that it did whether I recorded it or not."

How did you analyze the data?

"Initially, I had wanted to collect this data to analyze the construction of arguments. That's to say, the context (a talk radio show) was not going to be a major factor in the same way as the telephone was often not considered a major factor in early conversation analytic work using data from telephone conversations. But once I began working on the transcription, it quickly became clear that this was not the best way forward. Certainly, as I'd hoped, the conversations between callers and hosts contained arguments; but the arguments themselves were formatted in a recursive way by factors associated with the social identities of the participants (host/caller) and by the institutional processes of the show (the need for several calls to be processed in a given time frame, for example). In other words, the arguments revealed recursive features of the interactional practice of arguing, but at the same time, each argument was managed along with the recursive features of its singular interactional frame, a "call." To deal adequately with these omnirelevant factors, the study became an exercise in the analysis of institutional discourse: the structure of arguments *on a talk radio show*."

What was the value of CA for making recommendations from your work?

"Because this study was driven from the beginning by my 'blue skies' interest in the structural features of argument as a conversational practice, I never thought of any policy recommendations that would emerge from it. There are some argumentative devices described in that work that, it's sometimes been suggested to me, might act as 'techniques' that could be taught to foreign learners of English, for example, to help them recognize, construct, or counter argumentative claims they might encounter from native speakers. I haven't pursued this myself, and in any case I think that arguments are such rapid fire and often off-the-cuff interactional events that thinking about which particular device to use in which specific situation might in fact be counterproductive. But as in all cases of the possible application of CA findings, the value of the approach stems from its insistence on dealing with the actual detail of the data we find in front of us, whether it goes along with anyone's presumptions about what might be found there or it does not."

An Example From Adult Psychiatry Research

Conversation analytic work has made a considerable contribution to a range of institutional settings in health care. A large volume of applied CA research has focused on health care communication, and many scholars have focused on specific conditions in both physical and mental health. Dr. Laura Thompson has examined mental health using CA, particularly exploring the communication between individuals diagnosed with *schizophrenia* and psychiatrists.

> **Schizophrenia** is a form of psychosis classified as a mental illness. People experiencing schizophrenia may not be able to separate their thoughts from reality and can experience delusions and hallucinations.

The data for the project were taken from outpatient settings and assertive outreach clinics across three centers, and included 36 psychiatrists and 134 patients with schizophrenia or schizoaffective disorder. It is well established that much of institutional talk is made up of question–answer sequences; therefore, question design has been of central concern for those practicing applied CA. Thompson and her colleagues have studied question design in relation to clinical interactions with individuals diagnosed with schizophrenia, arguing that psychiatrists need to go beyond the simplicity of dichotomizing open and closed questions, and pay more attention to the nuances of the interaction. Thompson, Howes, and McCabe (2016) and Thompson and McCabe (2016) noted that psychiatrists' questions are a conversational mechanism by which they can achieve clinical objectives and manage the therapeutic alliance, with this relying heavily upon question design.

Declarative questions are questions phrased as a statement, but with a questioning intonation. For example: You mean it was blue?

Tag questions are short questions that are "tagged" onto the end of a statement. For example: You were feeling sad, were you?

Using CA, Thompson et al. (2016) developed a coding taxonomy of question designs, noting that it was common for psychiatrists to use yes/no auxiliary questions, wh-questions, ***declarative questions***, and ***tag questions***.

In this body of research, Thompson et al. (2016) sought to identify the systematic practices through which the psychiatrist and the patient performed and recognized social action in talk. They argued that illuminating such discursive practices enables the field of psychiatry to define "good" communication in schizophrenia, and by focusing on psychiatrists' questions, they were able to illustrate how therapeutic alliance is achieved. They provided recommendations to psychiatrists around how to communicate in practice more efficiently and effectively.

In related work, Thompson and McCabe (2016) focused specifically on the functions of declarative questions. They demonstrated using applied CA that declaratives may be a closed style of questioning but that they are more nuanced than this type of question implies. By paying closer attention to how declarative questions are asked by psychiatrists, Thompson and McCabe were able to show that declarative questions can support attentiveness to the client's stance, confirm understandings of the patient experience, and effectively close down topics and change them.

For example: Thompson and McCabe (2016) examined so-prefaced declaratives and how they functioned as formulations for the psychiatrist. Consider the following example quoted directly from page 405 of their book chapter.

```
PAT:    =I watch telly::: and (.) cook something and (0.4)
        then m- washing and (0.4) tidy the 'ouse up you
        know.
DOC:    ↑Yeah.
        (3.4) ((Doctor writes in notes))
DOC:    So: you're quite happy being on your o:::wn?
PAT:    I'm quite happy doctor yea:h yea:h.
```

Thompson and McCabe (2016) demonstrated in their analysis of this extract that the psychiatrist used a declarative question as a formulation of the patient's experience. This declarative question is illuminated as so-prefaced—"so you're quite happy being on your own?" They noted that this declarative therefore invites confirmation from the patient and is presented as a simple summary, giving the psychiatrist an opportunity to discard the less relevant material about mundane activities (like watching television) to focus on emotional work—happiness. From this example, you should be able to see how a declarative question performs a specific function in this interactional sequence and how this is more sophisticated than the simple open–closed question dichotomy suggests. By using applied CA, authors can examine this kind of phenomenon in more detail.

If you plan to undertake an applied CA study in a health care setting, there is a significant body of CA literature. The work of Thompson and her colleagues is a useful example of applied CA in adult psychiatry. We thus encourage you to read these two references:

1. Thompson, L., Howes, C., & McCabe, R. (2016). The effect of questions used by psychiatrists on therapeutic alliance and adherence. *British Journal of Psychiatry, 209*(1), 40–47.

2. Thompson, L., & McCabe, R. (2016). "Good" communication in schizophrenia: A conversation analytic definition. In M. O'Reilly & J. N. Lester (Eds.), *The Palgrave handbook of adult mental health: Discourse and conversation studies* (pp. 394–418). Basingstoke, England: Palgrave Macmillan.

We also invited Dr. Laura Thompson to participate in an interview to share about her research process. Her responses can be found in Box 12.2.

BOX 12.2
INTERVIEW WITH DR. LAURA THOMPSON ⟨?⟩

Dr. Laura Thompson is a lecturer in occupational health psychology at the Centre for Sustainable Working Life, Birkbeck University. Dr. Thompson has research interests in using applied CA to solve real-world problems in institutional settings. Broadly, she focuses on well-being and social interaction in occupational and mental health contexts.

What motivated you to undertake research on psychiatry and schizophrenia?

"The frequently episodic nature of schizophrenia, and the complex symptoms involving changes in perception, means sustained contact with mental health services is often required. I was interested in how communication in psychiatrist–patient consultations forms the vehicle for achieving clinical

(Continued)

(Continued)

objectives, whether developing therapeutic goals and assessing symptom severity or deciding on appropriate treatment. These conversations may be complicated (e.g., by the nature of symptoms), but it is important we understand how they "work" and the various challenges along the way. I was motivated by the idea that to understand what is *effective* communication, we must first examine the *actual* practices that psychiatrists and patients use in consultations. However, I could find very little research on how psychiatrists interact in situ. Psychiatrists can help patients to share power and responsibility through their conversations (e.g., by involving them in treatment decisions). But only by looking at practices in a naturalistic, interactional setting can we consider how they may, or may not, advance the values of patients. Using conversation analysis to analyze video-recorded psychiatric consultations offered a useful methodological framework for this research problem."

What decisions did you make about recording equipment and why?

"The key decision was to use a digital camcorder that provided visual acuity and a good-quality audio recording (essential for a fine-grained interactional analysis) but meanwhile was small and noninvasive to prevent patients and psychiatrists feeling uncomfortable. The camcorder also needed to be user-friendly and straightforward to operate: Should patients become distressed about being recorded at any point, various psychiatrists would need to end the recording."

What were the main challenges in recruitment?

"My research involved a secondary analysis of data gathered from various studies including a randomized controlled trial assessing a communication skills training intervention for psychiatrists (McCabe et al., 2016). One of the main issues in recruitment for this study was approaching patients prior to their consultations in a public waiting room in an outpatient clinic—trying to navigate a private conversation to explain the study while ensuring that they did not feel pressured or imposed on in any way. This challenge was discussed with the clinical team, and it was hence agreed that psychiatrists would speak to patients first to introduce the study, giving them a chance to decline before we approached them. It was also important that only those patients who were well enough to give fully informed consent were approached. As such, the psychiatrist reviewed his or her patient list in advance to exclude any inappropriate patients."

What was the value of CA for making recommendations to psychiatrists from your work?

"Using CA enabled me to look at the nuances of psychiatric communication. In doing this, I was able to see that many of the taken-for-granted assumptions about what constitutes "good" communication need refining. Conceptualizing good communication in psychiatry has been hindered by a lack of conceptual clarity. Abstract ideals of patient centeredness and shared decision making are, quite rightly, widely endorsed but do not easily translate into specific practices conducive to training. Using CA allowed me to look at important practices (e.g., psychiatrists' questions and treatment recommendations) as social *actions*—and the systematic practices by which these actions are designed and understood in their local sequential context. From this, it was possible to develop interactionally sensitive recommendations for clinicians that account for some of the contingencies of actual practice."

An Example From Mediation Research

It is quite common in modern society for individuals to come into conflict, and there are a whole range of situations, such as family disputes, consumer disputes, and neighborhood disputes. An institutional response to this is ***mediation***.

Mediation is a process of resolving disputes to prevent them from going to court and involves a neutral individual (a mediator) who facilitates agreement between the two parties.

Mediation has been a focus for applied CA researchers, and in recent work by Sikveland and Stokoe (2016), a collection of 100 calls from five mediation centers and 200 calls from five community services were collated for analysis. The focus of the work was to examine how mediators design their talk, which often proposes common ground between the two parties. In calls to the mediation services, they demonstrated that first the call taker explained what mediation is. They found that mediators tend to ask solution-focused questions and examined how mediators do the institutional work required of the context.

For example: By paying close attention to the call sequences, Sikveland and Stokoe (2016) observed that mediators work to show mediation as a strong recommendation for the caller rather than as a requirement, with callers showing an uptake of willingness to engage. Consider the following example quoted directly from page 242 of their article.

```
M    They- (0.3) always suggest mediation
     (0.2)
C    Yes.
M    First.
C    Ye[s. ]
M      [thhh.]Is that s[someth]ing you have tried.
C                      [Yes.]
         (0.4)
C        No. No, =
M    .h[hh- ]
C      [Noth]ing
         (0.3)
M    = Is that something you would be willing to [do. ]=
C                                                [I would-]
C    I would be willing to do it. =ye[s. ]
```

Through their analysis, Sikveland and Stokoe (2016) noted that the mediator worked to establish whether the caller had previously tried mediation before moving to the question about willingness to try it. They observed that the caller used a yes/no interrogative, which they argued was the caller proposing willingness. They concluded their article arguing that formulations are central to the mediation process, and as this scaffolds clients to promote agreement it is a way to move forward without giving direct advice.

> *What this means:* It is helpful to pay attention to the performative nature of talk to look at the social actions.

In other work, Stokoe (2011) focused on translating her CA research in mediation and police settings to develop a communication skills training method to deliver evidence-based training to professionals. This method, the conversation analytic role-play method, (CARM), was described by the author as an approach to training that is adaptable to a wide range of institutional settings and one that is crucially grounded in research about what is effective in conversation rather than in stereotyped and popular assumptions about how talk works. Particularly beneficial in CARM is its use of naturally occurring conversational examples, which grounds the method in real practice. This provides a foundational evidence base to the claims made. Stokoe's research was used to train salespeople, doctors, police officers, hostage negotiators, and medical receptionists as well as mediators.

(!) **The CARM approach provides an excellent example of the benefits of CA research for institutional practice.**

An applied CA piece of work examining institutional settings where conflict can arise has the potential to allow analysts to make important recommendations for practice based on what they have observed in the data. The use of naturally occurring data provides the basis for the analytic claims made. We encourage you to read the following two references:

1. Sikveland, R. O., & Stokoe, E. (2016). Dealing with resistance in initial intake and inquiry calls to mediation: The power of "willing." *Conflict Resolution Quarterly, 33*(3), 235–253.

2. Stokoe, E. (2014). The conversation analytic role-play method (CARM): A method for training communication skills as an alternative to simulated role-play. *Research on Language and Social Interaction, 47*(3), 255–265.

To understand the scope of Professor Stokoe's work, we invited her to participate in an interview in which she shared details about her applied CA research. Her responses can be found in Box 12.3.

BOX 12.3
INTERVIEW WITH PROFESSOR ELIZABETH STOKOE

Elizabeth Stokoe is a professor of social interaction in the Department of Social Sciences at Loughborough University. Professor Stokoe undertakes conversation analytic research across public, private, and third-sector organizations, and, as reported in this chapter, in mediation. She developed the conversation analytic role-play method, which won a WIRED Innovation Fellowship in 2015. She has also undertaken many public engagement events and activities, including performing at Latitude Festival and New Scientist Live, and given TEDx and Royal Institution lectures, all with the aim of informing the public about how conversation analysts study social interaction.

What were the challenges of doing CA research in mediation?

"It was hard, initially, to get mediators to agree to record themselves with clients. They were anxious, as many professionals are, about client confidentiality—though, of course, as researchers we work ethically with recorded materials and always anonymize them. However, mediators' reluctance to record mediation itself created an opportunity to collect and study initial telephone inquiries to services. Mediators were less concerned about these data being part of a research study as, for them, the calls were not yet part of the mediation process. What I found was that many mediators failed to engage potential clients in these calls, but I could also identify what worked to convert callers to clients. This was essential to the very existence of services—without clients, they would not attract funding."

What kind of transcription practices did you use?

"When working with large data sets (and I often work with thousands of recordings and quick turnaround CARM projects), I always have verbatim transcripts produced first. I use this to begin to identify potential phenomena of interest, which I will then transcribe using the Jefferson system."

What ethical decisions did you need to make?

"I do think about the organizations I agree to work with and the possible misuse of research findings—like any other researcher and any other type of research. Because almost all of my research now underpins a CARM workshop as one of the outcomes, I train police officers, medics, salespeople, and many others to use the practices that I have identified work well—but to their ends. So I need to decide whether or not I am happy to help police negotiators, doctors, or mediators."

How were the practical recommendations made to the practitioners?

"The recommendations are built into CARM workshops, although I try not to make recommendations in the first instance. I show practitioners different ways they, say, describe the mediation process, or make an appointment with patients, or persuade suicidal persons in crisis to stay calm. I show them the outcome of different ways of doing these actions, and they learn directly what works and what is less effective by my exposing their tacit expertise (or lack of it)."

An Example From Child Mental Health

Applied CA has been successful in examining children's talk in a range of institutional settings and exploring how children are engaged in the institutional task at hand. A good example of this is in the field of child mental health, where children and families undergo an initial ***mental health assessment***.

Children and their families are usually referred by the general practitioner when there are suspected difficulties. These assessments are the initial appointment for families whereby mental health practitioners (sometimes working in pairs) from various disciplines (such as psychiatry, psychology, mental health nursing) engage the family by asking them questions about the child's symptoms and behavior. During this assessment, the practitioner(s) assesses for risks and considers the most appropriate next steps, such as treatments (Mash & Hunsley, 2005). The institutional requirements of the assessment tend to focus on gathering relevant information; therefore, the questions posed to the individual (and his or her family) are generally centered around that institutional agenda (Thompson & McCabe, 2016).

● **Mental health assessments** are carried out by mental health practitioners, and their purpose is to screen for mental health difficulties in the child (Parkin, Frake, & Davison, 2003).

Specifically, Dr. Michelle O'Reilly (second author of this book) and her colleague Dr. Khalid Karim have examined child mental health and engaging children and families in child mental health assessments using CA. This work was a collaborative partnership between academics (Michelle O'Reilly, Ian Hutchby, Jessica Nina Lester, and Victoria Stafford) and clinical practitioners (Khalid Karim, child and adolescent psychiatrist, and Nikki Kiyimba, senior clinical psychologist). The collaboration with practicing clinical professionals was especially important in promoting an applied approach to CA. The project included 28 families attending specialist mental health services in the United Kingdom. Each assessment was conducted by at least two mental health practitioners including psychiatry, psychology, mental health nursing, psychotherapy, occupational therapy, and learning disability backgrounds. Children were aged from 6 to 17 years old, with an average age of 11 years. Each assessment lasted approximately 90 minutes.

A core way in which clinical practitioners worked to engage children in the assessment process was using questions. By paying close attention to the design of the question and the nature of the response, the authors could make practical recommendations for those working in the field by showing examples of what happens when questions were framed in different ways. One example of this was a focus on how clinical practitioners ask questions about self-harm and suicidal ideation (a required part of the risk assessment; O'Reilly, Kiyimba, & Karim, 2016). In this article, they made a simple observation that in less than half of the cases, the child/adolescent was asked a question about self-harm and suicidal ideation, but the CA revealed how this question was asked in the 13 cases it was. The authors demonstrated that there were two main styles: an incremental approach—building up the conversation from inquiries about emotions to suicidal ideation—and externalizing the question as being a requirement of the institutional setting.

For example: O'Reilly (2016) suggested that externalizing the question as a requirement of the setting worked to minimize any potential negative impact that asking a question about self-harm or suicidal ideation may have. Consider the following example extract directly quoted from page 484 of the article.

```
Prac: This is a question we have to ask everybody an' I'm
      sure that you've been asked it before (1.38) when you
      feel (0.92) a bit frustrated or a bit sad (0.63) an'
      I know that you've punched walls before have you ever
      thought about (0.41) really hurting yourself
YP:   no
```

In their analysis of this extract, O'Reilly, Kiyimba, and Karim (2016) argued that asking children about self-harm behavior as a risk assessment question is potentially accountable, evidenced by the way in which clinicians treat it. They showed that clinicians sought to normalize asking this question and externalized their reason for asking it with phrases like "we have to ask everybody," indicating a lack of choice, an institutional agenda, and demonstrating that this individual child has not been singled out for the question. They argued that in this way, the context is oriented to and the question is designed in a more socially accepted way, which functions as a basis for asking about self-harm more directly. From this example, you should be able to see how sometimes the basis for a question being asked is stated in such a way as to manage accountability of the asking of that question, and how questions themselves can create trouble for the asker. By using CA, the authors could examine how questions about self-harm and suicide were asked in mental health assessments and explore this in sequential and interactional detail.

A second focus on questions in this setting was an exploration of the child's understanding of his or her presence in the setting (Stafford, Hutchby, Karim, & O'Reilly, 2016). The child's knowledge about his or her role in the assessment process and the reasons for being assessed has important implications for the trajectory and agenda of the appointment. Stafford and colleagues showed that when children were directly asked by the clinical practitioner for the reasons they believed they were there, a range of reasons were offered. The authors demonstrated that in some cases children used candidate diagnoses, sometimes they offered vague lay descriptions, but mostly they made claims to insufficient knowledge.

If you plan to undertake a study in child mental health, or even child physical health settings, there is a large amount of CA literature in this area. The work of O'Reilly, Karim, and their colleagues is a useful example of applied CA in child mental health. We thus encourage you to read these two references:

1. O'Reilly, M., Kiyimba, N., & Karim, K. (2016). "This is a question we have to ask everyone": Asking young people about self-harm and suicide. *Journal of Psychiatric and Mental Health Nursing, 23,* 479–488.

2. Stafford, V., Hutchby, I., Karim, K., & O'Reilly, M. (2016). "Why are you here?" Seeking children's accounts of their presentation to CAMHS. *Clinical Child Psychology and Psychiatry, 21*(1), 3–18.

To better appreciate the perspectives of clinical practitioners using applied CA in their work and how this can be a useful approach for those working in practice as well as academia, Dr. Karim has written specifically about some of the benefits and challenges of using CA from a practice-based perspective, particularly in the field of medicine, and we recommend you read:

1. Karim, K. (2015). The value of conversation analysis: A child psychiatrist's perspective. In M. O'Reilly & J. N. Lester (Eds.), *The Palgrave handbook of child mental health: Discourse and conversation studies* (pp. 25–41). Basingstoke, England: Palgrave Macmillan.

We invited Dr. Karim to participate in an interview, and his responses are shared in Box 12.4.

BOX 12.4
INTERVIEW WITH DR. KHALID KARIM

Dr. Khalid Karim is a consultant child and adolescent psychiatrist with Leicestershire Partnership NHS Trust and a senior teaching fellow at the University of Leicester. Dr. Karim has research interests in neurodevelopmental conditions such as autism spectrum disorder and attention deficit (hyperactivity) disorder. Broadly, he is interested in child mental health and has recently begun to use applied CA in his research.

What motivated you to use applied conversation analysis in your research?

"Conversation analysis was not part of my training and was completely unknown to me until I worked with another academic (Michelle O'Reilly) who is passionate about this area. My initial response was quite skeptical, even being a psychiatrist where I know the use of words is important. However, I was surprised to find how much had been published using applied CA, and there were some very useful papers which I could use in my actual practice. A good example of this was the work on *any* and *some* by John Heritage and colleagues, which I use in lots of different settings from teaching to clinical work. The critique of active listening by Ian Hutchby was very interesting, and it showed that commonly used phrases like *active listening* are assumed as being understood by everyone, but this is not necessarily the case. Clinical applications such as the work by Markus Reuber on seizures was fascinating and showed that this rarely appreciated marginalized research method had something to offer to the wider clinical community but was unfortunately relatively ignored. Seeing the link between the ways in which words can be analyzed using this method and actual tangible outcomes has enabled me to see the benefit of applied CA as a credible tool in improving patient care—if we take the time to use it and think about the outcomes."

Why can it be helpful to involve practitioners as co-investigators, collaborators, or advisers on an applied CA project?

"Despite being a clinical academic and enjoying the interplay between being an active researcher, teacher, and jobbing clinician, it is still patently clear on this enormous gulf between the research that is done and the implementation of it into clinical practice. The joke generally is that it takes 10 years for work to translate from research to the workplace. Many clinicians who are not involved in research still view it as an ivory tower, and the less well known the research method, and the less accessible the material is to read, the less likely it is to be implemented in practice. Despite my position, it is still essential to involve those who are working as practitioners and patients, and in my case their families, to ground what is being suggested in reality. In this way, the research will have some meaning to the wider community and will demonstrate benefits. This will also raise the profile of this research approach if it is seen as useful by the wider public and other colleagues."

How can CA be seen as a useful methodology for practitioners who want to do some research of their own?

"Most practitioners are a little bit research averse, particularly due to the other pressures of their jobs and because doing research can cause a lot of anxiety. Therefore, people tend to revert to methods they are familiar with, often from their undergraduate days, which unfortunately rarely contain applied CA. Even if it was spoken about, individuals rarely took part. Thus, three things need to be achieved. First, they need to see the value of this type of research, and therefore, showing good examples of applied work is essential. Second, they will need a lot of support to even start in this area, particularly as the literature can seem a little daunting. Third, they need considerable time to both obtain and analyze the data. This is not always easy, but recognizing the value of talk in our interactions is something that needs to be appreciated to a much greater extent."

Future Directions of Applied CA

While we have carved out some of the historical moments, key trends, and core practices related to applied CA, we recognize that what we have offered is an overview. We thus encourage readers to engage in continued study. In addition, we recognize that the area of applied CA research is relatively young and there remains much to be done at the level of methodology, theory, and practice. Like van Dijk (2006), we acknowledge that "scholarship is constantly changing, that fashions, theories and methods come and go, and that originality and renewal typically take place at the boundary of different disciplines or approaches or by combining different theories and methods" (p. 7). As such, we call for those of you working in fields perhaps not represented in our writing of this book and/or working in areas less familiar with CA to begin envisioning possibilities for pursuing applied CA research. We believe that applied CA offers analysts as well as various stakeholders a unique and relevant way to make sense of everyday life, and, in some cases, work to change taken-for-granted interactional practices.

Applied CA is an important approach that is growing in popularity among academic scholars and those who work in fields of practice. In the future, there is great potential for CA's methodology to be integrated with external assessments from certain client groups, such as patients in health care (Drew, Chatwin, & Collins, 2001). Drew et al. (2001) recognized that researchers could combine the detailed analysis of communication in practical settings such as medicine with other qualitative methods such as interviewing patients about their expectations of such interactions so that comparisons may be made. Drew et al. argued that such a mixing of qualitative methods approaches (see O'Reilly & Kiyimba, 2015, for some discussion of this) may add a novel dimension to how medics understand the conditions for patient satisfaction. Furthermore, CA work is starting to be used to underpin quantitative evaluations (e.g., see Stivers & Majid, 2007) and to inform interventions to enhance health care (e.g., Sheon, Lee, & Facente, 2010), health communication practices (e.g., Heritage & Robinson, 2011; O'Reilly, Lester, & Muskett, 2017; Stivers, 2002), understanding of legal settings and processes (Auburn & Lea, 2003), and communication training for mediators and police (Stokoe, 2014), to name just a few.

We argue that applied CA has a bright future as the benefits and applications of it become more central to a range of disciplines. The growing number of CA studies has generated important and significant knowledge about the verbal and embodied communication practices and their consequences in relation to many areas of practice, such as health care and education (Parry & Land, 2013). There are a growing number of practice-based journals accepting articles using CA approaches and showcasing the important messages that facilitate practitioners in their daily business. By reaching out directly to those who work in practice, researchers can demonstrate the benefits of the approach but also impart some guidance on how to undertake this kind of work, hopefully encouraging practitioners to undertake their own CA work. Indeed, there are many practitioners in the field undertaking CA work and encouraging their peers to do so, and we provide just a few examples (some also have academic roles that we do not show here):

- Elizabeth Bromley, Adult Psychiatrist

- Katie Denman, Clinical Psychologist

- Sushie Dobbinson, Lead Forensic Speech & Language Therapist

- Khalid Karim, Consultant Child and Adolescent Psychiatrist

- Nikki Kiyimba, Senior Clinical Psychologist

- Tom Muskett, Speech and Language Therapist

- Anssi Peräkylä, Psychotherapist

- Markus Reuber, Consultant Neurologist

- Tom Strong, Family Therapist

However, while applied CA is growing and appealing to practitioners more and more, many studies are still framed in terms of sociological and linguistic concerns or theories, and the evidence has been largely confined to academic fields (Parry & Land, 2013). Parry and Land (2013) noted that CA knowledge and understanding from applied research should not be unavailable to practitioners working in the field, and this is a position we strongly agree with and hope this book helps practitioners to undertake their own applied CA work.

Indeed, we ourselves work in the fields of mental health research and education, and in so doing have partnered with practitioners in those fields to make our CA more applicable to those in practice. By working directly with practitioners, we envision that the learning process is bidirectional as we impart knowledge about the benefits of applied CA and simultaneously learn much more about the worlds we are observing. We strongly encourage this kind of partnership, which can serve to work to promote the impacts of applied CA research, spread the word about the value of applied CA, and ensure that you too learn from the experience.

Chapter Summary

In this chapter, we shared four empirical examples of applied CA research. Drawing from diverse fields, these examples illustrate well how applied CA research can be applied in diverse and meaningful ways. Within our discussion, we included interviews with key scholars. In doing so, we sought to provide real-world, practical understandings of the applied CA research and offer concrete ideas to consider when developing your own applied CA research studies. We concluded the chapter by pointing to several future possibilities of engaging in applied CA research. We summarize the key learning points in the next box.

Learning Points From Chapter 12

- There are myriad empirical examples of applied CA research, including those focused on radio talk, mental health, and mediation.

- Applied CA has the potential to make important and useful recommendations for practically oriented disciplines.

- There are many fields in which applied CA research has yet to be applied.

Conclusions

Across the book, we have sought to offer a practical guide for designing and carrying out an applied CA research study. In doing so, we have assumed that this book is one of many resources that you might access. In Chapter 1, we introduced CA generally and applied CA more particularly. In doing so, we provided an abbreviated history of CA and noted the varying ways that applied CA has been conceptualized (Antaki, 2011). While the focus of this book is not on the foundational principles or building blocks of CA but rather practical considerations for doing an applied CA study, we would be remiss to not at least mention some of the basic principles and building blocks of CA. Thus, in Chapter 2, we discussed some of the basic ideas central to CA. Chapters 3 and 4 offered important considerations for planning an applied CA study and engaging in ethical decision making. Chapters 5 through 7 introduced the core activities involved in designing and carrying out an applied CA study, which included a discussion of planning for and collecting data, transcribing data, and analyzing data. Notably, we devoted an entire chapter to discussing the ways in which digital tools can support researchers carrying out an applied CA study, with Chapter 8 introducing some key digital tools for supporting data collection, transcription,

and analysis. Chapter 9 offered practical insights related to establishing quality within a qualitative study, noting specific considerations for an applied CA research study. While discussions related to establishing quality in applied CA research are somewhat limited in the traditional CA literature base, we believe that it is a critical consideration when designing and carrying out an applied CA research study. Further, given this book's focus on an *applied* approach to CA, we devoted Chapter 10 to discussing the very notion of evidence in qualitative research generally and applied CA research specifically. In Chapter 11, we highlighted the various ways in which applied CA research might be disseminated and sought to offer practical advice for graduate students. Finally, in this chapter, we have provided multiple examples of applied CA research and pointed to possibilities for future directions of this kind of research.

Throughout the book, we have highlighted the value and the potential for practice-based impact of applied CA research. While we have pointed to the scholarship of several key CA scholars, we recognize that what we have shared here is partial and indeed positional. Thus, we encourage you to explore further literature that might be most pertinent to the work that you are interested in pursuing.

Recommended Readings

We recommend you engage with the work of those who practice in applied fields as well as do CA research. Such an engagement will help you see some of the benefits of applied CA research as related to informing practice.

- Dobbinson, S. (2016). Conversations with an adult with features of autism spectrum disorder in secure forensic care. In M. O'Reilly & J. N. Lester (Eds.), *The Palgrave handbook of adult mental health: Discourse and conversation analysis* (pp. 441–459). Basingstoke, England: Palgrave Macmillan.

This chapter is a useful example of a specific application of applied CA to exploring autism spectrum disorder in a clinical setting. Dobbinson is a practitioner, and thus this chapter offers useful insights into how a practitioner explored the clinical world using applied CA.

- Karim, K. (2015). The value of conversation analysis: A child psychiatrist's perspective. In M. O'Reilly & J. N. Lester (Eds.), *The Palgrave handbook of child mental health: Discourse and conversation studies* (pp. 25–41). Basingstoke, England: Palgrave Macmillan.

In this chapter, Karim provides an overview of CA from the perspective of a medical doctor examining the potential benefits of the approach and providing a refreshing and interesting view of the approach. Notably, as a child psychiatrist, Karim offers a practical view of how applied CA research might inform and shape the everyday practices of a practitioner.

- Streeck, U. (2010). A psychotherapist's view of conversation analysis. In A. Peräkylä, C. Antaki, S. Vehvilainen, & I. Leudar (Eds.). *Conversation analysis and psychotherapy* (pp. 173–187). Cambridge, England: Cambridge University Press.

This is a similar type of contribution to the one written by Karim (2015), as Streeck is a psychotherapist who describes the utility of CA. Specifically, Streeck provides a personal view of the usefulness of CA and considers the benefits of this methodological approach.

• References •

Abiddin, N. Z., Hassan, A., & Ahmad, A. R. (2009). Research student supervision: An approach to good supervisory practice. *Open Education Journal, 2*(1), 11–16.

American Association of University Professors. (2000). *Institutional review boards and social science research.* Retrieved from https://www.aaup.org/report/institutional-review-boards-and-social-science-research

Anastas, J. (2004). Quality in qualitative evaluation: Issues and possible answers. *Research on Social Work Practice, 14*(1), 57–65.

Angen, M. (2000). Evaluating interpretive inquiry: Reviewing the validity debate and opening the dialogue. *Qualitative Health Research, 10*(3), 378–395.

Angus, D., Rintel, S., & Wiles, J. (2013). Making sense of big text: A visual-first approach for analysing text data using Leximancer and Discursis. *International Journal of Social Research Methodology, 16*, 261–267.

Antaki, C. (2011). Six kinds of applied conversation analysis. In C. Antaki (Ed.), *Applied conversation analysis: Intervention and change in institutional talk* (pp. 1–4). Hampshire, England: Palgrave Macmillan.

Antaki, C., Billig, M. G., Edwards, D., & Potter, J. A. (2003). Discourse analysis means doing analysis: A critique of six analytic shortcomings. *Discourse Analysis Online, 1.* Retrieved from http://extra.shu.ac.uk/daol/articles/open/2002/002/antaki2002002-paper.html

Antaki, C., & O'Reilly, M. (2014). Either/or questions in child psychiatric assessments: The effect of the seriousness and order of the alternatives. *Discourse Studies, 16*(3), 327–345.

Armstrong, D., Gosling, A., Weinman, J., & Marteau, T. (1997). The place of inter-rater reliability in qualitative research: An empirical study. *Sociology, 31*(3), 597–606.

Ashcroft, R. (2003). The ethics and governance of medical research: What does regulation have to do with morality? *New Review of Bioethics, 1*(1), 41–58.

Atkinson, J. M. (1982). Understanding formality: Notes on the categorization and production of "formal" interaction. *British Journal of Sociology, 33*, 86–117.

Atkinson, J. M., & Drew, P. (1979). *Order in court: The organisation of verbal interaction in judicial settings.* London, England: Macmillan.

Atkinson, J. M., & Heritage, J. (1999). Jefferson's transcript notation. In A. Jaworski & N. Coupland (Eds.), *The discourse reader* (pp. 158–166). London, England: Routledge.

Atkinson, P. (2015). *For ethnography.* Los Angeles, CA: Sage.

Auburn, T., Hay, W., & Wilkinson, T. (2011). The place of an advice and support service in a magistrates' court. *Probation Journal, 58*(2), 112–125.

Auburn, T., & Lea, S. (2003). Doing cognitive distortions: A discursive psychology analysis of sex offender treatment talk. *British Journal of Social Psychology, 42*(2), 281–298.

Baker, C. C. (2002). Ethnomethodological analyses of interviews. In J. Gubrium & J. Holstein (Eds.), *Handbook of interviewing: Context and method* (pp. 777–795). Thousand Oaks, CA: Sage.

Barbour, R. (2001). Checklists for improving rigour in qualitative research: A case of the tail wagging the dog? *British Medical Journal, 322*(7294), 1115–1117.

Bartgis, J., & Bigfoot, D. (2010). *Evidence-based practice and practice-based evidence: What are they? How do we know if we have one?* Washington, DC: National Council of Urban Indian Health.

Berger, P. L., & Luckmann, T. (1966). *The social construction of reality: A treatise on the sociology of knowledge.* Garden City, NY: Anchor Books.

Bilmes, J. (1988). The concept of preference in conversation analysis. *Language in Society, 17,* 161–181.

Bishop, L. (2007). A reflexive account of reusing qualitative data: Beyond primary/secondary dualism. *Sociological Research Online, 12*(3), 2.

Blaxter, L., Hughes, C., & Tight, M. (2001). *How to research* (2nd ed.). Buckingham, England: Open University Press.

Bolden, G., & Robinson, J. (2011). Soliciting accounts with *why*-interrogatives in conversation. *Journal of Communication, 61,* 94–119.

Boote, D. N., & Beile, P. (2005). Scholars before researchers: On the centrality of the dissertation literature review in research preparation. *Educational Researcher, 34*(6), 3–15.

Bottorff, J. L. (1994). Using videotaped data recordings in qualitative research. In J. M. Morse (Ed.), *Critical issues in qualitative research methods* (pp. 244–261). London, England: Sage.

Bourne, P. (2005). Ten simple rules for getting published. *PLoS Computational Biology, 1*(5). Retrieved from https://doi.org/10.1371/journal.pcbi.0010057

Braun, V., & Clarke, V. (2006). Using thematic analysis in psychology. *Qualitative Research in Psychology, 3*, 77–101.

Brun-Cottan, F. (1990). Talk in the workplace: Occupational relevance. *Research on Language & Social Interaction, 24*(1-4), 277–297.

Burgess, R. (1981). Keeping a research diary. *Cambridge Journal of Education, 11*(1), 75–83.

Burr, V. (2003). *Social constructionism* (2nd ed.). London, England: Routledge.

Butler, C., Potter, J., Danby, S., Emmison, M., & Hepburn, A. (2010). Advice implicative interrogatives: Building "client centred" support in a children's helpline. *Social Psychology Quarterly, 73*(3), 265–287.

Caelli, K., Ray, L., & Mill, J. (2003). "Clear as mud": Toward greater clarity in generic qualitative research. *International Journal of Qualitative Methods, 2*(2). Retrieved from https://doi.org/10.1177/160940690300200201

Chen, Y-Y., Shek, D., & Bu, F-F. (2011). Applications of interpretive and constructionist research methods in adolescent research: Philosophy, principles and examples. *International Journal of Adolescent Medicine and Health, 23*(3), 129–139.

Chomsky, N. (1957). *Syntactic structures*. The Hague, Netherlands: Mouton & Co.

Cicourel, A.V. (1981). Notes on the integration of micro- and macro-levels of analysis. In K. Knorr-Cetina & A.V. Cicourel (Eds.), *Advances in social theory and methodology: Toward an integration of micro- and macro-sociologies* (pp. 51–80). London, England: Routledge & Kegan Paul.

Clarke, K. (2009). Uses of a research diary: Learning reflectively, developing understanding and establishing transparency. *Nurse Researcher, 17*(1), 68–76.

Clayman, S. (2013). Turn-construction units and the transition-relevance place. In J. Sidnell & T. Stivers (Eds.), *The handbook of conversation analysis* (pp. 150–166). West Sussex, England: Blackwell.

Cleary, M., & Walter, G. (2004). Apportioning our time and energy: Oral presentation, poster, journal article or other? *International Journal of Mental Health Nursing, 13*, 204–207.

Collingridge, D., & Gantt, E. (2008). The quality of qualitative research. *American Journal of Medical Quality, 23*(5), 389–395.

Corden, A., & Sainsbury, R. (2006). Exploring "quality": Research participants' perspectives on verbatim quotations. *International Journal of Social Research Methodology, 9*(2), 97–110.

Craswell, G. (2005). *Writing for academic success: A postgraduate guide*. London, England: Sage.

Creswell, J. (2013). *Qualitative inquiry and research design: Choosing among five approaches* (3rd ed.). London, England: Sage.

Cunningham, S. (2004). How to . . . write a paper. *Journal of Orthodontics, 31*, 47–51.

Davidson, J., & di Gregorio, S. (2011). Qualitative research and technology: In the midst of a revolution. In N. K. Denzin & Y. S. Lincoln (Eds.), *The Sage handbook of qualitative research* (4th ed., pp. 627–643). Thousand Oaks, CA: Sage.

Davies, D., & Dodd, J. (2002). Qualitative research and the question of rigor. *Qualitative Health Research, 12*(2), 279–289.

de Certeau, M. (1984). *The practice of everyday life* (S. F. Rendall, Trans.). Los Angeles: University of California Press.

Demuth, C. (2018). Generalization from single cases and the concept of double dialogicality. *Integr Psych Behav, 52*, 77–93.

Dey, I. (1993). *Qualitative data analysis: A user-friendly guide for social scientists*. London, England: Routledge.

Dickerson, P., & Robins, B. (2015). Looking or spotting: A conversation analytic perspective on interaction between a humanoid robot, a co-present adult, and a child with an ASC. In M. O'Reilly & J. N. Lester (Eds.), *The Palgrave handbook of child mental health: Discourse and conversation studies* (pp. 59–78). Basingstoke, England: Palgrave Macmillan.

Dickerson, P., & Robins, B. (2017). Conversation analysis with children with an autism spectrum disorder and limited verbal ability. In M. O'Reilly, J. N. Lester, & T. Muskett (Eds.), *A practical guide to social interaction research in autism spectrum disorders* (pp. 167–192). Basingstoke, England: Palgrave Macmillan.

Dickson-Swift, V., James, E., Kippen, S., & Liamputtong, P. (2009). Researching sensitive topics: Qualitative research as emotion work. *Qualitative Research, 9*(1), 61–79.

Dixon-Woods, M., Shaw, R., Agarwal, S., & Smith, J. (2004). The problem of appraising qualitative research. *Quality Safety & Health Care, 13*, 223–225.

Drew, P. (2013). Turn design. In J. Sidnell & T. Stivers (Eds.), *The handbook of conversation analysis* (pp. 131–149). West Sussex, England: Blackwell.

Drew, P. (2015). Conversation analysis. In J. Smith (Ed.), *Qualitative psychology* (3rd ed., pp. 133–159). London, England: Sage.

Drew, P., Chatwin, J., & Collins, S. (2001). Conversation analysis: A method for research into interactions between patients and health-care professionals. *Health Expectations, 4*(1), 58–70.

Drew, P., & Hepburn, A. (2015). Absent apologies. *Discourse Processes, 53*(1-2). doi:10.1080/0163853X.2015.1056690

Drew, P., & Heritage, J. (Eds.). (1992). *Talk at work: Interaction in institutional settings.* Cambridge, England: Cambridge University Press.

Drew, P., Heritage, J., Lerner, G., & Pomerantz, A. (2015). Introduction. In G. Jefferson (Ed.), *Talking about troubles in conversation* (pp. 1–26). New York, NY: Oxford University Press.

Duncan, R., Drew, S., Hodgson, J., & Sawyer, S. (2009). Is my mum going to hear this? Methodological and ethical challenges in qualitative health research with young people. *Social Science and Medicine, 69*(11), 1691–1699.

Dunn, L., Kim, D., Fellows, I., & Palmer, B. (2009). Worth the risk? Relationship of incentives to risk and benefit perceptions and willingness to participate in schizophrenia research. *Schizophrenia Bulletin, 35*(4), 730–737.

Easterby-Smith, M., Golden-Biddle, K., & Locke, K. (2008). Working with pluralism: Determining quality in qualitative research. *Organizational Research Methods, 11*(3), 419–429.

Eddy, D. (2011). History of medicine: The origins of evidence-based medicine—A personal perspective. *American Medical Association Journal of Ethics, 1*, 55–60.

Edwards, D., & Potter, J. (1992). *Discursive psychology.* London, England: Sage.

Egbert, M., Yufu, M., & Hirataka, F. (2016). An investigation of how 100 articles in the *Journal of Pragmatics* treat transcripts of English and non-English languages. *Journal of Pragmatics, 94*, 98–111.

Ekström, M. (2009). Announced refusal to answer: A study of norms and accountability in broadcast political interviews. *Discourse Studies, 11*(6), 681–702.

Ensign, J. (2003). Ethical issues in qualitative health research with homeless youths. *Journal of Advanced Nursing, 43*(1), 43–50.

Esposito, A. (2013). Neither digital or open. Just researchers: Views on digital/open scholarship practices in an Italian university. *First Monday, 18*(1).

European Commission. (2010). *European textbook on ethics in research.* Brussels, Belgium: Publications Office of the European Union.

Evans, D. (2003). Hierarchy of evidence: A framework for ranking evidence evaluating healthcare interventions. *Journal of Clinical Nursing, 12*, 77–84.

Fincham, B., Scourfield, J., & Langer, S. (2008). The impact of working with disturbing secondary data: Reading suicide files in a coroner's office. *Qualitative Health Research, 18*(6), 853–862.

Fink, A. (2005). *Conducting research literature reviews: From the Internet to paper* (2nd ed.). London, England: Sage.

Finlay, L. (2002). "Outing" the researcher: The provenance, process, and practice of reflexivity. *Qualitative Health Research, 12*, 531–545.

Finlay, L. (2003). The reflexive journey: Mapping multiple routes. In L. Finlay & B. Gough (Eds.), *Reflexivity: A practical guide for researchers in health and social sciences* (pp. 3–20). Oxford, England: Blackwell.

Flewitt, R. (2005). Conducting research with young children: Some ethical considerations. *Early Child Development and Care, 175*(6), 552–565.

Fox, N. (2003). Practice-based evidence: Towards collaborative and transgressive research. *Sociology, 37*(1), 81–102.

Francis, J., Johnston, M., Robertson, C., Glidewell, L., Entwistle, V., Eccles, M., & Grimshaw, J. (2010). What is adequate sample size? Operationalising data saturation for theory-based interview studies. *Psychology & Health, 25*(10), 1229–1245.

Freeman, M., deMarrais, K., Preissle, J., Roulston, K., & St. Pierre, E. (2007). Standards of evidence in qualitative research: An incitement to discourse. *Educational Researcher, 36*(1), 25–32.

Freshwater, D., Cahill, J., Walsh, E., & Muncey, T. (2010). Qualitative research as evidence. Criteria for rigour and relevance. *Journal of Research in Nursing, 15*(6), 497–508.

Freud, S. (1915). *Introductory lectures in psychoanalysis* (G. S. Hall, Trans.) [2013 Kindle edition]. Digireads.com.

Garfinkel, H. (1967). *Studies in ethnomethodology.* Englewood Cliffs, NJ: Prentice Hall.

Garfinkel, H. (2002). *Ethnomethodology's program: Working out Durkheim's aphorism.* Lanham, MD: Rowman & Littlefield.

Georgaca, E. (2014). Discourse analytic research on mental distress: A critical overview. *Journal of Mental Health, 23*(2), 55–61.

Georgaca, E., & Avdi, E. (2009). Evaluating the talking cure: The contribution of narrative, discourse, and conversation analysis to psychotherapy assessment. *Qualitative Research in Psychology, 6,* 233–247.

Gergen, K. J. (1985). The social constructionist movement in modern psychology. *American Psychologist, 40*(3), 266.

Gergen, K. (2004). Old-stream psychology will disappear with the dinosaurs; Kenneth Gergen in conversation with Peter Mattes and Ernst Schraube. *Forum: Qualitative Social Research, 5*(3).

Gergen, K. J., & Gergen, M. M. (1991). From theory to reflexivity in research practice. In F. Steier (Ed.), *Method and reflexivity: Knowing as systemic social construction* (pp. 76–95). London: Sage.

Gibbs, G. R., Friese, S., & Mangabeira, W. C. (2002). The use of new technology in qualitative research: Introduction. *Forum: Qualitative Social Research, 3*(2). Retrieved from http://nbn-resolving.de/urn:nbn:de:0114-fqs020287

Giles, D. C., Stommel, W., Paulus, T. M., Lester, J. N., & Reed, D. (2015). Microanalysis of online data: The methodological development of "digital CA." *Discourse, Context, & Media, 7,* 45–51.

Gillies, V., & Edwards, R. (2005). Secondary analysis in exploring family and social change: Addressing the issue of context. *Forum: Qualitative Social Research, 6*(1). Retrieved from http://www.qualitative-research.net/index.php/fqs/article/view/500/1077

Goffman, E. (1959). *The presentation of self in everyday life.* London, England: Penguin.

Goffman, E. (1983). The interaction order. *American Sociological Review, 48*(1), 1–17.

Golafshani, N. (2003). Understanding reliability and validity in qualitative research. *The Qualitative Report, 8*(4), 597–606.

Gomoll, A., Hmelo-Silver, C. E., Šabanović, S., & Francisco, M. (2016). Dragons, ladybugs, and softballs: Girls' STEM engagement with human-centered robotics. *Journal of Science Education & Technology, 25*(6), 899–914.

Goodwin, C. (2000). Action and embodiment within situated human interaction. *Journal of Pragmatics, 32*(10), 1489–1522.

Goodwin, C. (2003). Conversational frameworks for the accomplishment of meaning in aphasia. In C. Goodwin (Ed.), *Conversation and brain damage* (pp. 90–116). Oxford, England: Oxford University Press.

Goodwin, M. H. (2007). Participation and embodied action in preadolescent girls' assessment activity. *Research on Language and Social Interaction, 40*(4), 353–375.

Green, J., Franquiz, M., & Dixon, C. (1997). The myth of the objective transcript: Transcribing as a situated act. *TESOL Quarterly, 31*(1), 172–176.

Green, L. (2008). Making research relevant: If it is an evidence-based practice, where's the practice-based evidence? *Family Practice, 25*(1), i20–i24.

Greenhalgh, T. (1997). How to read a paper: The Medline database. *British Medical Journal, 315,* 180–185.

Griffin, C. (2007). Being dead and being there: Research interviews, sharing hand cream and the preference for naturally occurring data. *Discourse Studies, 92,* 246–269.

Grimshaw, A. (1982). Sound-image data records for research on social interaction: Some questions and answers. *Sociological Methods and Research, 11,* 121–144.

Grossman, J., & Mackenzie, F. (2005). The randomised controlled trial: Gold standard, or merely standard? *Perspectives in Biology and Medicine, 48*(4), 516–534.

Gubrium, J., & Holstein, J. (2008). The constructionist mosaic. In J. Holstein & J. Gubrium (Eds.), *Handbook of constructionist research* (pp. 3–12). New York, NY: Guilford Press.

Hagen, P., Robertson, T., Kan, M., & Sadler, K. (2005, November). Emerging research methods for understanding mobile technology use. In *Proceedings of the 17th Australia Conference on Computer-Human Interaction: Citizens Online: Considerations for Today and the Future* (pp. 1–10). Computer-Human Interaction Special Interest Group (CHISIG) of Australia.

Hall, M., Gough, B., & Seymour-Smith, S. (2012). "I'm METRO, NOT gay!" A discursive analysis of men's accounts of makeup use on YouTube. *Journal of Men's Studies, 20*(3), 209–226.

Hammersley, M. (1997). Qualitative data archiving: Some reflections on its prospects and problems. *Sociology, 31*(1), 131–142.

Hammersley, M. (2007). The issue of quality in qualitative research. *International Journal of Research and Method in Education, 30*(3), 287–305.

Hammersley, M. (2010a). Reproducing or constructing? Some questions about transcription in social research. *Qualitative Research, 10*(5), 553–569.

Hammersley, M. (2010b). Can we re-use qualitative data via secondary analysis? Notes on some terminological and substantive issues. *Sociological Research Online, 15*(1), 1–7.

Harris, M. (1976). History and significance of the emic/etic distinction. *Annual Review of Anthropology, 5,* 329–350.

Hayashi, M. (2013). Turn allocation and turn sharing. In J. Sidnell & T. Stivers (Eds.), *The handbook of conversation analysis* (pp. 167–190). West Sussex, England: Blackwell.

Headland, T. (1990). A dialogue between Kenneth Pike and Marvin Harris on emics and etics. In T. Headland, K. Pike, & M. Harris (Eds.), *Emics and etics: The insider/outsider debate. Frontiers of anthropology* (Vol. 7, pp. 13–27). Newbury Park, CA: Sage.

Heath, C. (1997). The analysis of activities in face to face interaction using video. In D. Silverman (Ed.), *Qualitative research: Theory, method and practice* (pp. 183–200). London, England: Sage.

Heath, C. (2004). Analysing face-to-face interaction: Video, the visual and material. In D. Silverman (Ed.), *Qualitative research: Theory, method and practice* (2nd ed., pp. 266–282). London, England: Sage.

Heath, C., & Hindmarsh, J. (2002). Analysing interaction: Video, ethnography and situated conduct. In T. May (Ed.), *Qualitative research in action* (pp. 99–121). London, England: Sage.

Heath, C., Hindmarsh, J., & Luff, P. (2010). *Video in qualitative research: Analysing social interaction in everyday life.* London, England: Sage.

Heath, C., & Luff, P. (2013). Embodied action and organizational activity. In J. Sidnell & T. Stivers (Eds.), *The handbook of conversation analysis* (pp. 283–307). West Sussex, England: Blackwell.

Heaton, J. (1998). Secondary analysis of qualitative data. *Social Research Update, 22.*

Hedgecoe, A. (2008). Research ethics review and the sociological research relationship. *Sociology, 42*(5), 873–886.

Hedgecoe, A. (2009). "A form of practical machinery": The origins of Research Ethics Committees in the UK, 1967–1972. *Medical History, 53*(3), 331–350.

Hepburn, A. (2004). Crying: Notes on description, transcription, and interaction. *Research on Language and Social Interaction, 37,* 251–290.

Hepburn, A., & Bolden, G. (2013). The conversation analytic approach to transcription. In J. Sidnell & T. Stivers (Eds.), *The handbook of conversation analysis* (pp. 57–76). West Sussex, England: Blackwell.

Hepburn, A., & Bolden, G. B. (2017). *Transcribing for social research.* London, England: Sage.

Hepburn, A., & Potter, J. (2007). Crying receipts: Time, empathy, and institutional practice. *Research on Language and Social Interaction, 40*(1), 89–116.

Hepburn, A., & Potter, J. (2011). Designing the recipient: Resisting advice resistance in a child protection helpline. *Social Psychology Quarterly, 74*(2), 216–241.

Hepburn, A., & Wiggins, S. (2005). Size matters: Constructing accountable bodies in NSPCC helpline interaction. *Discourse and Society, 16*(5), 625–645.

Hepburn, A., Wilkinson, S., & Butler, C. (2014). Intervening with conversation analysis in telephone helpline services: Strategies to improve effectiveness. *Research on Language and Social Interaction, 47*(3), 239–254.

Heritage, J. (1984). A change-of-state token and aspects of its sequential placement. In J. M. Atkinson & J. Heritage (Eds.), *Structures of social action: Studies in conversation analysis* (pp. 299–345). Cambridge, England: Cambridge University Press.

Heritage, J. (1988). Explanations as accounts: A conversation analytic perspective. In C. Antaki (Ed.), *Analyzing everyday explanation: A casebook of methods* (pp. 127–144). London, England: Sage.

Heritage, J. (2004). *Garfinkel and ethnomethodology.* Cambridge, England: Polity Press.

Heritage, J. (2005). Conversation analysis and institutional talk. In K. Fitch & R. Sanders (Eds.), *Handbook of language and social interaction* (pp. 103–149). Mahwah, NJ: Erlbaum.

Heritage, J. (2011). Conversation analysis: Practices and methods. In D. Silverman (Ed.), *Qualitative research* (3rd ed., pp. 208–230). London, England: Sage.

Heritage, J. (2015). Well-prefaced turns in English conversation: A conversation analytic perspective. *Journal of Pragmatics, 88,* 88–104.

Heritage, J., & Atkinson, J. M. (1984). Introduction. In J. M. Atkinson & J. Heritage (Eds.), *Structures of social action:*

Studies in conversation analysis (pp. 1–15). Cambridge, England: Cambridge University Press.

Heritage, J., & Greatbatch, D. (1986). Generating applause: A study of rhetoric and response at party political conferences. *American Journal of Sociology, 92*(1), 110–157.

Heritage, J., & Robinson, J. D. (2011). "Some" versus "any" medical issues: Encouraging patients to reveal their unmet concerns. In C. Antaki (Ed.), *Applied conversation analysis* (pp. 15–31). Hampshire, England: Palgrave Macmillan.

Herring, S. (1996). Linguistic and critical analysis of computer-mediated communication: Some ethical and scholarly considerations. *The Information Society, 12*(2), 153–168.

Herring, S. C. (2007). A faceted classification scheme for computer-mediated discourse. *Language@Internet, 4*(1), 1–37.

Higgs, J., & Jones, M. A. (2000). Will evidence-based practice take the reasoning out of practice? In J. Higgs & M. A. Jones (Eds.), *Clinical reasoning in the health professions* (2nd ed., pp. 307–315). Oxford, England: Butterworth Heineman.

Hoagwood, K., Burns, B., Kiser, L., Ringeisem, H., & Schoenwald, S. (2001). Evidence-based practice in child and adolescent mental health services. *Psychiatric Services, 52*(9), 1179–1189.

Hopper, R. (1990). Ethnography and conversation analysis after Talking Culture. *Research on Language & Social Interaction, 24*(1-4), 161–171.

Hunter, D. (2008). The ESRC research ethics framework and research ethics review at UK universities: Rebuilding the tower of Babel REC by REC. *Journal of Medical Ethics, 34*(11), 815–820.

Hutchby, I. (2001). Witnessing: The use of first-hand knowledge in legitimating lay opinions on talk radio. *Discourse Studies, 3*(4), 481–497.

Hutchby, I. (2005). Children's talk and social competence. *Children and Society, 19*, 66–73.

Hutchby, I. (2007). *The discourse of child counselling.* Amsterdam, Netherlands: John Benjamins.

Hutchby, I. (2011). Non-neutrality and argument in the hybrid political interview. *Discourse Studies, 13*(3), 349–366.

Hutchby, I., & Wooffitt, R. (2008). *Conversation analysis* (2nd ed.). Cambridge, England: Polity Press.

Irvine, A., Drew, P., & Sainsbury, R. (2013). "Am I not answering your questions properly?" Clarification, adequacy and responsiveness in semi-structured telephone and face-to-face interviews. *Qualitative Research, 13*(1), 87–106.

Jefferson, G. (1984). On the organization of laughter in talk about troubles. In J. M. Atkinson and J. Heritage (Eds.), *Structures of social action: Studies in conversation analysis* (pp. 346–369). Cambridge, England: Cambridge University Press.

Jefferson, G. (1986). Notes on "latency" in overlap onset. *Human Studies, 9*(2/3), 153–183.

Jefferson, G. (2004a). Glossary of transcript symbols with an introduction. In G. H. Lerner (Ed.), *Conversation analysis: Studies from the first generation* (pp. 13–31). Amsterdam, Netherlands: John Benjamins.

Jefferson, G. (2004b). At first I thought. In G. H. Lerner (Ed.), *Conversation analysis: Studies from the first generation.* Amsterdam, Netherlands: John Benjamins.

Karim, K. (2015). The value of conversation analysis: A child psychiatrist's perspective. In M. O'Reilly & J. N. Lester (Eds.), *The Palgrave handbook of child mental health: Discourse and conversation studies* (pp. 25–41). Basingstoke, England: Palgrave Macmillan.

Kasper, G. (2000). Data collection in pragmatics research. In H. Spencer-Oatley (Ed.), *Culturally speaking: Managing rapport through talk across cultures* (pp. 316–341). London, England: Continuum.

Kearney, M. (2001). Levels and applications of qualitative research evidence. *Research in Nursing and Health, 24*, 145–153.

Kilbourn, B. (2006). The qualitative doctoral dissertation proposal. *Teachers College Record, 108*(4), 529.

Kimmel, M. (2012). Optimizing the analysis of metaphor in discourse: How to make the most of qualitative software and find a good research design. *Review of Cognitive Linguistics, 10*(1), 1–48.

Kirk, J., & Miller, M. L. (1986). *Reliability and validity in qualitative research.* London, England: Sage.

Kitzinger, C. (2005). Heteronormativity in action: Reproducing the heterosexual nuclear family in "after hours" medical calls [Special Section: Language Interaction and Social Problems]. *Social Problems, 52*(4), 477–498.

Kitzinger, C. (2008). Developing feminist conversation analysis. *Human Studies, 31*, 179–208.

Kitzinger, C. (2013). Repair. In J. Sidnell & T. Stivers (Eds.), *The handbook of conversation analysis* (pp. 229–256). West Sussex, England: Blackwell.

Kiyimba, N. (2016). Using discourse and conversation analysis to study clinical practice in adult mental health. In M. O'Reilly & J. N. Lester (Eds.), *The Palgrave handbook of adult mental health: Discourse and conversation studies* (pp. 45–63). Basingstoke, England: Palgrave Macmillan.

Kiyimba, N., Lester, J. N., & O'Reilly, M. (in press). *Collecting naturally-occurring data*. London, England: Springer.

Kiyimba, N., & O'Reilly, M. (2016a). The value of using discourse and conversation analysis as evidence to inform practice in counselling and therapeutic interactions. In M. O'Reilly & J. N. Lester (Eds.), *The Palgrave handbook of adult mental health: Discourse and conversation studies* (pp. 520–539). Basingstoke, England: Palgrave Macmillan.

Kiyimba, N. & O'Reilly (2016b). An exploration of the possibility for secondary traumatic stress amongst transcriptionists: A grounded theory approach. *Qualitative Research in Psychology, 13*(1), 92–108.

Konopasek, Z. (2008). Making thinking visible with ATLAS.ti: Computer-assisted qualitative analysis as textual practices. *Forum: Qualitative Social Research, 9*(2). Retrieved from http://nbn-resolving.de/urn:nbn:de:0114-fqs0802124

Kvale, S. (1996). *Interviews: An introduction to qualitative research interviewing*. Thousand Oaks, CA: Sage.

Kvale, S. (2008). *Doing interviews*. London, England: Sage.

Lapadat, J. (2000). Problematizing transcription: Purpose, paradigm and quality. *International Journal of Social Research Methodology, 3*(3), 203–219.

Lapadat, J., & Lindsay, A. (1999). Transcription in research and practice: From standardization of technique to interpretive positioning. *Qualitative Inquiry, 5*(1), 64–86.

Latour, B. (1988). The politics of explanation: An alternative. In S. Woolgar (Ed.), *Knowledge and reflexivity: New frontiers in the sociology of knowledge* (pp. 155–176). London, England: Sage.

Lester, J., & O'Reilly, M. (2015). Is evidence-based practice a threat to the progress of the qualitative community? Arguments from the bottom of the pyramid. *Qualitative Inquiry, 21*(7), 628–632.

Lester, J. N., & Paulus, T. (2011). Accountability and public displays of knowing in an undergraduate computer-mediated communication context. *Discourse Studies, 13*(5), 671–686.

Lester, J. N., & Paulus, T. M. (2015). "I'm not sure I even know": Therapists' tentative constructions of autism.

Review of Disability Studies: An International Journal, 11(3), 1–18.

Lett, J. (1990). Emics and etics: Notes on the epistemology of anthropology. In T. Headland, K. Pike, & M. Harris (Eds.), *Emics and etics: The insider/outsider debate. Frontiers of anthropology* (Vol. 7, pp. 127–142). Newbury Park, CA: Sage.

Levinson, S. C. (1992). Activity types and language. In P. Drew & J. Heritage (Eds.), *Talk at work: Interaction in institutional settings* (pp. 66–100). Cambridge, England: Cambridge University Press.

Lewis, J., & Ritchie, J. (2003). Generalising from qualitative research. In J. Ritchie & J. Lewis (Eds.), *Qualitative research practice: A guide for social science students and researchers* (pp. 263–286). London, England: Sage.

Lincoln, Y., & Guba, E. (1985). *Naturalistic inquiry*. Beverly Hills, CA: Sage.

Lochmiller, C. R., & Lester, J. N. (2017). *An introduction to educational research: Connecting methods to practice*. Thousand Oaks, CA: Sage.

Lucas, K. (2010). *A waste of time? The value and promise of researcher completed qualitative data transcribing*. Northeastern Educational Research Association Conference proceedings, Paper 24. Retrieved from http://digitalcommons.uconn.edu/nera_2010/24

Luff, P., & Heath, C. (2012). Some "technical challenges" of video analysis: Social actions, objects, material realities and the problems of perspective. *Qualitative Research, 12*(3), 255–279.

Lynch, M. (1985). *Art and artifact in laboratory science: A study of shop work and shop talk*. London, England: Routledge & Kegan Paul.

Lynch, M. (2000). Against reflexivity as an academic virtue and source of privileged knowledge. *Theory, Culture and Society, 17*(3), 26–54.

Macbeth, D. (2001). On "reflexivity" in qualitative research: Two readings, and a third. *Qualitative Inquiry, 7*(1), 26–54.

Machi, L., & McEvoy, B. (2012). *The literature review: Six steps to success* (2nd ed.). London, England: Corwin.

Madill, A., Widdicomb, S., & Barkham, M. (2001). The potential of conversation analysis for psychotherapy research. *The Counseling Psychologist, 29*, 413–434.

Magnuson, S., Wilcoxon, S. A., & Norem, K. (2000). A profile of lousy supervision: Experienced counselors' perspectives. *Counselor Education and Supervision, 39*, 189–202.

Mahon, A., Glendinning, C., Clarke, K., & Craig, G. (1996). Researching children: Methods and ethics. *Children and Society, 10,* 145–154.

Marks, D. (2002). *Perspectives on evidence-based practice.* London, England: Health Development Agency, Public Health Evidence Steering Group.

Mash, E., & Hunsley, (2005). Developing guidelines for the evidence-based assessment of child and adolescent disorders [Special section]. *Journal of Child and Adolescent Psychology, 34,* 362–379.

Mason, J. (2007). "Re-using" qualitative data: On the merits of an investigative epistemology. *Sociological Research Online, 12*(3), 3.

Mavrikis, M., & Geraniou, E. (2011). Using qualitative data analysis software to analyse students' computer-mediated interactions: The case of MiGen and Transana. *International Journal of Social Research Methodology, 14,* 245–252.

Maynard, D. W. (1988). Language, interaction and social problems. *Social Problems, 35,* 311–334.

Maynard, D. W. (2003). *Conversational order in everyday talk and clinical settings.* Chicago, IL: University of Chicago Press.

Maynard, D., & Clayman, S. (2003). Ethnomethodology and conversation analysis. In L. Reynolds & N. Herman-Kinney (Eds.), *Handbook of symbolic interactionism* (pp. 173–202). Lanham, MD: AltaMira Press.

Maynard, D., Clayman, S., Halkowski, T., & Kidwell, M. (2010). Toward an interdisciplinary field: Language and social interaction research at the University of California, Santa Barbara. In W. Leeds-Hurwitz (Ed.), *The social history of language and social interaction research* (pp. 313–333). Cresskill, NJ: Humana Press.

Maynard, D., & Peräkylä, A. (2003). Language and social interaction. In J. Delamater (Ed.), *Handbook of social psychology* (pp. 233–257). New York, NY: Kluwer Academic Press.

Mays, N., & Pope, C. (2000). Quality in qualitative health research. In C. Pope & N. Mays (Eds.), *Qualitative research in health care* (pp. 89–102). London, England: BMJ Books.

Mazeland, H. (2006). Conversation analysis. In *Encyclopaedia of language and linguistics* (2nd ed., Vol. 3, pp. 153–162). Oxford, England: Elsevier Science.

McCabe, R. (2006). Conversation analysis. In M. Slade & S. Priebe (Eds.), *Choosing methods in mental health research: Mental health research from theory to practice* (pp. 24–46). London, England: Routledge.

McCabe, R., John, P., Dooley, J., Healey, P., Cushing, A., Kingdon, D., Bremner, S., and Priebe, S. (2016). "Training to enhance psychiatrist communication with patients with psychosis (TEMPO): cluster randomised controlled trial." *The British Journal of Psychiatry* 209, no. 6., 517–524.

McCrone, P., Dhanasiri, S., Patel, A., Knapp, M., & Lawton-Smith, S. (2008). *Paying the price: The cost of mental health care in England to 2026.* London, England: The Kings Fund.

McHoul, A. (1978). The organisation of turns at formal talk in the classroom. *Language in Society, 7,* 183–213.

McLellan, E., MacQueen, K., & Neidig, J. (2003). Beyond the qualitative interview: Data preparation and transcription. *Field Methods, 15*(1), 63–84.

McNeill, P. (1997). Paying people to participate in research: Why not? A response to Wilkinson and Moore. *Bioethics, 11*(5), 390–396.

McNeill, T. (2006). Evidence-based practice in an age of relativism: Toward a model for practice. *Social Work, 51*(2), 147–156.

Mehan, H. (1979). *Learning lessons: Social organization in the classroom.* Cambridge, MA: Harvard University Press.

Meredith, J., & Potter, J. (2013). Conversation analysis and electronic interactions: Methodological, analytic and technical considerations. In H. L. Lim & F. Sudweeks (Eds.), *Innovative methods and technologies for electronic discourse analysis* (pp. 370–393). Hershey, PA: IGI Global.

Meyrick, J. (2006). What is good qualitative research? A first step towards a comprehensive approach to judging rigour/quality. *Journal of Health Psychology, 11*(5), 799–808.

Moccia, P. (1988). A critique of compromise: Beyond the methods debate. *Advances in Nursing Science, 10,* 1–9.

Mondada, L. (2007). Commentary: Transcript variations and the indexicality of transcribing practices. *Discourse Studies, 9*(6), 809–821.

Mondada, L. (2013). The conversation analytic approach to data collection. In J. Sidnell & T. Stivers (Eds.), *The handbook of conversation analysis* (pp. 32–56). West Sussex, England: Blackwell.

Moore, N. (2006). The contexts of data: Broadening perspectives in the (re)use of qualitative data. *Methodological Innovations Online, 1,* 2.

Moore, N. (2007). (Re)using qualitative data. *Sociological Research Online, 12,* 3.

Morse, J. (2006a). The politics of evidence. *Qualitative Health Research, 16*(3), 395–404.

Morse, J. (2006b). It is time to revise the Cochrane criteria [Editorial]. *Qualitative Health Research, 16*(3), 315–317.

Morse, J., Barrett, M., Mayan, M., Olson, K., & Spiers, J. (2002). Verification strategies for establishing reliability and validity in qualitative research. *International Journal for Qualitative Methods, 1*(2), 1–19.

Murray, R. (2006). *How to write a thesis* (2nd ed.). Berkshire, England: Open University Press.

Murthy, D. (2008). Digital ethnography: An examination of the use of new technologies for social research. *Sociology, 42*(5), 837–855.

Nadin, S., & Cassell, C. (2006). The use of a research diary as a tool for reflexive practice: Some reflections from management research. *Qualitative Research in Accounting and Management, 3*(3), 208–217.

Nevile, M. (2015). The embodied turn in research on language and social interaction. *Research on Language and Social Interaction, 48*(2), 121–151.

Ngui, E., Khasakhala, L., Ndetei, D., & Weiss Roberts, L. (2010). Mental disorders, health inequalities and ethics: A global perspective. *International Review of Psychiatry, 22*(3), 235–244.

Nutley, S., Powell, A., & Davies, H. (2013). *What counts as good evidence? Provocation paper for the Alliance for Useful Evidence*. Retrieved from https://www.alliance4usefulev idence.org/assets/What-Counts-as-Good-Evidence-WEB .pdf

Ochs, E. (1979). Transcription as theory. In E. Ochs & B. Schiefflin (Eds.), *Developmental pragmatics* (pp. 43–72). New York, NY: Academic Press.

O'Leary, Z. (2014). *The essential guide to doing your research project* (2nd ed.). London, England: Sage.

Onwuegbuzie, A., & Leech, N. (2007). Sampling designs in qualitative research: Making the sampling process more public. *The Qualitative Report, 12*(2), 238–254.

O'Reilly, M. (2005). Active noising: The use of noises in talk, the case of onomatopoeia, abstract sounds and the functions they serve in therapy. *Text, 25*(6), 745–761.

O'Reilly, M. (2006). Should children be seen and not heard? An examination of how children's interruptions are treated in family therapy. *Discourse Studies, 8*(4), 549–566.

O'Reilly, M. (2007). Who's a naughty boy then? Accountability, family therapy and the "naughty" child. *The Family Journal: Counseling and Therapy for Couples and Families, 15*(3), 234–243.

O'Reilly, M. (2008a). "What value is there in children's talk?" Investigating family therapists' interruptions of parents and children during the therapeutic process. *Journal of Pragmatics, 40*, 507–524.

O'Reilly, M. (2008b). "I didn't violent punch him": Parental accounts of punishing children with mental health problems. *Journal of Family Therapy, 30*, 272–295.

O'Reilly, M., & Dogra, N. (2017). *Interviewing children and young people for research*. London, England: Sage.

O'Reilly, M., & Karim, K. (2016, July). *An investigation of the reality of clinical assessments with children and families: Question design and child-centered practices*. Paper presented at Children and Young People's Mental Health Conference, Northampton, England.

O'Reilly, M., Karim, K., Stafford, V., & Hutchby, V. (2015). Identifying the interactional processes in the first assessments in child mental health. *Child and Adolescent Mental Health, 20*(4), 195–201.

O'Reilly, M., & Kiyimba, N. (2015). *Advanced qualitative research: A guide to contemporary theoretical debates*. London, England: Sage.

O'Reilly, M., Kiyimba, N., & Karim, K. (2016). "This is a question we have to ask everyone": Asking young people about self-harm and suicide. *Journal of Psychiatric and Mental Health Nursing, 23*, 479–488.

O'Reilly, M., & Lester, J. (2014, June). Epistemic claims to psychiatric matters in child mental health settings: Children's claims to knowledge regarding their mental health experiences and professionals' renegotiation of the problem. In T. Stivers (Chair), *Symposium: Knowledge management in institutional interaction*. Symposium conducted at the International Society for Conversation Analysis Fourth Annual Conference, Los Angeles, California.

O'Reilly, M., & Lester, J. N. (2016). Building a case for a good parent identity in a systemic environment: Resisting blame and accounting for children's behaviour. *Journal of Family Therapy, 38*(4), 491–511.

O'Reilly, M., & Lester, J. N. (2017). *Examining mental health through social constructionism: The language of mental health*. London, England: Palgrave Macmillan.

O'Reilly, M., & Lester, J. (in press). Building a case for good parenting in a family therapy systemic environment: Resisting blame and accounting for children's behaviour. *Journal of Family Therapy*.

O'Reilly, M., Lester, J., & Muskett, T. (2016). Children's claims to knowledge regarding their mental health experiences and practitioners' negotiation of the problem. *Patient Education and Counseling, 99*, 905–910.

O'Reilly, M., Lester, J., & Muskett, T. (Eds.). (2017). *A practical guide to social interaction research in autism spectrum disorders*. Basingstoke, England: Palgrave Macmillan.

O'Reilly, M., Lester, J., Muskett, T., & Karim, K. (2017). How parents build a case for autism spectrum disorder during initial assessments: "We're fighting a losing battle." *Discourse Studies, 19*(1), 69–83.

O'Reilly, M., & Parker, N. (2013). Unsatisfactory saturation: A critical exploration of the notion of saturated sample sizes in qualitative research. *Qualitative Research, 13*(2), 190–197.

O'Reilly, M., & Parker, N. (2014). *Doing mental health research with children and adolescents: A guide to qualitative methods*. London, England: Sage.

O'Reilly, M., Parker, N., & Hutchby, I. (2011). Ongoing processes of managing consent: The empirical ethics of using video-recording in clinical practice and research. *Clinical Ethics, 6*, 179–185.

O'Reilly, M., Ronzoni, P., & Dogra, N. (2013). *Research with children: Theory and practice*. London, England: Sage.

Parker, N., & O'Reilly, M. (2012). "Gossiping" as a social action in family therapy: The pseudo-absence and pseudo-presence of children. *Discourse Studies, 14*(4), 1–19.

Parker, N., & O'Reilly, M. (2013). "We are alone in the house": A case study addressing researcher safety and risk. *Qualitative Research in Psychology, 10*(4), 341–354.

Parkin, A., Frake, C., & Davison, I. (2003). A triage clinic in a child and adolescent mental health service. *Child and Adolescent Mental Health, 8,* 177–183.

Parry, O., & Mauthner, N. S. (2004). Whose data are they anyway? Practical, legal and ethical issues in archiving qualitative research data. *Sociology, 38*(1), 139–152.

Parry, R., & Land, V. (2013). Systematically reviewing and synthesizing evidence from conversation analytic and related discursive research to inform healthcare communication practice and policy: An illustrated guide. *BMC Medical Research Methods, 13*, 69–82.

Patton, M. (2002). *Qualitative evaluation and research methods* (3rd ed.). Thousand Oaks, CA: Sage.

Paulus, T. (2016, July). *Digital tools for qualitative research*. Two-day workshop for the 13th Annual Qualitative Research Summer Intensive, The Odum Institute and ResearchTalk, Inc., Chapel Hill, NC.

Paulus, T., & Lester, J. (2016). ATLAS.ti for conversation and discourse analysis. *International Journal of Social Research Methodology, 19*(4), 405–428.

Paulus, T. M., & Lester, J. N. (2017, May). *Creating a qualitative researcher identity with social media*. Paper presented at the Thirteenth International Congress of Qualitative Inquiry, Urbana-Champaign, IL.

Paulus, T. M., Lester, J. N., & Britt, V. G. (2013). Constructing hopes and fears around technology: A discourse analysis of introductory qualitative research texts. *Qualitative Inquiry, 19*(9), 639–651.

Paulus, T., Lester, J., & Dempster, P. (2014). *Digital tools for qualitative research*. London, England: Sage.

Paulus, T., Warren, A., & Lester, J. N. (2016). Applying conversation analysis methods to online talk: A literature review. *Discourse, Context & Media, 12*, 1–10.

Payne, G., & Williams, M. (2005). Generalization in qualitative research. *Sociology, 39*(2), 295–314.

Pelose, G. C. (1987). The functions of behavioral synchrony and speech rhythm in conversation. *Research on Language and Social Interaction, 20*(1-4), 171–220.

Peräkylä, A. (1997). Reliability and validity in research based on tapes and transcripts. In D. Silverman (Ed.), *Qualitative research: Theory, method and practice* (pp. 201–220). London, England: Sage.

Peräkylä, A. (2011). Validity in research on naturally occurring social interaction. In D. Silverman (Ed.), *Qualitative research* (3rd ed., pp. 365–382). London, England: Sage.

Pomerantz, A. (1984). Agreeing and disagreeing with assessments: Some features of preferred/dispreferred turn shapes. In J. M. Atkinson & J. Heritage (Eds.), *Structures of social action: Studies in conversation analysis* (pp. 57–101). Cambridge, England: Cambridge University Press.

Pomerantz, A. (1990). On the validity and generalizability of conversation analytic methods: Conversation analytic claims. *Communication Monographs, 57*(3), 231–235.

Pomerantz, A., & Fehr, B. J. (1997). Conversation analysis: An approach to the study of social action as sense making practices. In T. A. van Dijk (Ed.), *Discourse as social interaction* (pp. 64–91). London, England: Sage.

Potter, J. (1996a). *Representing reality: Discourse, rhetoric, and social construction*. London, England: Sage.

Potter, J. (1996b). Discourse analysis and constructionist approaches: Theoretical background. In J. T. E. Richardson (Ed.), *Handbook of qualitative research methods for psychology and the social sciences* (pp. 125–140). Leicester, England: British Psychological Society.

Potter, J. (1997). Discourse analysis as a way of analysing naturally occurring talk. In D. Silverman (Ed.),

Qualitative research: Theory, method and practice (pp. 144–160). London, England: Sage.

Potter, J. (2001). Wittgenstein and Austin. In M. Wetherell, S. Taylor, & S. Yates (Eds.), *Discourse theory and practice: A reader* (pp. 39–46). London, England: Sage.

Potter, J. (2002). Two kinds of natural. *Discourse Studies, 4*(4), 539–542.

Potter, J. (2003). Discursive psychology: Between method and paradigm. *Discourse & Society, 14*(6), 783–794.

Potter, J. (2010). Contemporary discursive psychology: Issues, prospects, and Corcoran's awkward ontology. *British Journal of Social Psychology, 49*(4), 657–678.

Potter, J., & Hepburn, A. (2005). Qualitative interviews in psychology: Problems and possibilities. *Qualitative Research in Psychology, 2*, 1–27.

Potter, J., & Hepburn, A. (2010). Putting aspiration into words: "Laugh particles," managing descriptive trouble and modulating action. *Journal of Pragmatics, 42*(6), 1543–1555.

Potter, J., & Wetherell, M. (1987). *Discourse and social psychology.* London, England: Sage.

Prior, M. T. (2016). *Emotion and discourse in L2 narrative research.* Bristol, England: Multilingual Matters.

Psathas, G. (1990). *Interactional competence.* Washington, DC: University Press of America.

Psathas, G., & Anderson, T. (1990). The practices of transcription in conversation analysis. *Semiotica, 78*(1/2), 75–99.

Punch, K. (2000). *Developing effective research proposals.* London, England: Sage.

Rapley, T. (2012). The (extra)ordinary practices of qualitative interviewing. In J. F. Gubrium, J. A. Holstein, A. B. Marvasti, & K. D. McKinney (Eds.), *The SAGE handbook of interview research: The complexity of the craft* (pp. 541–554). Los Angeles, CA: Sage.

Ravitch, S., & Carl, N. M. (2016). *Qualitative research: Bridging the conceptual, theoretical and methodological.* London, England: Sage.

Ravitch, S., & Riggan, M. (2012). *Reason & rigor: How conceptual frameworks guide research.* Thousand Oaks, CA: Sage.

Rawls, A. (1989). Language, self, and social order: A reformulation of Goffman and Sacks. *Human Studies, 12*(1/2), 147–172.

Reddington, E., & Waring, H. Z. (2015). Understanding the sequential resources of doing humor in the language classroom. *Humor: International Journal of Humor Research, 28*(1), 1–23.

Ridley, D. (2012). *The literature review: A step-by-step guide for students.* London, England: Sage.

Roberts, F., & Robinson, J. (2004). Interobserver agreement on first-stage conversation analytic transcription. *Health Communication Research, 30*(3), 376–410.

Robinson, J. (2007). The role of numbers and statistics within conversation analysis. *Communication Methods and Measures, 1*(1), 65–75.

Robinson, J. D., Tate, A., & Heritage, J. (2016). Agenda-setting revisited: When and how do primary-care physicians solicit patients' additional concerns? *Patient Education and Counseling, 99*(5), 718–723.

Rolfe, G. (1998). The theory-practice gap in nursing: From research-based practice to practitioner-based research. *Journal of Advanced Nursing, 28*(3), 672–679.

Rolfe, G. (2006). Validity, trustworthiness and rigour: Quality and the idea of qualitative research. *Journal of Advanced Nursing, 53*(3), 304–310.

Roulston, K. (2006). Close encounters of the "CA" kind: A review of literature analysing talk in research interviews. *Qualitative Research, 6*(4), 515–534.

Roulston, K. (2010). *Reflective interviewing: A guide to theory and practice.* London, England: Sage.

Roulston, K. (2017). *Social studies of interviewing: Contributions from ethnomethodologically informed analyses.* Presentation at the International Congress of Qualitative Inquiry, University of Illinois, Urbana-Champaign, IL.

Rycroft-Malone, J., Harvey, G., Seers, K., Kitson, A., McCormack, B., & Titchen, A. (2004). An exploration of the factors that influence the implementation of evidence into practice. *Issues in Clinical Nursing, 13*, 913–924.

Sackett, D. (1986). Rules of evidence and clinical recommendations on the use of antithrombotic agents. *Chest, 89*, 2s–3s.

Sackett, D., Rosenberg, W., Gray, J., Haynes, R., & Richardson, W. (1996). Evidence based medicine: What it is and what it isn't. *British Medical Journal, 312*, 71–72.

Sacks, H. (1972). On the analyzability of stories by children. In J. J. Gumperz & D. Hymes (Eds.), *Directions in sociolinguistics: The ethnography of speaking* (pp. 337–353). Cambridge, England: Cambridge University Press.

Sacks, H. (1987). On the preferences for agreement and contiguity in sequences in conversation. In G. Button & J. R. Lee (Eds.), *Talk and social organisation* (pp. 54–69). Clevedon, England: Multilingual Matters.

Sacks, H. (1992). *Lectures on conversation* (Vols. I & II, edited by G. Jefferson). Oxford, England: Blackwell.

Sacks, H. (1995). *Lectures on conversation*. Oxford, England: Blackwell.

Sacks, H., Schegloff, E., & Jefferson, G. (1974). A simplest systematic for the organization of turn-taking for conversation. *Language, 50,* 696–735.

Sandelowski, M. (1993). Rigor or rigor mortis: The problem of rigor in qualitative research revisited. *Advances in Nursing Science, 16*(2), 1–8.

Sandelowski, M. (1995). Sample sizes in qualitative research. *Research in Nursing and Health, 18*(2), 179–183.

Sandelowski, M., & Barroso, J. (2002). Reading qualitative studies. *International Journal of Qualitative Methods, 1*(1), 74–108.

Schegloff, E. (1979). The relevance of repair to syntax-for-conversation. *Syntax and Semantics, 12,* 261–286.

Schegloff, E. (1987). Analyzing single episodes of interaction: An exercise in conversation analysis. *Social Psychology Quarterly, 50*(2), 101–114.

Schegloff, E. (1993). Reflections on quantification in the study of conversation. *Research on Language and Social Interaction, 26,* 99–128.

Schegloff, E. A. (1996). Confirming allusions: Toward an empirical account of action. *American Journal of Sociology, 102*(1), 161–216.

Schegloff, E. A. (1997). Practices and actions: Boundary cases of other-initiated repair. *Discourse Processes, 23*(3), 499–545.

Schegloff, E. (1998). Reply to Wetherell. *Discourse & Society, 9*(3), 413–416.

Schegloff, E. (1999). Discourse, pragmatics, conversation, analysis. *Discourse Studies, 1*(4), 405–435.

Schegloff, E. (2003). On conversation analysis: An interview with Emanuel A. Schegloff. In S. Cmejrkova & C. Prevignano (Eds.), *Discussing conversation analysis: The work of Emanuel Schegloff* (pp. 11–55). Philadelphia, PA: John Benjamins.

Schegloff, E. A. (2007a). A tutorial on membership categorization. *Journal of Pragmatics, 39*(3), 462–482.

Schegloff, E. A. (2007b). *Sequence organization in interaction: A primer in conversation analysis.* Cambridge, England: Cambridge University Press.

Schegloff, E., Jefferson, G., & Sacks, H. (1977). The preference for self-correction in the organization of repair in conversation. *Language, 53*(2), 361–382.

Schegloff, E., & Sacks, H. (1973). Opening up closings. *Semiotica, 8,* 289–327.

Schwabe, M., Howell, S., & Reuber, M. (2007). Differential diagnosis of seizure disorders: A conversation analytic approach. *Social Science and Medicine, 65*(4), 712–724.

Schwandt, T. (1996). Farewell to criteriology. *Qualitative Inquiry, 2*(1), 58–72.

Schwandt, T. (1997). *Qualitative inquiry: A dictionary of terms.* Thousand Oaks, CA: Sage.

Seedhouse, P. (2004). Conversation analysis methodology. *Language Learning, 54*(S1), 1–54.

Sheon, N., Lee, S., & Facente, S. (2010). From questionnaire to conversation: A structural intervention to improve HIV test counseling. *Patient Education & Counseling, 81,* 468–475.

Shrum, W., Duque, R., & Brown, T. (2005). Digital video as research practice: Methodology for the millennium. *Journal of Research Practice, 1*(1), M4.

Sidnell, J. (2010). *Conversation analysis: An introduction.* West Sussex, England: Blackwell.

Sidnell, J. (2013). Basic conversation analytic methods. In J. Sidnell & T. Stivers (Eds.), *The handbook of conversation analysis* (pp. 77–99). West Sussex, England: Blackwell.

Sidnell, J., & Stivers, T. (Eds.). (2013). *The handbook of conversation analysis.* West Sussex, England: Blackwell.

Sikveland, R. O., & Stokoe, E. (2016). Dealing with resistance in initial intake and inquiry calls to mediation: The power of "willing." *Conflict Resolution Quarterly, 33*(3), 235–253.

Silverman, D. (1997). *Discourses of counselling: HIV counselling as social interaction.* London, England: Sage.

Silverman, D. (1998). *Harvey Sacks: Social science and conversation analysis.* Cambridge, England: Polity Press.

Silverman, D. (2006). *Interpreting qualitative data: Methods for analysing talk, text and interaction* (3rd ed.). London, England: Sage.

Silverman, D. (2009). *Doing qualitative research* (3rd ed.). London, England: Sage.

Silverman, D. (2013). *Doing qualitative research: A practical handbook*. London, England: Sage.

Skukauskaite, A. (2012). Transparency in transcribing: Making visible theoretical bases impacting knowledge construction from open-ended interview records. *Forum: Qualitative Social Research, 13*(1). Retrieved from http://www.qualitative-research.net/index.php/fqs/article/view/1532/3330

Smith, B. (1999). Ethical and methodologic benefits of using a reflexive journal in hermeneutic-phenomenologic research. *Journal of Nursing Scholarship, 31*(4), 359–363.

Smith, J. (1990). Goodness criteria: Alternative research paradigms and the problem of criteria. In E. Guba (Ed.), *The paradigm dialog* (pp. 167–187). London, England: Sage.

Speer, S. (2002). "Natural" and "contrived" data: A sustainable distinction? *Discourse Studies, 4*(4), 511–525.

Speer, S., & Hutchby, I. (2003). From ethics to analytics: Aspects of participants' orientations to the presence and relevance of recording devices. *Sociology, 37*(2), 315–337.

Spencer, L., Ritchie, J., Lewis, J., & Dillon, L. (2003). *Quality in qualitative evaluation: A framework for assessing research evidence.* London, England: Government Chief Social Researcher's Office, Prime Minister's Strategy Unit. Retrieved from http://webarchive.nationalarchives.gov.uk/20140619055846/http://www.civilservice.gov.uk/wp-content/uploads/2011/09/a_quality_framework_tcm6-38740.pdf

Stafford, V., Hutchby, I., Karim, K., & O'Reilly, M. (2016). "Why are you here?" Seeking children's accounts of their presentation to CAMHS. *Clinical Child Psychology and Psychiatry, 21*(1), 3–18.

Staller, K. (2013). Epistemological boot camp: The politics of science and what every qualitative researcher needs to know to survive in the academy. *Qualitative Social Work, 12*(4), 395–413.

Stein, A. (2010). Sex, truths, and audiotape: Anonymity and the ethics of public exposure in ethnography. *Journal of Contemporary Ethnography, 39*(5), 554–568.

Stenbacka, C. (2001). Qualitative research requires quality concepts of its own. *Management Decision, 39*(7), 551–555.

Stewart, B. (2015). In abundance: Networked participatory practices as scholarship. *International Review of Research in Open & Distributed Learning, 16*(3).

Stiles, W. (1993). Quality control in qualitative research. *Clinical Psychology Review, 13*, 593–618.

Stivers, T. (2002). Presenting the problem in pediatric encounters: "Symptoms only" versus "candidate diagnosis" presentations. *Health Communication, 14*(3), 299–338.

Stivers, T. (2015). Coding social interaction: A heretical approach in conversation analysis? *Research on Language and Social Interaction, 48*(1), 1–19.

Stivers, T., & Majid, A. (2007). Questioning children: Interactional evidence of implicit bias in medical interviews. *Social Psychology Quarterly, 70*(4), 424–441.

Stivers, T., & Robinson, J. (2006). A preference for progressivity in interaction. *Language in Society, 35*(3), 367–392.

Stokoe, E. (2008). Categories, actions and sequences: Formulating gender in talk-in-interaction. In K. Harrington, I. Litosseliti, H. Sauntson, & J. Sunderland (Eds.), *Gender and language research methodologies* (pp. 139–157). New York, NY: Palgrave Macmillan.

Stokoe, E. (2010). "I'm not gonna hit a lady": Conversation analysis, membership categorization and men's denials of violence towards women. *Discourse & Society, 21*(1), 59–82.

Stokoe, E. (2011). Simulated interaction and communication skills training: The conversation analytic role-play method. In C. Antaki (Ed.), *Applied conversation analysis: Intervention and change in institutional talk* (pp. 119–139). Hampshire, England: Palgrave Macmillan.

Stokoe, E. (2012). Moving forward with membership categorization analysis: Methods for systematic analysis. *Discourse Studies, 14*(3), 277–303.

Stokoe, E. (2014). The conversation analytic role-play method (CARM): A method for training communication skills as an alternative to simulated role-play. *Research on Language and Social Interaction, 47*(3), 255–265.

Stokoe, E., Hepburn, A., & Antaki, C. (2012). Beware the "Loughborough School" of social psychology? Interaction and the politics of intervention. *British Journal of Social Psychology, 51*, 486–496.

Stommel, W., & Koole, T. (2010). The online support group as a community: A micro-analysis of the interaction with a new member. *Discourse Studies, 12*(3), 357–378.

Stommel, W., & Van der Houwen, F. (2013). Formulations in "trouble" chat sessions. *Language@Internet, 10.*

Streeck, J., Goodwin, C., & LeBaron, C. (2011). Embodied interaction in the material world: An interaction. In J. Streeck, C. Goodwin, & C. LeBaron (Eds.), *Embodied interaction: Language and body in the material world* (pp. 1–28). Cambridge, England: Cambridge University Press.

Streeck, U. (2010). A psychotherapist's view of conversation analysis. In A. Peräkylä, C. Antaki, S. Vehvilainen, & I. Leudar (Eds.), *Conversation analysis and psychotherapy* (pp. 173–187). Cambridge, England: Cambridge University Press.

Strong, T., Busch, R., & Couture, S. (2008). Conversational evidence in therapeutic dialogue. *Journal of Marital and Family Therapy, 34*(3), 388–405.

Suchman, L. (1987). *Plans and situated actions: The problem of human-machine communication.* New York, NY: Cambridge University Press.

Suchman, L., & Jordan, B. (1990). Interactional troubles in face-to-face survey interviews. *Journal of the American Statistical Association, 85*(409), 232–253.

Svirydzenka, N., Aitken, J., & Dogra, N. (in press). Research and partnerships with schools. *Social Psychiatry and Psychiatric Epidemiology.*

Swisher, A. K. (2010). Practice-based evidence. *Cardiopulmonary Physical Therapy Journal, 21*(2), 4.

Talmy, S. (2010). Qualitative interviews in applied linguistics: From research instrument to social practice. *Annual Review of Applied Linguistics, 30*, 128–148.

Taylor, R. (2007). Reversing the retreat from Gillick? R (Axon) v Secretary of State for Health. *Child and Family Law Quarterly, 19*(1), 81–97.

Taylor, S. (2001). Locating and conducting discourse analytic research. In M. Wetherell, S. Taylor, & S. Yates (Eds.), *Discourse and data.* London, England: Sage.

ten Have, P. (1990). Methodological issues in conversation analysis. *Bulletin of Sociological Methodology/Bulletin de Méthodologie Sociologique, 27*(1), 23–51.

ten Have, P. (1999). *Doing conversation analysis: A practical guide.* London, England: Sage.

ten Have, P. (2001). Applied conversation analysis. In A. McHoul & M. Rapley (Eds.), *How to analyse talk in institutional settings: A casebook of methods* (pp. 3–11). London, England: Continuum.

ten Have, P. (2007). *Doing conversation analysis: A practical guide* (2nd ed.). London, England: Sage.

Themessl-Huber, M., Humphris, G., Dowell, J., Macgillivray, S., Rushmer, R., & Williams, B. (2008). Audio-visual recording of patient–GP consultations for research purposes: A literature review on recruiting rates and strategies. *Patient Education & Counseling, 71*, 157–168.

Thompson, D., Kirkman, S., Watson, R., & Stewart, S. (2005). Improving research supervision in nursing. *Nurse Education Today, 25*, 283–290.

Thompson, L., Howes, C., & McCabe, R. (2016). The effect of questions used by psychiatrists on therapeutic alliance and adherence. *British Journal of Psychiatry, 209*(1), 40–47.

Thompson, L., & McCabe, R. (2016). "Good" communication in schizophrenia: A conversation analytic definition. In M. O'Reilly & J. N. Lester (Eds.), *The Palgrave handbook of adult mental health: Discourse and conversation studies* (pp. 394–418). Basingstoke, England: Palgrave Macmillan.

Thorne, S. (2009). The role of qualitative research within an evidence-based context: Can metasynthesis be the answer? *International Journal of Nursing Studies, 46*, 569–575.

Timmermans, S., & Berg, M. (2003). *The gold standard: The challenge of evidence-based medicine and standardization in health care.* Philadelphia, PA: Temple University Press.

Tong, A., Sainsbury, P., & Craig, J. (2007). Consolidated criteria for reporting qualitative research (COREQ): A 32-item checklist for interviews and focus groups. *International Journal for Quality in Health Care, 19*(6), 349–357.

Tracy, S. J. (2010). Qualitative quality: Eight "big-tent" criteria for excellent qualitative research. *Qualitative Inquiry, 16*(10), 837–851.

Tseliou, E. (2013). A critical methodological review of discourse and conversation analysis studies of family therapy. *Family Process, 52*(4), 653–672.

Turner, J. (2013). Hierarchy of evidence. In M. Gellman & J. R. Turner (Eds.), *Encyclopaedia of behavioral medicine* (pp. 963–964). New York, NY: Springer-Verlag.

van Dijk, T. A. (2006). Introduction: Discourse, interaction and cognition. *Discourse Studies, 8*(1), 5–7.

Vannini, P. (Ed.). (2012). *Popularizing research: Engaging new genres, media, and audiences.* New York, NY: Peter Lang.

Varga, M. A., & Paulus, T. M. (2014). Grieving online: Newcomers' constructions of grief in an online support group. *Death Studies, 38*(7), 443–449.

Veletsianos, G., & Kimmons, R. (2012). Assumptions and challenges of open scholarship. *International Review of Research in Open and Distributed Learning, 13*(4), 166–189.

Wakin, M., & Zimmerman, D. H. (1999). Reduction and specialization in emergency and directory assistance calls. *Research on Language and Social Interaction, 32*, 409–437.

Walen, M., & Zimmerman, D. H. (1987). Sequential and institutional contexts in calls for help. *Social Psychology Quarterly, 50*, 172–185.

Walker, G. (2013). Phonetics and prosody in conversation. In J. Sidnell & T. Stivers (Eds.), *The handbook of conversation analysis* (pp. 455–474). West Sussex, England: Blackwell.

Waring, H. Z. (2014). Managing control and connection in the language classroom. *Research in the Teaching of English, 49*(1), 52–74.

Watt, D. (2007). On becoming a qualitative researcher: The value of reflexivity. *The Qualitative Report, 12*(1), 82–101.

Wetherell, M. (1998). Positioning and interpretative repertoires: Conversation analysis and post-structuralism in dialogue. *Discourse & Society, 9*(3), 387–412.

Wiggins, S. (2014). Adult and child use of *love, like, don't like* and *hate* during family mealtimes: Subjective category assessments as food preference talk. *Appetite, 80,* 7–15.

Wilkinson, R. (2015). Conversation and aphasia: Advances in analysis and intervention. *Aphasiology, 29*(3), 257–268.

Williams, M. (2000). Interpretivism and generalization. *Sociology, 34*(2), 209–224.

Willig, C. (2008). *Introducing qualitative research in psychology* (2nd ed.). Buckingham, England: Open University Press.

Woods, D., & Dempster, P. (2012). Tales from the bleeding edge: The qualitative analysis of complex video data using Transana. *Forum: Qualitative Social Research, 12*(1). Retrieved from http://www.qualitative-research.net/index.php/fqs/article/view/1516/ 3120

Wooffitt, R. (1992). *Telling tales of the unexpected: The organisation of factual discourse.* Hemel Hempstead, England: Harvester Wheatsheaf.

Zein, H. (2013). *The alignment between a paradigm and an approach in studying the media discourse of guerrillas in the Middle East: A case of social constructionism and critical discourse analysis.* Presentation at the International Conference on Communication, Media, Technology and Design, Famagusta, North Cyprus.

Zimmerman, D. H. (1984). Talk and its occasion: The case of calling the police. In D. Schiffrin (Ed.), *Meaning, form, and use in context: Linguistic applications* (pp. 210–228). Georgetown University Roundtable on Language and Linguistics. Washington, DC: Georgetown University Press.

Zimmerman, D. H. (1992a). The interactional organization of calls for emergency assistance. In P. Drew & J. Heritage (Eds.), *Talk at work: Social interaction in institutional settings* (pp. 418–459). Cambridge, England: Cambridge University Press.

Zimmerman, D. H. (1992b). Achieving context: Openings in emergency calls. In G. Watson & R. M. Seiler (Eds.), *Text in context: Contributions to ethnomethodology* (pp. 35–51). Newbury Park, CA: Sage.

• Index •